8 Prepare a final outline which shows clearly the relationship of subordinate points to your central idea and to each other.

9 Develop language which frees and strengthens the ideas of the speech.

Delivery

1 Free and strengthen ideas through physical poise, alertness, directness, and spontaneity.

2 From the foundation of an alert body, use adequate action and gesture to reinforce ideas, or to describe them further for increased clarity.

3 From the foundation of an alert body, develop a voice loud enough and distinct enough to be heard and understood by everyone in the room.

4 Develop a warm, human control over variety in pitch, timing, and intensity which makes it easy for listeners to attend to ideas, to understand them, and to respond to them willingly.

5 Make all delivery techniques subordinate to your desire to communicate ideas to the audience.

SPEECH

idea and delivery

Galveston Community College Library
Galveston, Texas

Presented by

Dr. James O. Ross

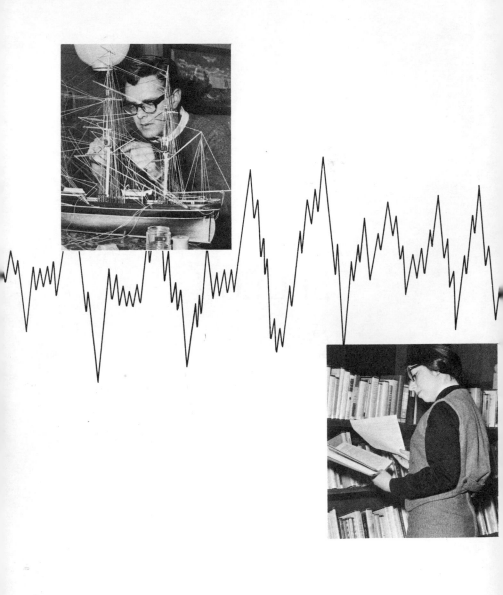

SPEECH

idea and delivery

SECOND EDITION

CHARLES W. LOMAS · RALPH RICHARDSON
The University of California at Los Angeles

HOUGHTON MIFFLIN COMPANY · BOSTON

For permission to use copyrighted material not acknowledged elsewhere
in the text, we wish to thank the following publishers:

W. W. Norton & Company, Inc., for a quotation from
Harry Overstreet, *The Mature Mind*. Copyright 1949 by
W. W. Norton & Company, Inc.

D. C. Heath and Company, for a quotation from John
Dewey, *How We Think*. Copyright 1910 by D. C. Heath
and Company.

PREFACE

In preparing the second edition of *Speech: Idea and Delivery*, I have tried to maintain the same student-centered approach that characterized the first edition. The first business of a beginning speech class is making good speeches; the second is learning to discriminate between good and bad speeches made both by fellow students and by speakers in everyday affairs outside the classroom. This book, like its predecessor, is designed to accomplish these ends.

Yet experience has suggested some changes. Two wholly new chapters have been added, dealing respectively with oral reading and discussion. The material of the opening chapters has been reorganized to clarify basic concepts and bring the student more quickly to the making of speeches based on the acquisition of new ideas. The chapters dealing with supporting material and delivery have been enlarged. Mark Twain's speech, "New England Weather," has been added to the Appendix as an example of a speech to entertain. With some reluctance, we have eliminated the cartoons, which suggested to some readers a flippancy toward the preparation and delivery of speeches which we did not intend. In their place, we have included a series of maxims by prominent speakers, writers, rhetoricians, and men in public life dealing with the concepts developed in the text. We hope that they will prove thought-provoking for the readers of this book.

I am indebted to Professor Martin P. Andersen for helpful criticism of the new chapter on group discussion, and to Professor Donald Hargis for similar suggestions concerning the chapter on oral reading. My colleague, Ralph Richardson, has been prevented by the press of other duties from working actively on the revision, but he has offered many suggestions which have been incorporated into the new book.

CHARLES W. LOMAS

CONTENTS

FIRST PRINCIPLES

1 APPROACHING A COURSE IN SPEECH

A speech class is a laboratory for the study and mastery of the skills of communication.

EFFECTIVE SPEECH serves both a private and a public good. In a world where many ideas and insights are exchanged through talk, the ability to speak well is a private good to the individual who possesses the skill; it is a public good when it meets the communicative needs of a democratic society as they occur in government, commerce, community activities, education, and entertainment.

For your individual benefit and for the public benefit deriving from your improved skill you are offered a course in effective speaking. You have the guidance of a trained instructor, the aids in theory and practice provided by this text, and the opportunity to learn to speak by speaking, as well as by observing the efforts of your fellow students.

A College Class In Speech

Joining a group of undergraduates in learning to speak more effectively can be pleasant and worth-while. You will undoubtedly improve your ability to marshal facts and ideas and to present them convincingly. Since you will get to know your fellow students better than is possible in most college courses, you will form many friendships and thus experience personal and social growth as well. If you are timid, you should gain in self-confidence. If you are brash, the reactions of your classmates should make you aware that you have much to learn. In short, you should emerge from this experience better equipped to meet the challenges of the world around you.

In this class you will be both a learner and a practitioner of the art of speech. To the extent that you have assignments, receive a few lectures, are criticized and formally evaluated, this is a class and you are a student. But you are also a speaker before a living audience. You have an opportunity, even an obligation, to try to affect the attitudes and ideas of those who listen to you. Thus your speech class is actually society in miniature.

The People in Your Class

No two speech classes are quite alike. Differences stem from variations in geography and background, numbers, age and sex distribution, and the methods and beliefs of the instructor. Beyond this, there is an elusive factor sometimes called "class personality," a statistical accident of the human equations produced by chance in registration and enrollment. Yet despite these many variables, enough predictable developments will occur to justify some preliminary observations about a class in speech. These may give you a helpful and early insight into what to expect.

Your fellow students, probably numbering between ten and twenty-five, may have widely different reasons for entering the class. Most of them will have enrolled through interest and free will. Some are here because they have to be. A misguided few may be in search of easy grade-points. But in the main, those who are looking forward to professions in teaching, law, public service, or entertainment and mass communication will know well the need to seek effectiveness in speech. Others may believe that skill in oral communication is necessary in business, commerce, and industry, where a clear and quick exchange of information is often imperative. At this stage in their education there will be some who have not yet chosen a profession. Even so, they may realize that in the broad range of social living and community activities the ability to speak well is often invaluable. At some later date, they may be home-owners protesting a change in a zoning law, committee chairmen offering a report, or the organizers of some neighborhood drive.

On the other hand, an occasional individual may enroll with a purpose in mind which is beneficial neither to himself nor to his fellow students. There is, first, the infrequent student who is carried away by his own glibness or enamored of his pear-shaped tones. It may be, as an impatient instructor once remarked, that such a student finds it cheaper to take the course than to rent a hall. Perhaps so, yet both his skills and his interests can be directed toward constructive purposes. With guidance, and the cooperation of the class, he will soon cease to regard himself as being on the verge of an eloquence hitherto unknown in the world and will begin, instead, to speak with the genuine purpose of improving his skills and satisfying the wishes of his audience.

The second type of student, equally rare, represents another extreme. This is the student who stubbornly claims that "It's not how you say it but what you say that counts." Such an attitude, we believe, is largely a result of fear. The individual who is unsure either of his ideas or of his speech is more likely to question speech, and to imply the existence of competitive roles between speech and ideas. Yet there need be no such competition. Ideas are increased in usefulness when they are spoken in a way others can understand and follow. Thus in good speaking, knowledge and communication are made to complement each other, as we suggest in our title — *Speech: Idea and Delivery*. When the student who once resisted speech as a required course realizes the importance of this complementary function, he will no longer believe that communication is "the silent exchange of noble thoughts between disembodied souls." Rather, he will conclude, "If my ideas are good, they deserve my best delivery."

Your Class and You

This course will begin with a realistic appraisal of legitimate speech goals, with an appraisal of your needs, and with an exploration of your purposes and attitudes. If, like many of your fellow students, you have been dissatisfied with your efforts to speak before an audience, you now have a laboratory or clinical situation where you, your classmates, and your instructor may set about to discover the cause and the cure of the trouble. Thus in your progress through the course you and the others in your class may

Speech is . . . that through which we clarify our ideas and beliefs: putting these out into the public medium of language, we discover whether or not they make sense.

— H. A. OVERSTREET

expect to arrive at a state of mind and competence where you carry off the speaking situation with confidence and poise.

Of course, not all the members of your class will arrive at the same level of confidence and proficiency. Speech, like other media of communication, has some of the qualities of an art form, and by implication, art suggests a limitless quest. There is no magic formula by which each college undergraduate can be transformed into a Demosthenes, a Webster, or a Churchill. Short of a miracle unlikely to occur through using any textbook, no such formula will ever be found. Yet the serious study of speech will improve the communicative abilities of any student. And all progress, heartening and impressive as it may be, will reflect the endless quest for perfection in the art of communication — and the rewards of its pursuit.

Your Ethos: Integrity, Intelligence, and Good Will

Centuries ago, Aristotle wrote that, other things being equal, audiences respond to those whose character, intelligence, and good will they trust. Among Roman rhetoricians, it was an axiom that an orator was a good man skilled in speaking. In this respect, nothing has changed by the passage of centuries. In your class, and in the speaking you will do after you leave college, your success will be measured in large part by the level at which your audience evaluates your integrity, your intelligence, and your good will. Writers on rhetoric call this *ethos* or *ethical persuasion*.

Of course, you cannot, merely by enrolling in a speech class, change your nature overnight, or suddenly remove discordant elements from your personality. Yet there are elements of ethos which are clearly within the control of even a beginning speaker and should become a matter of continuing concern to him.

INTEGRITY. If you cannot change all the elements of your character or personality as you might choose, you can at least decide that whatever you say to your classmates from the platform will be soundly based in fact and will represent your best judgment. We do not, of course, rule out deliberate nonsense for the purpose of entertaining your listeners; but when you speak with a serious purpose, your audience will quickly sense whether you are vitally concerned with what you are saying, or whether you are going through the motions of giving a speech to satisfy a class requirement. To the extent that they doubt your sincerity, to the degree that they do not feel you believe in the validity of your ideas, they will discount them and consider your speech a windy waste of time.

KNOWLEDGE AND INTELLIGENCE. Audiences prefer to listen to speeches by those whom they believe to be better informed than themselves on the subject in question. Your classmates will not be the exception. They will not be pleased with speeches which they themselves could have given on a half hour's notice. They will expect you to bring new information and to interpret your facts with intelligence and discernment.

GOOD WILL. If you are to be effective, your audience must also believe that you respect them and have their best interests at heart in what you say. A politician with a long record of hostility to public education would not be heard with patience by the National Education Association, no matter how accurately or intelligently he might present a case to show that additional taxes should not be levied to raise teachers' salaries. A student who does not respect his classmates because they know less than he about physics, or law, or religion, or modern art will soon find that they react to him with

Ethos is the combination of integrity, intelligence, and good will which reflects human concern, creates trust, and results in ethical persuasion.

equal contempt. He will not easily persuade them to learn more about his specialty.

Your good will toward your listeners is in part in what you say — your awareness of their attitudes and beliefs. You cannot change those attitudes unless you show that you understand them and respect the right of your listeners to hold them. But in part your good will is reflected in non-verbal ways as well. Do you appear brash and over-confident? Or do you pretend to a humility unbecoming one who presumes to be a leader? Are you friendly — or aggressive? Even your dress and grooming will be interpreted by your listeners as reflecting your attitude toward them. In the intimate atmosphere of the classroom the impressions you create in these matters are cumulative. Good or bad, they will be much stronger at the end of the course than at the beginning.

Your Assignments and Responsibilities: Speaking

The specific nature of assignments and responsibilities will be determined by your instructor and adapted to individual and class needs. But the main activity of the class will be speaking. Some assignments may involve group discussion or committee activity. You may be asked to read aloud to improve the flexibility of your voice or to develop your skill in interpreting the ideas of others. Some speeches will be short, some long; some will involve major research, and some may be presented impromptu to teach you to think on your feet or to develop delivery skills. The important thing is that you try to master each new speaking skill as you are introduced to it, and then to build on that foundation a sound structure of additional skills. In this way your growth as a speaker will be continuous and you will minimize the tensions which are inevitably associated with adjustment to new situations.

LANGUAGE AND THOUGHT

If the way in which men express their thoughts is slipshod and mean, it will be very difficult for their thoughts themselves to escape being the same. If it is high flown and bombastic, a character for natural simplicity and truthfulness cannot long be maintained.

— HENRY ALFORD

Your instructor may ask you to present an outline for each speech as evidence of your preparation to speak. The form and extent of this evidence will vary with the type of speech and the wishes of your instructor. Whatever form it takes, your outline helps your instructor evaluate your work by giving him some insight into the nature of your preparation. But it is even more important to you, for it places you under strong compulsion to think and to evaluate your thoughts before you attempt to speak.

Your Assignments and Responsibilities: Listening

As a listener in your speech class you have a dual responsibility. You are, first of all, a member of the audience which makes possible a speaking situation. Secondly, you are an assistant to your instructor as an evaluator and critic of the speeches of your classmates.

Your Role as Audience

Be present. Regardless of whether your instructor has a policy of enforcing attendance, you have a responsibility to your classmates to furnish them with the same audience you yourself need to do your best speaking. It is dispiriting to a speaker to see empty spaces where his classmates should be. Neither he nor you can do the best speaking in the absence of an audience.

Give courteous attention. At a later stage in his development as a speaker a student may profit from being subjected to inattention or heckling. But few beginning speakers can cope with the problem of disciplining an audience and compelling them to listen. Even if a classmate gives a bad speech, give him courteous attention. Do not doodle — or knit. If you wish to take a few notes, do so inconspicuously. Remember that even a good speaker may be disconcerted by looking around the room and seeing nothing but the tops of heads.

Try to understand and evaluate. Start with the expectation that the speaker will say something worth listening to. As you listen, try to determine what his central idea is. Let it stimulate your own thinking for or against his point of view, but do not daydream. Even if you find the speech dull or lacking in merit, you will profit from analyzing the reasons for its failure and resolving not to repeat the mistakes when your turn comes.

Respond freely. Do not establish classroom barriers to response. If you wish to applaud, do so. If the speech is funny, laugh. Except for a verbal reply, react as you would in conversation.

Your Role as Critic

Evaluate the speech as a whole. Recall the subtitle of this book, *Idea and Delivery.* Because matters of delivery, grammar, and mechanics of speech are more obvious and easier to isolate, it is easy to forget that the purpose of speaking is to communicate an idea. The idea and its development are central and should be analyzed fully in the criticisms offered.

Evaluate constructively. Probably no speech given in your class will be wholly bad. Recognize this, and give encouragement to the speaker by pointing out his strength as well as his weakness. On the other hand, even constructive criticism must sometimes tear down. Where weakness exists, point it out clearly and suggest how it may be remedied.

Concentrate on the immediate assignment. In your criticism, ask whether the speaker succeeded in demonstrating skills which were emphasized in the assignment. Did he do so without sacrificing those stressed earlier? Do not emphasize failures in matters not yet discussed in class even though you are aware of them.

Profit from the mistakes of others. Other things being equal, it is fair to expect those who speak on the fourth day of a round of speeches to do better than those who speak on the first day. If you have been an effective critic of others, you should not make the same mistakes yourself when your turn comes.

Learn to apply your critical skills outside class. When you have finished the work of this course, you ought to be able to listen to the speeches of lecturers, preachers, politicians, and community leaders with greater appreciation and greater objectivity. You should listen to a good speech for its artistic excellence as well as for the worth of its ideas. You should be better able to analyze windy nonsense for what it is. Your training in critical evaluation of the speeches given in class should help you to recognize ideas which are accurately stated, adequately supported, and clearly reasoned. In short, you should be better able to exercise the functions of good citizenship.

To help you develop critical skill, we have phrased many of our chapter summaries in the form of advice to the critic. Read these carefully before any speeches are given, and review the earlier suggestions as the course progresses. At the end of the semester you will have a critical framework for evaluating your classmates' speeches, your own, and those heard off-campus and in later life.

Working With Your Instructor

Your instructor's ability to help you, and your ability to receive help, depend upon your recognition of a basic fact: he is seeking not only to present you with a body of facts and principles but also to start you out in the learning of an art. A teacher of history, Spanish, or physics deals with a specific subject matter; your speech instructor has, in a sense, a more complex problem, for his subject matter is you. Yet he will not trespass upon your innate personal dignity, your beliefs, or your basic personality. They are yours, and your instructor will be neither a puppeteer nor a pseudo-psychiatrist. Rather, his chief desire is to help you become what you are to the fullest extent. These responsibilities he can better discharge if you work with him willingly and cooperatively. Do not feel personally affronted if, on occasion, he seems to take an unenthusiastic view of your efforts. Accept his criticism and his help in the spirit in which he gives it; the only thing he wants is to make you a more effective speaker. He will criticize you and others, not to make all of you speak like him, but to speak well within the context of your individual characteristics and potentialities. This is his job. If you help him do it well, you will receive much benefit.

Communication: The Goal of Speaking

There are many different kinds of speaking situations. Some are informal, as in conversation, or in a parent's reading *The Three Bears* to his children. Some are partly structured, as in a planned group discussion. Still others are of a more formal type, as in the oral interpretation of poetry or public speaking. In each of these situations, the speaker's purpose may vary. Sometimes he may seek to inform his listeners, sometimes to persuade or entertain. But whatever the structure of the group or the speaker's purpose, every speaking situation is an effort on the part of one human being to communicate his thoughts or feelings to others.

The Nature of Communication

We believe that you and our society need skills, not in exhibitory speech but in *communicative speech* — in the sense that *communication is a process of recreating or establishing in another person's thinking those ideas which you want him to have in common with you.* The term "idea," as used at this point, is to be taken broadly. We have in mind *items of information* as well as *opinions, feelings,* and *beliefs.*

In communicating, that is, in establishing your ideas with other people, you must make those ideas *interesting* (deserving of attention), *clear,* and *believable.* As a simple illustration of how these

Communication is easy for the quarterback who has a ready-made audience which is attentive, able to understand, and predisposed to accept.

qualities operate to make ideas communicable, consider the huddle of a football team during the quarterback's call of the signal for the next play. Let us say that he names "one-A-six," which may be a fullback spinner off left tackle. In making this call, the quarterback is assured of the presence of the three necessary elements of communication. In the first place, he has *attention*. All members of the team want to know the call. The huddle is closed and compact. He is heard, or if he is not heard, any member missing the call will be sure to ask him to repeat it. What the quarterback has to say is "interesting" and he has undivided attention. *Attention (the result of interest) is a primary need in any attempt to communicate.* In the second place, the quarterback's meaning is *clear*. The team, trained and drilled, fully understands the call. Every man, upon hearing the words "one-A-six," knows the play it calls for, and knows his individual responsibility. There is no confusion, no lack of clarity in meaning which could prevent complete communication. *Understandability (clarity of meaning) is a second essential to communication.* Third, and last, because the team is disciplined and the quarterback is in a position of responsibility and authority, his decision is *accepted* and its worth *believed*. In the twenty-five seconds a team has to get the ball into play, there is no time for a roundtable discussion. All the players, being limited in time and having the common goal of victory, will want to believe that what their chief strategist calls for is best and will work. *Believability, then, is the last essential to communication.*

Communication is relatively simple for the quarterback in the huddle situation. He has a ready-made audience which is attentive, able to understand, and predisposed to believe or accept.

COMMUNICATION AND SPEECH PURPOSE. Let us, however, look ahead in this class to some occasion on which you may speak about the automatic transmission on one of the current new cars. Obviously, your speaking situation will be more complex than the quarterback's because you will have to work to create the elements of communication, whereas in the situation he faced they were already present. The elements can be named with equal simplicity: you will want your ideas to be interesting, clear, and believable no matter what may be your broad purpose in speaking. But as your purpose changes, these elements will vary in importance to you and to your speech. If your main purpose is to have your audience understand *how* such a transmission operates, yours may be called *a speech to inform,* and you will be mainly concerned with clarity. But one can be clear without being listened to or believed. Thus your total communicative responsibility in a speech

A TWO-WAY PROCESS . . .

Communication requires interchange between speaker and audience. Both have a responsibility. It is not difficult to see which speaker and which audience is doing its part.

to inform is to be clear in a manner which is also interesting and believable. On the other hand, your purpose may be to have each listener believe that he should buy the new Futuramobile because of its fine automatic transmission. If so, you are making *a speech to persuade* — or as some prefer to call it, a speech *to convince.* Your communicative responsibility is then to make your ideas believable or acceptable to your hearers, and this you can hardly do if your hearers are inattentive or do not understand. Again, your purpose might be *to entertain* your hearers with a light speech on the frightening complexities or "gimmicks" of the new transmission. Thus you will need most of all to be interesting, and the interest may rest solely in the facetious clarity and believability of your ideas. In short, *you may do communicative speaking for many purposes: to inform, to persuade or convince, to stimulate or inspire, or to entertain.* Yet none of the larger ends can be achieved unless your communicative means are interesting, clear, and believable.

A Plan for Developing Communicative Skill

During the coming weeks you will be trying with the help of your instructor and your classmates to develop your communicative skill. To aid you in this, we have organized this book around the five objectives listed below. You will note that the first three deal largely with ideas and their forms, which are the substance of good speech; that the fourth is concerned with delivery, the audible and visible format of speech; and that the fifth seeks to aid you in applying your skill to specialized forms of communication.

Thus you will want the skills which enable you to:

1. Discover ideas which can be developed from your own experience, personal investigation, and research reading.
2. Direct your ideas to a specific audience by selecting clear, interesting, and believable materials, and adapting them to the responses of your listeners.
3. Organize or arrange ideas for maximum speech effectiveness, and word them in a style which has simplicity and energy.
4. Present ideas to audiences in a manner which helps communication by the effective use of voice and body.
5. Adapt each of these skills to the special needs of group discussion and oral reading.

Throughout the book we shall seldom tell you what *not* to do, preferring to put the emphasis on positive techniques. But one word of caution is in order: Do not be concerned too early with exact or absolute rules. Consider a sport such as golf. The unfortunate penalty for driving a ball out of bounds is two strokes — especially if your opponent is watching and is inclined to enforce the rules. Yet merely avoiding an infraction or penalty does not lead to skill in any sport; one might conceivably nudge the ball around the course with a tablespoon and never go out of bounds. Clearly the pursuit of rules as ends in themselves leads to no mastery of the game. Rather, it is the application of skills, such as a free swing and follow through, which produces competence. These skills are the legitimate means whose mastery leads to the ultimate objective. Similarly, in speaking, your energies should be positively directed toward the skills which you must employ to gain your purpose of communication.

While you are acquiring the ability to organize ideas, to support your points, and to deliver your speech with the rhetorical equivalent of the free swing and the follow through, you must remember that your central purpose is communication. You are dealing with dynamic ideas and living people, not with static words and inanimate objects, or with absolute rules. You are truly communicative only when you think as you speak. Thus you use your voice and your body to deliver an idea, and your mind to make both idea and delivery fit the interests, knowledge, and attitudes of the people who are listening to you.

A Point of View About Speech

We began this chapter by suggesting that effective speech serves both a public and a private good. Most of the chapter has dealt with private values. But a moment's reflection will tell you that a democratic government does not work well without able spokesmen for both sides of controversial issues. Ours is a government by talk, from grass roots discussion groups to mass meetings in Hollywood Bowl or Madison Square Garden. We make decisions in collective bargaining conferences by talk; we select our representatives on the basis of their stated views on issues; juries confine or release prisoners after listening to speeches by attorneys. Can you imagine Abraham Lincoln attaining national leadership without his skill in debate? In what way might your life be different at this moment if Winston Churchill and Franklin D. Roosevelt had not been able to speak in critical days the words their nations could believe and follow? Every citizen of a democratic state has a stake in maintaining freedom of speech and making it work by developing his ability to contribute to the intelligent discussion of public issues.

To be sure, as we have said, your speech class is but a small segment of a broader society. In it there may be no occasion for speeches of world import. But it doubtless will have in it young men and women of integrity and sincerity, of force of character, coupled with a moving and communicative directness of speech, who will favorably affect the behavior of the whole group and who will give it leadership toward goals of value to the class, the school, and the community.

This much we have said about the public values of skills in speech on the assumption that those skills would be ethically used by honest men. Unfortunately, as we all know, this is not always true. As there have been skilled technicians dedicated to safecracking, so also there have been dishonest and unethical speakers of great talent. The problem is in the speaker and not in speech-making, as Aristotle pointed out centuries ago. Unfortunately, the skilled charlatans cannot be quickly reformed. Saints cannot be made eloquent and sinners mute by legislation. Rather, in a free society speech should be free and the auditors discriminating. Persons whose ideas have merit will, we all hope, acquire skill in public speech. Those whose ideas do harm should lose their effectiveness, not by being muzzled but by being faced with audiences immunized against their blandishments. Better still, it may be hoped that ethical education will decrease the number of speakers with dishonest methods and harmful ideas. Perhaps in your own class you may find a student whose

---

TWO VIEWS OF THE VALUE OF CONTROVERSY

Whoever is afraid of submitting any question, civil or religious, to the test of free discussion, is more in love with his own opinion than with truth.

— THOMAS WATSON

Where all think alike, no one thinks very much.

— WALTER LIPPMANN

A PUBLIC GOOD . . .

Effective speech serves not only a private good. Consider the impact of these public speakers on national and international affairs. The free world owes much to their dedication and skill.

method mirrors some national specialist in irresponsible speech and bogus supporting material. Do not be impressed; if possible, reform him.

Your class is set up as a learning situation, yet you should not think of your speeches as mechanical exercises. When it is your turn, be well prepared, know the response you want, and speak to win it — just as others will seek to win responses and approval from you. In it all, keep your dual responsibilities clearly in mind — to plan carefully for your own speeches and to listen attentively to those of your classmates. Thus you have, while still a student, a balance between learning and doing. You are, in part, an intellectually subsidized member of society; in part you are a free member of society, moving within it and having an impact on it even while a student of speech. We urge you to believe that your progress in the class and your personal gain from it will be enhanced if you regard your work not merely as so many assignments enforced by your instructor and this text, but as part of a genuine speaker-audience situation created under favorable laboratory conditions for the study and mastery of the skills of communication.

2 THE SPEAKER AND HIS SUBJECT:

Basic Concepts in Speech Preparation

The more personal knowledge you have about the subject for a speech, the more likely is the audience to accept your idea.

DURING THE NEXT FEW MONTHS in this class you will deliver six or eight prepared speeches as well as several impromptu ones. Beyond this you will hear between one hundred and two hundred talks by your fellow students. Many of these, let us hope all, will be pleasant and satisfying for both the speaker and the listener. If some are empty or tiresome, it will be a challenge to your instructor, to the speaker, and to the members of the class to discover the reasons for failure and to seek ways of improving later efforts. Sometimes speeches are unsatisfactory because the speaker obviously has nothing to say. Sometimes they are dull because of poor planning and inadequate preparation for speaking. Sometimes the speaker does not quite understand the nature of oral communication and is unable to speak directly and confidently to an audience. Several of these barriers to effective speaking will disappear when you know how to answer these questions:

1. Where can I find the materials from which to choose subjects for speeches?
2. How can I develop these subjects into good speeches?

3. How can I create and maintain a communicative relationship with my audience in the delivery of these speeches?

To the first two questions, this chapter offers some preliminary answers, while Chapter 3 will make some initial suggestions to help you with the beginner's problems in delivery. Later chapters will deal with these questions in depth.

Choosing a Subject

The best speeches are not born in an hour or two of preparation the night before a speech is to be given. Although a number of truly great speeches, like Webster's *Reply to Hayne,* have been given on relatively short notice, they were not the product of the moment. Webster spoke the day after Hayne had addressed the Senate, but the material of the speech represented his whole philosophy of government, developed not overnight but from a lifetime of experience and deliberation. The actual preparation time which Lincoln gave to the *Gettysburg Address* has been grossly misrepresented in fiction and legend. But even if it were true that he scrawled it on the back of an old envelope as he traveled to Gettysburg, the ideas of the speech were the product of three years of soul-searching meditation on the meaning of the war between the states. Each of these speeches was the inevitable product of a lifetime of experience adapted to a specific occasion and audience.

Full-Time Thinking

Like any other worth-while idea, a great speech is the *product* of what has been informally called "full-time thinking." Full-time thinking is easy to define, but not so easy to do. It is responding to experience thoughtfully, relating new facts and ideas to old, seeing relationships — in short, being aware, and using time rather than wasting it. It is the habit of thinking now rather than waiting until later. The full-time thinker turns an assignment over in his mind even when he is not formally working on it, with the result that facts and ideas begin to cluster about his subject like filings around a magnet. A ten-minute streetcar ride may provide a dozen illustrations and comments for a speech on advertising (or on Christmas, social inequality, or any of a dozen other topics). A walk across campus may yield a telling paragraph on fraternities, college politics, student-faculty relations, or the habits of squirrels. The full-time thinker keeps his eyes and his mind open, and he uses bits and scraps of time. When he sits at his desk "to work" he is thus many steps ahead of the game.

The full-time thinker also learns to distinguish between productive thought and the false coin of reverie, pipe-dreams, and wool-gathering. Real thinking is hard work, whereas reverie is fatally pleasant and so becomes a favorite refuge when problems get too difficult. In reverie, the free association of ideas which float and veer with every mental breeze and tide, we can make ourselves as brilliant and the world as pleasant as we like. It is all too easy to let the mind slip off a difficult problem onto something more or less allied — from that to something else, and so on, until we are a thousand mental miles from the job at hand, time has fled, and nothing has been done. The unwary can be deceived that this pleasant occupation is thinking, and it is, of a sort; but it accomplishes nothing, and the full-time thinker sees it for what it is.

Full-time thinking can help to relieve you of one anxiety which many students feel, that they have nothing to say that is worth saying. It can also help you to recognize what is worth saying. Few students ever have a subject or a body of information which is original, in the strict sense, to base a speech on. Many contribute the originality of their own conclusions, observations, and organization, and the excitement they have felt upon thinking a thing through for themselves. If you are to find and develop ideas which will be interesting to you and to others, it is important to know what originality is, how far you can hope to attain it, and how to recognize it when you see it.

True originality of fact or idea is rare. Only one man in the world's history wrote *Hamlet,* discovered penicillin, or formulated the law of gravity. Somewhat more frequently, two or more minds, working with the ideas and information available in their time, reach similar conclusions independently. It is probable that many men discovered the use of fire and invented the wheel, and each was original if not unique. The most striking case of simultaneous discovery on record involved two scientists. In 1858, one year before Darwin was ready to publish the theory of evolution we associate with his name, he received a communication from Alfred Russel Wallace setting forth exactly the same theory. Neither had known the trend of the other's thought. Both were original and brilliant thinkers, though Wallace reached a tentative conclusion on rather slight evidence, whereas Darwin had worked for years and built up a mass of supporting fact.

Humbler ranges of originality are within the scope of all. A student is always "discovering" facts previously unknown to himself, and often to his listeners. Suppose you are the only student in your class who has visited Yosemite National Park. Your experience is hardly original, but it is unique in the group. You then have an excellent chance to portray the majestic grandeur of Halfdome or the exciting man-made spectacle of the nightly "firefall" from a cliff high over the valley, and your portrayal may recreate in your hearers some of the feelings you experienced during your visit to the Park. In this sense you can be original, for your subject is new to your listeners, and no one can ever duplicate exactly your experience.

The whole process of your education consists of adding to your stock of information, and of learning to interpret facts in reasonable relationship to each other. In a limited sense, each time you take a new idea from observation, conversation, or reading, and incorporate it into the pattern of your thinking, you are being original. In a fuller degree, you are originating ideas when you think them out for yourself, even though you later discover that they are truths that walk the street. And of course, you may always hope to reach that high level of creativity in which you develop for the first time in history an idea which fits the needs of the society of which you are a part. But such attainment is for the few. Be content if ideas grow and develop in your mind as you perform experiments in the laboratory, read in the library, listen to professors, or engage in seminars or "bull sessions" with fellow students. Even though you do not originate them, ideas become your own to the extent that you combine and interrelate experiences in a growing pattern of thought. Perhaps this is what Voltaire meant when he wrote: "Ideas are like beards; men do not have them until they

ON ORIGINALITY

A good book is a Damascus blade made by the welding of old nails and horseshoes. Everything has seen service, and has been proved by wear and tear in the world for centuries, and yet now the article is brand new.

— RALPH WALDO EMERSON

grow up." When such ideas develop, you will want to speak. And all the thinking you have done will make speaking easier.

Sources of Ideas

In your first speeches you will discover that the subjects on which you talk best are those with which you have a personal identification and which grow out of your interests, knowledge, and experience. Thus if you are to find and develop your best subjects, you must explore the "raw materials" of your own experiences, attitudes, and beliefs, your special knowledge and particular interests, with the eagerness of a prospector and the accuracy of a surveyor. But there is no reason why your interests, knowledge, and experience must remain as they now are. For like the prospector who has removed all the valuable ore from one claim and moves on to new territory, you must continually seek to enlarge the breadth and depth of your own experience if your speeches are to reflect a maturing mind. Specifically, this means that the materials for the speeches you deliver during the term will be drawn from three major sources:

1. What you already know.
2. What you can learn in the next few months by general reading and observation.
3. What you can discover by specific research on a subject which interests you.

We suggest that you begin your speaking with what you already know, or with what you can readily discover by personal investigation. In Chapter 4, we will discuss in more detail the process of patient research designed to permit you to speak with authority in new areas.

A Plan For Preparing Speeches

You will save yourself time and energy if you have an orderly procedure to follow as you begin the preparation of your speeches. For your first speeches we recommend this four-step plan:

1. Determine your purpose in speaking.
2. Evaluate your present knowledge and compare it with what you think your audience knows or believes about your subject.
3. Test your ideas in conversation with as many people as you

can get to listen. Discard weak points or support them more fully. Alter your purpose if necessary.

4. Organize your material in outline form.

If you follow this procedure, you will discover that personal materials can be made into interesting and profitable speeches. Although you will need to add new steps to the plan in later speeches based upon specific research, no steps will be discarded. These four points will therefore be useful to you in every speech you prepare.

Determining Your Purpose in Speaking

You cannot speak intelligently to any audience unless you have a purpose in doing so. For each classroom assignment, your instructor will ask you to work toward some specific goal in your development as a speaker. Beyond this, you need to ask whether the things you plan to say are worth saying. Why speak at all? It is not enough to answer that you are fulfilling an assignment. Do you wish to convey information to an audience? If so, for what purpose? Of what use is the information? Is it genuine "news" to your listeners? Perhaps you wish to convince the audience of the truth of an idea. A worthy goal, but is there any good reason why others should think or feel as you do? Do you wish to stimulate or to entertain your hearers? If so, do the occasion and the mood of the audience justify such use of speaking time? Clearly it is not enough to know that you seek one of the general ends of speech: to inform, to convince, to stimulate, or to entertain. You should not speak unless you can give an intelligent and highly specific reply to a simple purpose question: Why am *I* speaking on *this subject* to *this audience?* A sound answer will give you self-confidence by justifying your belief that your remarks are worth the time of your hearers.

SPEAKER AND SUBJECT: "Why am *I* speaking on *this subject . . . ?*" The beginning speaker tends to assume that what he already knows is "not good enough" to be used in a speech. So he hurries to the library for the latest issue of a current magazine, hastily gobbles down the content of one article, and then stands before his classmates and recites facts and opinions he hardly understands himself. The student who is guilty of this kind of preparation does not have a right to speak. We do not, of course, oppose library research, but the procedure we have just described is neither good research nor good speaking. For one thing, it leaves the "I" entirely out of the performance. The student who prepares in this way can contribute nothing to the speech except a voice. His own experience is by-passed. Since he has not thought through the problem for himself, he cannot speak with any confidence that the material he parrots is worth the time the audience must give. He would do better to stand before the group and say, "My speech for today is found in the September issue of the *Reader's Digest,* beginning on the first page. I enjoyed reading the article and I think you would too," and having said this, sit down. Most listeners would rather read the article for themselves than listen to a weak paraphrase of it.

If the members of the audience could hear the author of the article himself, their reaction would be quite different. The speaker would then be talking about his own experience or personal research, and would be fully identified with his subject. From his own knowledge and reflection, he could attest the accuracy and validity of his ideas. The importance of this identification of the speaker with his subject is clearest when the speaker is a person with unusual knowledge or personal qualifications. No one can speak with such authority on the first solo flight across the Atlantic as Charles A. Lindbergh. The chief United States delegate to the United Nations is the best person to talk on what it is like to argue with the Russian representative. The more personal authority and experience the speaker brings to his subject the more effective he will be with most audiences.

What, then, of you, at age nineteen, with no Atlantic flight behind you and no encounters at the United Nations? Must you be forever silent because you have never "really lived"? Not at all, for in the act of surviving for nearly two decades, and having sufficient intelligence to gain admission to college, you have had experiences, acquired insights, developed attitudes, and learned skills about which you can speak well. Where have you been, for example, and what have you seen which might be of interest to others? What interesting people have you known? What attitudes and convictions move you deeply? What skills or unusual interests are you able to explain to your classmates? Each of these questions should suggest subjects on which you might speak with assurance. If you develop them with imagination and insight, you will have no difficulty with the first element of our preliminary purpose question, the fitness of the speaker to talk on the subject.

Subject and Audience *". . . on this subject to this audience?"* Even though you are sure the subject is right for you to talk on, you must still consider its suitability for your particular audience. When you speak, you and the audience enter into a tacit contract, the one to say something worth hearing, the other to give courteous attention. If you fulfill your obligation, most listeners will meet theirs. In order to carry out your share of the compact, however, you must make the audience a factor in determining your purpose. What elements in your subject are naturally interesting to the people who comprise your audience? To what extent do the factors which caused you to select the subject operate among your hearers? Do you have any personal prestige on this subject with this audience? Questions such as these are part of a preliminary evaluation, and your answers to them are only tentative. Nevertheless, at the stage of preparation when you are considering purpose, they are necessary approaches to the basic question: Why am I speaking on this subject to this audience?

Phrasing a Purpose Statement. Your answer to the purpose question can usually be incorporated in one or two sentences, or at the most a short paragraph. Here are some typical purpose statements:

Subject: Kansas Wheat Harvest
Audience: Students of an eastern university
Purpose: To explain the operation of a harvest combine to students whose experience is largely in the city. I am qualified to speak because I spent a summer working as a harvest hand.

Subject: Direct Election of the President
Audience: Students of a southern university
Purpose: To show southern students that their influence in national affairs would be diminished by direct election of the President. I am qualified to speak by detailed reading from many sources, and by personal interviews with my Senator and Representative.

These statements are not intended to provide a rigid form for your purpose sentences, but they may suggest ways of framing your ideas, both for personal speeches and for those based on specific research. Notice that in each statement the speaker, the subject, and the audience are given a place. Not until these three factors are included is your purpose statement complete.

Evaluating Your Present Knowledge

Phrasing your purpose statement is the first step in preparing a speech. But do not think of this preliminary statement as necessarily final. You may need to modify it after you have developed the possibilities of the subject. Your next step should be to take an inventory of your present information and beliefs on the subject of your choice. A simple listing of topic headings is a good beginning. What facts and opinions now in your possession are relevant to your purpose? At first you do not need to organize these into any particular system. You may even list some topics which do not at the moment seem particularly important. Get them down on paper and it will be easier to evaluate them.

Having made as exhaustive a list as possible, return to the preliminary analysis of the audience which you made when you first stated your purpose. By exploring this analysis further, you can determine whether you should speak on this subject to this audience at all. If you decide that you should, you may then determine the focus of your talk and the points which should be developed.

Let us suppose that you belong to a hiking club which visited the Mount Rushmore Memorial in the Black Hills of South Dakota. It should be obvious at once that a speech to your fellow hikers describing the visit would be unprofitable. You probably have nothing to say which each member of the audience could not report as well as you. But if you are obligated to speak to them on this subject you must extend your resources, perhaps by learning more about the Memorial. Who conceived the idea for this gigantic sculpture? How did the sculptor happen to choose the heads of these particular four Presidents, Washington, Lincoln, Jefferson, and Theodore Roosevelt? How was the project financed? What problems were overcome to execute the sculptures? If you know the answers and you are reasonably sure the other members of the club do not, you can profitably speak to your fellow hikers. On the other hand, an audience of school children who have never seen the Memorial might appreciate a descriptive treatment of what you saw and did.

The background details, so essential in a speech to your fellow hikers, would not be needed in a short talk to a group of school children. Basically, what we are saying is that you must know more than your audience about your subject, or more accurately, that you must know things about it which they do not.

For any speech, a careful estimate of the interests and knowledge of the audience will help to determine the focus of your idea. You may find, for example, that your hearers live in a very different sort of world from the one you wish to talk about. Under some circumstances, this is a real asset to the speaker. If you talk about the mountains to plainsmen, the sea to inlanders, or the prairie to city dwellers, the novelty of the contrast with their typical experience may furnish a theme which can be used profitably to develop an entire speech. These differences between audience and speaker may help you make your idea clear and interesting.

Often, however, there may be differences between speaker and audience which are barriers to communication. Perhaps you know so much about the subject that you forget how little the audience knows. You must rid yourself of technical vocabulary and verbal shortcuts if you want to make ideas clear to a non-technical audience. Or perhaps your beliefs contradict those of your hearers. If you are a Young Republican talking to a Young Democratic Club, you must deal with your political convictions in a very different way than if you were speaking to your fellow partisans. Instead of soliciting active support for Republican candidates, you need to seek more limited ends of tolerance and understanding for the goals your party seeks. The difference in purpose will modify both your central idea and the materials selected to make it clear and believable.

When you have determined what items are most likely to be effective with your audience, begin to arrange them in an order suitable for presentation. Some statements will immediately appear to be less important than others. Perhaps these may be treated as sub-points. Eventually you may emerge with three or four major points and numerous minor ones. Some of your original items may be eliminated as not relevant to your purpose, or as duplicating others. You should not regard this as a finished outline, however, for you need to test the validity of your analysis before you complete your preparation. One of the best ways of checking your thinking is by discussing your idea informally with your friends.

FINDING A SUBJECT . . .

Good subjects lie all around you, in things you see and do. Travel, an interesting job, a hobby, sports, the vast world of books — all can supply you with material for interesting speeches.

Testing Ideas in Conversation

"I rough out my thoughts in talk as an artist models in clay," wrote Oliver Wendell Holmes in *The Autocrat of the Breakfast Table.* "Spoken language is so plastic, — you can pat and coax, and spread and shave, and rub out and fill up, and stick on so easily, when you work that soft material, that there is nothing like it for modelling." Many beginning speakers fail completely to take advantage of the plastic nature of conversation. They make outlines, or write out speeches, and then practice them in private or impose them on their friends or families in what they imagine is finished form. This is not an efficient way to prepare a speech. A better way is to test your ideas in conversation with as many different people as will listen, preferably people with varied backgrounds.

Testing through conversation has several specific values. It makes you realize that giving a speech is a two-way process. Unless you put an audience to sleep, your hearers respond actively while you talk. They smile or frown, sit erect or fidget, applaud or sit on their hands. Preparation through conversation will help you anticipate these reactions and modify your speech by adjusting to them. These overt signs are indications of the thoughts your hearers are having as you speak. In the conversational situation, these responses will be openly voiced. If your listener does not understand, he will tell you so. You will then rephrase the concept, if necessary several times, until you have made it clear. If he thinks the idea is foolish or illogical, his spoken objections will give you a chance to defend your point. When you cannot do so, you will certainly revise or discard that portion of your material before you make the speech.

This picture was taken during a student conference on the United Nations. Is this a speech or a conversation? Do you think this speaker will be effective with a larger audience?

If your hearer agrees with you in conversation, his approval will give you confidence when you speak to a full audience. It is also possible that the conversational listener may have ideas on the subject himself, some of which would greatly improve your speech. You will therefore do well to turn listener yourself and borrow from the other person's fund of information. When you have done this with several people, you will have a better rounded speech than you started with. Of course you may also acquire some misinformation, and it is usually wise to check "facts" given you in conversation against reputable published sources. Nevertheless, your chances of enriching your speech by this process are good.

Planning the Final Outline

When you have tested ideas by discussing them informally with friends, you will be in a position to prepare the final outline from which to speak. In Chapter 6 we will discuss speech organization in detail. For the present, it is enough if your outline shows clearly the relationships among the ideas in your speech. In addition it should contain a clear and definite introduction of your idea, and an equally unmistakable conclusion. Write out your opening and closing sentences in full, even though you may change the phrasing at the actual moment of delivery. Thus you will not be at a loss for words at the beginning, or be left in the unenviable position of being unable to stop when your idea is exhausted. Usually your opening remarks in these early speeches should state the subject of your speech and predict its central theme. The wording should be easy and informal, not stereotyped. Do not say: "My subject for today is Yosemite National Park." Rather begin, "In the past three years I have visited eight national parks. Those of you who have seen any of them know that each park has its own special beauty and point of unusual interest. To my eyes, though, none is quite equal to Yosemite Valley." Or you may wish to begin the development of your idea with a narrative or descriptive section out of which your theme emerges. If you do this, however, be sure you do it purposefully. If the opening narrative does not make clear the nature of your central idea, you may only succeed in concealing it forever.

The conclusion to the speech should restate the central theme in such a way that your audience will remember it easily. Your hearers should recognize it as a conclusion without your telling them so.

Your instructor may ask you to submit a detailed preparation outline before you begin to speak. Or he may require it a day or two in advance. Either way, this outline is the evidence of your preparation, and it will enable your instructor to suggest more clearly how you may improve your next speech. The outline may be quite different from the notes you use while speaking (see pages 137–144). Moreover, you should not feel that the outline you hand in commits you irrevocably to the precise form which your speech must take. Often something in the speaking situation or the reaction of your audience will suggest variations from your plan which would make your speech more appropriate to the time and circumstance. If what you say makes sense, your instructor will not penalize you because it varies from your prepared outline.

The following format is suitable for the preparation outline for your first speech:

Subject:
Audience:
Purpose:

Outline

Introduction
    I. Opening sentence
    II. Outline of narrative or descriptive opening if used
    III. Statement of central theme if not included in opening sentence

Body
    I. First main point
      A.
      B. (etc.)
    II. Second main point (etc.)

Conclusion
    Restatement of central theme in a complete sentence

First Speeches: Your Own Experience

In earlier pages we suggested that every college student has at his disposal a fund of information which, when properly developed, can make interesting and stimulating speeches. No doubt many such ideas have already occurred to you. Still, it may be helpful to explore here some specific areas in which we believe you will find subjects of value to be developed either with knowledge you already have or through personal investigation.

Places and Objects

If you are a student at Brooklyn College, you cannot expect to interest your fellow students with a speech on "My Visit to Manhattan," unless something extraordinary occurred on the trip. If you attend Grinnell College in Iowa, a description of the beauty of the Iowa prairie would hardly be new to your classmates. But reverse the situations, and the opportunity for a skillful and imaginative treatment of your experience is much greater. You now have a chance to draw upon the contrasts between the normal experiences of your audience and those which you have had because of your trip or residence in a community unfamiliar to your hearers. It is still possible for you to bore your audience, but if you do, it is because you have not used enough imagination in developing the natural possibilities of your subject.

Objects, like places, derive their interest from both similarities and contrasts. You do not have to be an Edgar Allan Poe or a Jules Verne to find subject matter in the unusual. A university student in a freshman composition course once caught up the professor's favorite simile, "dull as ditchwater," and wrote a vivid description of the liveliness of "ditchwater" as seen under the revealing eye of the microscope. The unusual may turn out to be merely the unnoticed. On the other hand, you may know about some actual oddity unfamiliar to others in your class. Or you may have seen an unusual work of art, a rare book, or a house of distinctive architecture.

When places or objects are used as speech materials, look for contrasts and similarities between these things and the normal experiences of your audience. Find an early answer to the purpose question: Why am I speaking on *this subject* to *this audience?* Analyze factors which make the place or object unique. By using words which convey sense imagery — sight, sound, smell, touch — you may make a rural audience feel the press of bodies in the Times Square Subway Station at rush hour, or enable a city audience to smell new-mown hay in June or hear the snorting of hogs at feeding time. All these methods will help you make your idea clear and interesting to your listeners.

We have been discussing places and objects as speech subjects in themselves. A more common use of such materials in speeches is as support for a broader theme. Thus in a speech on city planning, you might state that there is no reason why a city waterfront must be ugly. To establish the truth of this statement, you could describe Chicago's lake shore as you saw it on your last visit to the city, or explain the change made by city planners in "the point" at Pittsburgh. In a sermon on the text, "Ye are the salt of the earth," Henry Van Dyke began by describing the properties of salt, such as its use for preservation and flavor. The body of his speech was the application of these properties to the qualities of Christian living. There are, of course, many more ways in which you may use place and object materials in speeches. At this point, your primary task is to learn to develop them clearly and interestingly. You will have no difficulty finding use for them in later assignments.

TYPICAL SUBJECTS

Times Square at Eleven
Paris (or any foreign city)
The Grand Canyon (or any national park)
Fisherman's Wharf in San Francisco
Boston's Charles River
Wisconsin Lake Country
Iowa in June
The Sunset Strip in Los Angeles
Pittsburgh at Night
The Ocean

The Rocky Mountains
The Battlefield of Vicksburg (or another historical spot)
A Rare Shell, Fossil, or Rock
Carving in Driftwood
A Close Look at a Housefly
Skyscraper University
The Shakespeare Folio
A Civil War Carbine
A Chess Set of Unusual Design
The Wright Brothers' First Airplane

Exercises

1. List as many interesting places or objects as you can about which you have personal knowledge. Select three of these for future development. For each of the three, list similarities and contrasts between what you are describing and the normal experiences of your audience. What senses can you appeal to? In what other ways can you make these things vivid to the audience?

2. Could any of these subjects be used as supporting material in developing a speech on a broader theme? What theme? How?
3. Prepare a five-minute speech about one of the three subjects you have chosen.
   a. Phrase a purpose statement in answer to the question: Why am I speaking on *this subject* to *this audience?* Your purpose may be simply to recreate an experience and share it with your audience, or you may be using place and object material for a broader purpose.
   b. Select details which implement your purpose in the most interesting and stimulating manner possible, utilizing the factors you analyzed in Exercise 1.

People

For many years a national magazine has carried a series of articles entitled, "The Most Unforgettable Character I've Met." Sometimes these character sketches have revealed warm humanity, sometimes droll comedy; occasionally they have stretched credulity. But generally they have been interesting, for nothing is so vital to people as people. The traits of human character revealed by the virtues and frailties of individual men and women offer excellent material to speakers, either as the entire subject matter of short speeches, or as illustrative material in longer ones. Great men like Lincoln are the subjects of endless anecdotes, so that it is frequently impossible to separate the genuine from the spurious.

Speakers need to cultivate the habit of observing the behavior of their fellow men, for direct personal knowledge is a fertile source from which useful illustrations may be derived. Some people go for years and never seem to meet an interesting person. Others can hardly leave their homes without observing some unusual trait of character. Much of the power of such famous speakers as Henry Ward Beecher and William Jennings Bryan lay in their ability to use the experience of ordinary people as illustrations for their speeches. An effective speaker may use such a story to illustrate a trait of character or an attitude toward life, or perhaps as an example of a practice in public life that he is condemning or praising. When Thomas E. Dewey was special prosecutor in New York charged with ferreting out racketeering, he reported regularly to the people of the city by radio on the progress of his campaign. In one of these speeches, he told in simple words the story of two of the racketeers and their victim. The story itself presented a dramatic and frightening picture of the rackets; it had added impact because Dewey knew personally the people he was discussing.

In developing speeches in which you use illustrations about people, the important thing is to highlight the character traits or incidents which make the story important to your purpose. Just as the deft touch of the caricaturist or the portrait painter changes a mere likeness to a character study, so may you emphasize events and traits of character which portray your subject to the audience as you see him. Irrelevant details should be omitted, and significant ones pointed up and enlarged upon to create in the minds of the hearers the picture you wish them to see.

Typical Subjects

The Man Next Door	Life with Mother
A Great Public Speaker	My Kid Sister (or brother)
A Favorite Teacher	A Courteous Bus Driver
My Boss	A "Good Sport" (or a poor loser)
The Most Unpleasant Person I Know	A Celebrity I Know
A Convincing Fictional Villain	A Spendthrift (or a penny pincher)
Life with Father	

Exercises

1. Select three people whose traits have impressed you either favorably or unfavorably. List your impressions of each. List also specific observations or events which gave you each impression. Do any of these people illustrate a general truth which might be used as a speech subject? How could you develop this idea?

2. Select the most interesting person of the three analyzed in Exercise 1 and prepare a five-minute speech about him, or about a general truth which he exemplifies.

   a. Phrase a purpose statement in answer to the question: Why am I speaking on *this subject* to *this audience?*

   b. Organize the speech around the traits he possesses or your impressions of those traits, explaining your impressions by citing examples of his behavior.

Attitudes and Convictions

In junior high school you may have been assigned a speech in an oral English class on the subject, "My Pet Peeve," or something of the sort. If so, this was done to stimulate you to talk with feeling and force. On the junior high school level this end was perhaps achieved. As you have matured, however, there are surely other subjects which have moved you to deeper feelings than the trivial irritation of a "pet peeve." What subjects draw fire in college "bull sessions"? What convictions seem to you to be important enough to defend vigorously in discussions with your family and friends? Since such subjects carry strong personal meaning to you, they can be made into excellent speeches. Bear in mind, however, that mere argument on such subjects is often pointless. If you set out to change the opinion of a friend when you and he both feel strongly, but on opposite sides of a question, you may end by losing both the argument and the friend. Approach such questions without attempting to force your opinions on others. Your goal is solely to win respectful attention to and understanding of your views from those who take opposite positions.

The greatest value in speaking on subjects of this type lies in the probability that if you hold an opinion deeply, you will forget yourself and speak with a confidence and directness you might not show in discussing topics less vital to you. Belief is a strong antidote for fear.

TYPICAL SUBJECTS

Why I Am a Republican (or a Democrat)	Why I Think a Public Official Is a Menace to the Country
Why I Am a Member of the —— Church	What My Family Means to Me Why I Prefer America
Why I Dislike Organized Religion	Why I Dislike Professional Patriots
Why I Prefer the Mountains, Sea, Forest, Prairie, etc.	Why I Read a Specific Magazine or Newspaper
Why I Respect a Public Official	

Exercises

1. Make a list of subjects on which you have strong convictions. Select three of these for development, and write down some of your reasons for your beliefs.
2. Select one of the three subjects for development into a five-minute speech.
   a. Phrase a purpose statement in answer to the question: Why am *I* speaking on *this subject* to *this audience?*
   b. Organize your ideas around not more than three or four main headings. Give examples from your experience or general knowledge to support each heading.

Processes

Do you have some unique knowledge or skill which is potentially interesting to the rest of the class? Are you an expert in some field? A hobby, perhaps? Do you play a musical instrument? Do you understand the intricacies of line play in football? Perhaps you know how to make a traction splint or administer artificial respiration. Have you ever learned how an automobile is built on the assembly line, or how steel is made or fabricated into I-beams or rails? Do you, because of studies in such fields as engineering, chemistry, or home economics, have special knowledge of a technical process or a scientific principle? An affirmative answer to any of these questions can start you on the development of a good speech.

The explanation of processes is an important part of teaching at all levels. It is effective only if you understand the process thoroughly and can give a step by step analysis and demonstration. If you have ever seen an army training film, you know that clear presentation of this kind of material involves both explanation and demonstration, frequently with the actual materials or with charts and pictures to represent them. Simple processes drawn from your daily experience, such as sports and hobbies, may be demonstrated directly. You will need to prepare charts for more complex activities.

Visual materials are valuable aids to understanding in many speeches, but you must be sure to use them effectively. Make certain that any visual materials you use can be seen by persons in the last row. Your study room may be deceptively small, and objects or charts which seem large at home may be quite meaningless beyond the first three rows when you speak. In presenting visual materials to an audience, do not turn your back on your listeners. Stand to one side and keep direct contact with the audience while you explain your chart. If visual materials are carefully prepared to make ideas clear and interesting, they will need a minimum of explanation.

No matter what the process you wish to explain, the essential element is clearness. Analyze the activity to determine the order of details which will make it easiest for your hearers to learn the process quickly. Do not leave out steps obvious to the expert but obscure to the beginner. Explain all technical words as you use them. Summarize your points frequently. If you develop your points clearly, many of your hearers should be able to give a similar explanation of the process when you have finished.

TYPICAL SUBJECTS

Team Play in Basketball
Tomato: Field to Ketchup
Milk Production on the Farm
Building a Barbecue
A Laboratory Experiment in
   Chemistry, Physics, or
   Electronics
Counting Calories: How to Plan
   a Diet

Solving a Complex Puzzle
Rebinding a Book
Tuning a Piano
Footwork in Tennis
The Infield in Baseball
A Tailor-made Bookcase
Logarithms on Lumber: The
   Slide Rule
Overhauling a Sailboat

Exercises

1. Make a list of processes you understand well enough to explain to others. Select two or three you know best, and make a list of technical terms you might use in the explanation. Define them.
2. Select one of the subjects listed in Exercise 1 and plan a five-minute speech explaining it to the class.
   a. Phrase a purpose statement in answer to the question: Why am I speaking on *this subject* to *this audience?*
   b. Open with a clear statement of exactly what the process is, defining terms as you introduce them.
   c. Explain the steps in the process in the order in which they are needed by the learner, using visual materials (objects

or charts and pictures) to make the process clear; define any new terms as you introduce them.

  d. Restate the process as a whole and indicate its importance to your hearers.

Approaching Speaking Through Group Discussion

In a later chapter we discuss in some detail the process of group discussion and analyze its problems and methods. Since discussion is a less formal activity than public speaking, you may wish to work jointly with three or four of your classmates to present a panel discussion as your first speaking assignment. If so, you may wish to read the discussion chapter now.

For an opening assignment, you probably will do better to limit your discussion to the simple sharing of information rather than to attempt the more complex type of problem-solving discussion. For this purpose you may find it possible to use the same four categories we have suggested for first speeches. Here are some suggestions.

TYPICAL SUBJECTS

Places and Objects

The Relative Advantages of the Small Town and the City
The Relative Advantages of the University and the College
What Students Can Gain from Summer Travel in Europe

People

The Characteristics of a Good Teacher
The Traits of Leadership

Attitudes and Convictions

Values and Limitations of the Honor System
The Future of Intercollegiate Athletics
Required Courses in Our College

Processes

What Makes a Good Photographer?
How to Watch a Football Game

Exercises

1. Select a subject on which the members of your group have some differences of opinion.
2. Each member of the group should prepare an outline of his own views within the general framework the group has agreed on. This framework should provide for a planned progression of ideas.
3. Using the panel format (see pages 252–253), present the ideas to the class through the informal exchange of views among the panel members.

Criticizing First Speeches

An important part of every speech course is the opportunity students have to act as critics of their classmates. This process can be immensely valuable to both speakers and critics if it is approached intelligently. As a speaker you can learn to accept criticism and profit from it; as a critic you can see in others the skills you need to emulate, or the errors you need to avoid. In addition, cultivation of the habit of critical listening will help you listen more objectively to speeches given outside the classroom. Here are some general rules for critical analysis which may make the process more valuable.

1. Criticism does not mean annihilation. Remember that your classmates are learners, as you are. They will make mistakes which should be pointed out, but as human beings they will also need encouragement. Totally destructive criticism is harmful both to the person who gives it and the person who receives it.

2. Criticism should include a contribution. Indicate not only what was wrong, but how a specific change would have made the speech more effective. Be specific in pointing out both good and bad features.

3. Direct the major part of your criticism toward the skill with which the speaker met the aims of the particular assignment. For the speeches covered in this assignment, ask these questions:

a. Did the speaker have a clear-cut purpose, suited to himself, his subject, and his audience? Was the subject worth the time given to it? Would changes in purpose or development have made it more worth-while?

b. Was the plan of the speech clear and easy to follow?

4. Remember that you will be evaluated by these standards your-self. Plan your own speech, therefore, to meet the criticisms before they are given. Your progress will be rapid if you meet the require-ments of each assignment in turn.

3 THE SPEAKER AND HIS AUDIENCE:

Basic Concepts in Delivery

A mobile face and a skilled balance of formality and friendliness characterized the speeches of Franklin D. Roosevelt.

IN CHAPTER 1 we defined communication as the process of recreating or establishing in another person's thinking those ideas which we want him to have in common with us. We noted that those ideas, to be communicated, must be interesting, clear, and believable to the listeners. All of this depends upon a clear sense of purpose on the part of the speaker, and upon adequate preparation of his materials and organization of his ideas.

But it is in delivery that the whole process of preparation is put to the test. Only by standing in front of an audience and voicing the ideas you have prepared can you discover whether your preparation has been effective and your purpose has been achieved. You need not wait for a vote of the audience or the criticism of the instructor to know whether you have been successful. For public speaking is a two-way process, and with a little experience you can gauge the effect you have upon the audience without waiting for verbal comment. In part, your ability to do this depends upon your own attitude toward your listeners.

Establishing Positive Attitudes

Every speaker, no matter how experienced, occasionally suffers from what is sometimes called "stage fright." It is natural that such feelings should be more common and more intense with beginning speakers. But the excitement you feel, when you learn to control it, will be an asset rather than a liability. Properly channeled, your nervous tension will enable you to speak with energy and enthusiasm. Your goal, therefore, should not be to rid yourself of tension, but to divorce it from the irrational fears which cause some students to avoid speaking opportunities. Face the fact realistically that you have a learning situation before you. Within the limits of what is possible and wise your instructor will minimize the difficulties. And your classmates, despite any present misgivings you may have about them, will join you in making this learning situation as productive and pleasant as possible.

Contrary to the conviction of most beginning speakers, the members of the audience are not hostile and critical, but are usually friendly and receptive. What is your own attitude when you listen to a speaker? Would you rather he gave a poor speech which bored you to death or a good one which interested you? Obviously, unless you strongly oppose the cause he represents, you want him to be successful, for your comfort and enjoyment as a listener depend on his success. If this is your attitude toward other speakers, why should you, when it is your turn to speak, presume a different attitude among your hearers? It is irrational to believe that the audience is somehow different from the individuals who compose it. You are talking to people, not to a collective monster. Your attitude, therefore, should be exactly the one you would take toward any of the individuals who make up the group. So far as delivery is concerned, think of yourself as conversing with your listeners, while they in turn are responding to you, even though there may be no interruptions in which they can answer you.

The Conversational Mode of Delivery

Good delivery should resemble animated conversation about important ideas. There are, to be sure, certain obvious differences. In delivering a speech, you will be standing in front of an audience where your position lends prestige to what you say. The size of the audience, the size, shape, and acoustical properties of the room, the presence or absence of amplifying devices, and of a platform, desk, or podium, will all affect the loudness and rate of speaking. Movement and gesture will also need to be enlarged as the size of the room may dictate. But aside from these circumstantial differences, you will wish to retain the essential characteristics of good conversation when you speak to an audience.

Preparation and Delivery

The conversational mode is appropriate no matter what your manner of preparation and regardless of whether you speak with or without notes or manuscript. In an *impromptu speech,* delivered without specific preparation (as in debating a motion before a meeting of your club), the chances are good that you will demonstrate both the best and the worst qualities of conversation. You will have a vital sense of personal contact with your hearers, but you will probably have difficulty keeping your ideas in order and using the best language to express them. Most of your speaking in this class will be *extemporaneous,* meaning that you have done thinking and research, organized your ideas into a coherent outline, and practiced the wording of the speech without trying to memorize exact language. Your arrangement and wording will be better than in an impromptu speech, but your advance preparation may tempt you to withdraw from the audience and think only about what you are saying. The latter problem becomes more acute when you deliver a *manuscript* speech or a *memorized* one. In each case the problems of delivery will be different, but the goal should be the same: to simulate the best qualities of animated conversation. The refinements of delivery can wait. For the moment, concentrate your efforts on developing the conversational qualities of directness, physical alertness, and physical freedom.

Directness

As in conversation, you must not only speak to your listeners, but you must be aware of signs coming to you from them. Are they alert and listening? Do they seem to be enjoying what you are saying? Do they respond as you expected them to? Of course you cannot answer these questions unless you *look at* and *see* individuals

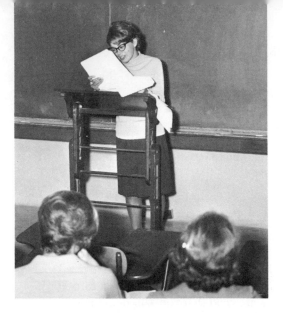

This speaker may have an excellent topic and may have prepared well, but she is failing to communicate with her audience because she is chained to her manuscript.

before you. If you spend most of your time looking at the floor or otherwise avoiding your audience, you cannot establish direct personal contact, nor can you get any idea what the members of the audience are thinking.

The sense of conversational directness can quickly be impaired by too much reliance on notes. In general, the less you have to use notes the more effective you will be. Speaking notes should be a good deal less detailed than the outline you hand in to your instructor, and should be very easy to read. Generally, they should contain only a few key words. If you can get along without any notes, so much the better; but memorize ideas rather than words. Your aim in speaking should be to rethink the ideas in your speech, not merely to remember them. Conversation is direct because you think as you talk and are eager to convey your ideas to your listeners. So in a speech you should sense at each moment just where you are in the pattern of your thought and be fully aware of the thought as a whole. Good delivery springs from a firm grasp of idea and a sincere wish to communicate. Only then can you be free to maintain contact with your listeners.

Obviously, good eye contact is of value both to the speaker and to his listeners. It enables the speaker to observe and adapt to the reactions of his audience. It enables the audience to listen with greater intentness and often with greater understanding. Remember that your hearers will tend to look where you do. If a window fascinates you, it will attract them. In addition, they will sense your lack of confidence in yourself and come to doubt your ability and mistrust the accuracy of your statements. The effective speaker has a direct and communicative delivery.

As you work for greater directness, you should, however, be on guard against several kinds of pseudo eye contact:

1. *Glaring.* Some speakers stare at individuals in the audience so intently as to cause them embarrassment. This is a favorite technique of high-pressure salesmen, who are interested in only one sale rather than steady patronage. It is not effective in public speaking.

2. *Shifting.* In contrast, some speakers shift their eyes from person to person so rapidly that no one in the audience ever feels noticed or involved in the act of communication. Although such a speaker sees many people, he does not have time to observe how they are reacting to his speech. In some respects he might almost as well look out the window.

3. *Vagueness.* It is quite possible to avoid too-rapid shifting and look in the general direction of the audience without being direct. Instead of consciously observing the reactions of the audience, a speaker may be desperately seeking to remember the next point in his outline. His listeners will sense his mental detachment when they fail to see purposive focusing in his eyes.

The Appearance of Confidence — Physical Alertness

You will find it easier to achieve a direct and communicative delivery if you discipline yourself to maintain the appearance of confidence. Your whole body should be physically alert when you speak. Too-relaxed muscles induce slumped posture, a drooping head, wandering eyes, and a dreary and monotonous voice. Indeed you will not only sound dull; you will actually be dull and lacking in confidence. On the other hand, an alert body will give you that sense of well-being which is essential to self-assured behavior.

Proper physical alertness in speaking is in many ways similar to the relaxed readiness of a good athlete. A football player, just before the ball is snapped, must not be tense, for he will be unable to move in whatever direction the play develops. But if his muscles are not alert and ready to respond, he will find himself stretched out on the ground while the play moves down the field. Similarly, an over-tense or a physically sluggish speaker cannot respond properly to his subject matter or to his audience. Moreover, he cannot acquire skill in the use of gesture and movement and in the portrayal of meaning by modifying the pitch, quality, and loudness of his voice, for these skills are all dependent upon over-all physical responsiveness.

Alert posture is essential to a physically responsive body. The expression "on your toes" has become synonymous with alertness because it suggests a body ready to respond from head to foot. You will feel and look more alert if you keep your weight slightly forward while you speak — not literally "on your toes," but far enough forward to make you feel that you are reaching *toward* the audience rather than backing away from it. A military posture is too rigid, and should be avoided as much as a sagging spine and a drooping head. Between these two extremes there is an adequate compromise so that you need not be uncomfortable in your posture. Feel free to be relaxed in the use of the lectern without depending on it for support. Place your hands in any comfortable position which does not look awkward to the audience, but do not freeze them there. Keep them ready for use when you need them for pointing, demonstrating, or gesturing for emphasis. Above all, think confidently of your ability and respond to that thought with your whole body. You will be surprised how quickly that confidence becomes a reality.

Spontaneity — Physical Freedom

When you have learned to be physically alert while you speak, you will have laid a solid foundation on which to build the quality of spontaneity. This quality involves competence in moving easily and naturally on the platform, in gesturing without tension, and in making the physical movements necessary to an expressive voice. The effective use of voice and gesture is a more advanced skill which we shall discuss in Chapter 7. Here we are concerned only with physical freedom, the ability and desire to move freely when it is appropriate to do so.

Of course physical freedom does not mean action unlimited, like that of the speaker described as having spoken "for two miles." You do not want to give the impression of a caged lion or a flailing windmill. Action should have a purpose in the speech — to make an idea clearer, to emphasize a significant point. When it is both purposeful and spontaneous, it makes the speech more effective and helps put the speaker at ease. As we noted earlier, standing before

*This speaker demonstrates
the presence of physical
alertness and spontaneity.
His audience will find it
difficult to reject his ideas.*

an audience is a highly stimulating experience. Like any venture into the unknown it sets up changes in body chemistry which enable you to react more quickly and with greater energy than usual. If you respond with an alert body and meaningful action, the stimulation will be pleasant and satisfying. On the other hand, if you bottle up your new energy either by having nothing worth saying or by suppressing physical action, you are likely to find yourself the victim of unwanted physical responses, such as shuffles, shifts, ear-scratching, or fidgety hands.

Do not be too afraid of overdoing meaningful movement while speaking. If your action is excessive, your instructor and your classmates can tone it down without hardship for you. It is much more difficult for them to make a lethargic speaker come alive. Some of the speech subjects suggested in Chapter 2 are especially well-suited to the use of action. If you analyze a process, describe an interesting place, or emphasize the importance of a strong conviction, use your hands and body to clarify and strengthen your ideas.

Exercises

1. *Directness*
   a. If you find it hard to look at individuals in the audience, call one of them by name and speak directly to him for two or three sentences. Then shift to another person and repeat the process.

    b. Without calling individuals by name, determine before you begin to speak that you are going to talk directly to five different people in the audience. Plan the order in which you will direct your attention toward them, and hold to your plan.

    c. As you speak, imagine that someone in the audience has asked you a question, the answer to which is found in your next point. Direct your answer to the imaginary questioner.

2. *Physical Alertness and Physical Freedom*

    a. Practice walking from your seat to the platform. Act as if you had a message for the audience. Reflect this feeling in your walk.

    b. Stand in front of the class with your arms resting on the lectern. Make yourself comfortable, but do not depend on the lectern for support. Have someone remove the lectern. Can you hold your position without losing balance?

    c. Stand in front of a full-length mirror and experiment with different postures. Find one that is comfortable, free from awkwardness, and alert in appearance and feeling. Try using this posture in your next speech.

    d. Using no language at all, practice demonstrating an idea in pantomime: (1) baby sitting; (2) first date; (3) pitcher throwing a home run ball; (4) how to eat Italian spaghetti; (5) how to use chop sticks; (6) Cauliflower McPugg's last fight; (7) the free throw that won the game; (8) the free throw that lost the game; (9) sewing on a button; (10) hanging wallpaper; (11) a photographer trying to take a picture of a large and unruly family; (12) any other idea that involves extensive action.

Using Audience Response

As you acquire experience in speaking you will learn to interpret cues which come to you from the audience. If you practice looking directly at your listeners, you will soon see that they respond to some ideas and reject others. You will learn to distinguish between

---

THE SPEAKER AND HIS AUDIENCE

Eloquence is in the assembly, not merely in the speaker.

— WILLIAM PITT

Effective communication involves both speaker and audience, each responding to the other in a very personal way. Obviously, this speech was highly successful.

nods of approval and nods of weariness. You will discover that some respond more readily than others. Of course, observing these audience reactions will help you in the preparation of your next speech because you will be aware of the factors most likely to win a favorable response from the class.

But you should also try to adjust to responses as you speak. Make your outline flexible enough to allow some variation. If the audience seems to accept a point, do not labor it but go on to the next. On the other hand, keep something in reserve if the audience seems reluctant to go along with your ideas. The more you speak, the easier such adjustments become, *provided* you begin now to try to make them. They do not come automatically without effort on your part.

Criticizing Delivery In First Speeches

In criticizing delivery avoid the temptation to treat delivery techniques as something apart from the content and organization of the speech. Before analyzing any technique, ask this basic question: Did the speaker's delivery enhance the idea, barely support it, or detract from it? *All criticism of delivery should be derived from your answer to this question.* Specifically, you may now ask:

1. Did the speaker look at and see members of the audience?
2. Did he appear to be aware of audience responses to his speech? Did he adjust to those responses?

3. Was the speaker physically alert? Did he make you feel that he was in earnest, sincerely interested in what he was saying?

4. Did the speaker move freely when it was appropriate to do so? Did he look as if he could not move freely? Did he move too much?

PART TWO·

FUNDAMENTALS OF SPEECH
PREPARATION AND DELIVERY

lifetime. Let us, then, enlarge the theme of the second chapter by noting the difference between "speaking on the things you know about," and "knowing things to speak about." The good speaker discusses ideas which are his own, and which audiences are willing to make their own. By increasing the value and number of your ideas, you are more likely to provide audiences with a basis for interest or belief.

Sources of New Ideas

This chapter seeks to outline a plan for increasing your store of general information, and a means of developing new ideas into successful speeches by reading and research. Any plan to acquire and speak about new ideas should relate your speech studies to the full context of your college education, where, it is assumed, your learning is moving ahead apace both in and out of class.

If only you could put a book under your pillow and wake in the morning with its contents in your head! But unless science invents intellectual osmosis, you must gain the knowledge and experience vital to effective speaking by reading, discussing, observing, and what in Chapter 2 we labelled "full-time thinking." Unfortunately this takes work.

We noted earlier how Webster and Lincoln drew upon personal experience, reading, and reflection to make their speeches significant. Like every speaker of merit, they made general preparation and creative thinking the business of a lifetime. A similar attitude, if not breadth of experience and skill, can be yours now. More than years, a mind moved by interest and curiosity is the crucial need of a good speaker. Of course interest and curiosity must be reinforced by disciplined study and thought. Specifically, your ability to become a speaker whose ideas win attention and respect depends upon your industry in personal investigation, in general reading, and the thinking you do based upon that investigation and reading.

In a sense the rest of this book aims to direct this thinking. You have already learned that it is not wise to speak until you can frame a clear and specific answer to the purpose question: "Why am I speaking on this subject to this audience?" In this and later chapters you will receive more help in choosing worthwhile subjects, finding, selecting, and organizing suitable materials, and choosing accurate and forceful language. As you learn to use these skills in speaking, you will learn to discipline your thought processes — to indulge in

Intellectual osmosis?

less unproductive reverie and idle sight-seeing among ideas. In short, you will learn to apply full-time thinking to the preparation of your speeches.

The next few pages suggest four areas rich in resources. They are the "hiding places" of good speech ideas. They are not unfamiliar or unusual; indeed they are as close as your classroom, your home, your library, and your next door neighbor. If you will dig deep into these resources, your well of ideas for speeches need never run dry.

Your Courses

Each course you take in college gives you access to new facts and helps you to interpret them. If you are a person of normal curiosity, many courses may also raise more questions than they answer. Among the unanswered questions you may find stimulating subjects for speeches. From your courses in the social sciences, philosophy, literature, mathematics, or science, pick an area which promises to interest you, and dig deeper than the "gentleman's C grade" requires. Discover facts which are not in your class lectures and required readings. Discuss your findings with your professor and your classmates.

Investigation, research reading, and analysis through thought and discussion will provide you with the basis for a topnotch speech. Your confidence in speaking and your mastery of the particular course material from which you draw the subject will both benefit. Trying to tell your classmates about Gresham's law in economics is a sure way to find out what you really know about the topic. It has all the benefits and therapeutic values of a written examination in an economics course, and can cause only half the damage if you do poorly. And if you do well, your next test in economics will show that good thinking in a speech course drives out bad thinking in an economics course — a variant suggested by Gresham's law, which states that "Bad money drives out good." There are equally good speech subjects in any course you take: an explanation of the Bernoulli effect in physics, or a defense of modern poetry from your course in literature. Let all courses work together through your speech course.

Your Community

Your home, your city, and your nation abound with ideas and issues you may either investigate personally or read about. Are there, for example, plans for a new freeway or turnpike near your home? If so, why? How will it affect real estate values? Will it change the character of your neighborhood? How do construction

Though it may not be a major construction project, whatever affects the welfare and progress of your community is a likely subject for a speech.

methods differ from those used in other freeways? Will construction give summer employment to your classmates? You can discover the answers to these and other questions by personal investigation. Meanwhile, if you read your daily newspaper, you will learn of events somewhat farther from your immediate home which will whet your curiosity. In metropolitan centers the major dailies will be discussing methods of combatting crime and juvenile delinquency, ways of improving the flow of traffic, the problem of smog. You will read about current political campaigns and proposals for dealing with issues in taxation, labor relations, housing, and social security. Any one of these topics, pursued through careful reading and adapted to local situations, could provide knowledge and insight for your audience.

Magazines and Books

For a long-range view of contemporary problems, add several weekly or monthly magazines to your program of reading. Among the monthly magazines, you will find *Harper's* and *The Atlantic Monthly* stimulating. You will not, of course, agree with all you find in the pages of any magazine or book, but part of the value of your reading lies in forcing you to reexamine your views in the light of challenges to what you now believe. Other interesting periodicals which emphasize comment on the contemporary social, intellectual, and political scene are *The Reporter, Commonweal, The Christian Century,* and the *Saturday Review.* Weekly magazines of news and opinion offer useful summaries of events, sometimes combined with analysis and editorial comment. Among these you may find value in *Life, Newsweek, Time,* and *U.S. News and World Report.* There are, of course, many other magazines which have some helpful articles, including such popular "slicks" as *The Saturday Evening Post* and *McCall's.* We do not wish to limit your reading to those we have named, but rather to list types of magazines most likely to suggest speech ideas. The only real limitations are that the articles be prepared by competent writers, and that they deal with significant material at a length great enough to help you enlarge the scope of your ideas.

Books present such a large and challenging area that we can only plead their values in general terms. But remember that, as Oliver Wendell Holmes put it, "The best of a book is not the thought which it contains, but the thought which it suggests."

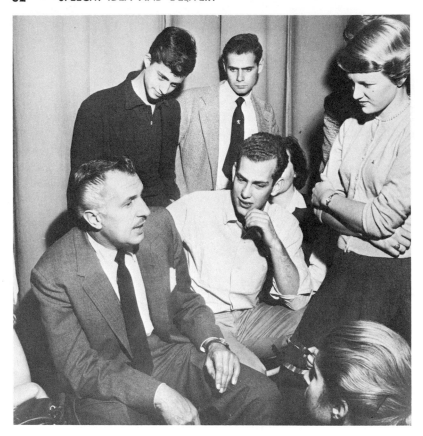

Conversations with interesting people can be the source of many speeches.

Conversation With Interesting People

There is, perhaps, no more pleasurable way of acquiring stimulating ideas than through conversation with able people. This, of course, you have always known. We mention it here as a fourth category only to remind you to use your next interesting listening session as a means of adding to the breadth of your knowledge. Listen, and reflect on how you might pursue some new idea even further in order that you might have a good subject to offer your audience.

In short, your courses, your community, books, and people surround you with a limitless storehouse of new and stimulating ideas. They are yours for the asking. But you must ask. Perhaps the most frustrating if not the most annoying problem faced by instructors of speech is the student who helplessly or defiantly says, "I just can't think of anything to talk about." It may be true that he has not thought of anything, but it is probably also true that he may not be trying to or perhaps does not know how. His quest for a subject is only an ill-disguised search for a ready-made speech. His concept of creativity is like that of the high school freshman who, upon reading Shakespeare, remarked, "I could've written that stuff if I'd only thought of it." The ability to think of it — not Shakespeare, perhaps, but an interesting and thoughtful speech — is the product of an alert mind in a person developing new idea resources for the interest and benefit of his audience and of himself.

Simple Research Speeches

A planned program of general reading will make it easier for you to select stimulating speech subjects, but it will not, of itself, provide adequate preparation for a particular speech. On most subjects of importance an analysis of your information and knowledge will reveal wide gaps. To fill these gaps you may conduct individual observations, consult directly with informed persons, or examine written materials and analyses prepared by experts. Later in this chapter we will show how these research processes may be employed in the preparation of a major speech. At this point, however, let us see what immediate use you can make of these techniques in preparing two relatively simple assignments.

SUBJECTS FOR CONVERSATION

"The time has come," the Walrus said,
"To talk of many things:
Of shoes — and ships — and sealing wax —
Of cabbages — and kings —
And why the sea is boiling hot —
And whether pigs have wings."

— LEWIS CARROLL

You may not get a speech subject from all of these suggestions, and we do not recommend the Walrus as a conversational companion. But conversations with informed people are almost never unprofitable.

A Speech Based on Observation and Interview

Speeches based exclusively on personal observation and interview are common in clubs, church groups, and other organizations which you belong to or may someday join. For example, a Parent-Teacher group, concerned for the safety of their children crossing the streets on the way to school, may instruct a member to interview the local police department in search of its plans or advice. A businessmen's luncheon group, thinking of sponsoring a boys' club, might ask a member to investigate the needs of the club and the responsibilities the group would have to assume. In either case, the report to the organization seeking advice will be a speech based on observation and interview. Thus the assignment we suggest here is the prototype of speeches you are likely to give often in college and after.

The number of subjects suited to speeches based on observation and interview is limited only by your own sensitivity to interesting possibilities. Every community has many individuals and organizations that would make good material for speeches. The suggestions below are only a beginning. For example, in addition to item six, which suggests speeches on such professions as teaching, law, medicine, and dentistry, there are dozens of little-known businesses and professions which might be investigated. Thumb through your local classified telephone directory. In ours we find such diverse occupations as antique dealer, travel agent, auctioneer, used car dealer, caterer, collection agent, exterminator, "fix-it" man, clinical laboratory specialist, landscape gardener, dealer in "horsemeat for human consumption," mover, printer, TV repairman, and many others. Any one of these could lead to an interesting interview and subsequently to a good speech.

Each of the subjects recommended below should suggest others to you if you will explore parallels with sufficient ingenuity.

Some Typical Subjects

1. How to Apply for a Job. Interview the personnel director of a business firm, an official of the local office of the state Department of Employment, or a member of your college placement bureau. If possible observe this person as he talks to job applicants.

2. Public Opinion in My Community. Conduct your own "Gallup Poll" in the vicinity of your home on the most explosive public issue you can find. Have a prepared list of questions, but allow the discussion to go beyond this list. How are your neighbors like others who must form opinions on this subject? Analyze these opinions and describe their significance.

3. *Athletics at Our College.* Interview the head coach and some of the players to learn the college policy toward athletic subsidy. Do not forget to be wisely skeptical.

4. *How an Organization Serves the Community.* Interview an official of the Community Chest, the Red Cross, the March of Dimes, the YMCA, the Cancer Clinic, a church, the American Civil Liberties Union, the Urban League, the Chamber of Commerce, or any other civic group. If possible, spend at least a half day observing the activities of the group.

5. *The Highway Department.* Interview an official of the Highway Department of your county to discover what plans are being made for the development of more adequate facilities. Visit the areas you are told about in the interview. (Or follow the same procedure with other agencies, such as the Police or Fire Commission, the City Planning Commission, the Department of Sanitation, etc.)

6. *The Profession of Teaching* (*Law, Medicine, Dentistry, etc.*). Interview an elementary teacher to discover what she does, what preparation is required, what salary she may receive, and other pertinent data. Observe her work for at least half a day.

7. *"Honest John."* Analyze the business methods of a high pressure used car salesman. Get a direct interview, or pose as a customer at several lots.

8. *Our College in the Next Ten Years.* Interview the college business manager, director of admissions, or other official. Find out what plans are being made for expansion, changes in curriculum, new buildings, etc.

9. *Buddhism* (or some other religious faith little understood in your community). Interview a Buddhist priest. Attend a Buddhist service. Tell the class about the basic tenets of the faith and the way it is practiced.

10. *Public Transportation.* Interview an official of your local bus company to find out what can be done to improve transportation to the campus. Ride on several bus lines to check what you learned in the interview.

11. *A Street Excavation: Why?* Interview the foreman on a street excavation job which has inconvenienced you. Get the facts about the project and the reasons for it.

THE TECHNIQUE OF THE INTERVIEW. When you request an interview, identify yourself and let the interviewee know you seek information for a speech before your fellow students. Unless you are inquiring into a highly controversial or confidential topic, he will usually welcome the publicity your talk will give to his work. When admitted, get to the point with vital questions which show your interest and supplement or fill the gaps in your knowledge. Beyond this, let the interview take an easy, natural course while you restrict note-taking to the minimum necessary to reconstruct the conversation after you leave. This will be possible only if you are thoroughly prepared for the interview by a careful analysis of information you already have. Do not expect your interviewee to do your thinking for you.

If it is appropriate to your subject; ask questions which show how the activities of the person interviewed affect the community; or inquire how students can help. The answers to these questions will give an audience-centered focus to your speech. Inquire also whether it is possible for you to supplement the interview with direct observation. One student spent an evening in a police patrol car — through permission, not compulsion — in his study of police methods. Several who interviewed the director of a community agency using volunteer help were put to work immediately. If you are offered such opportunities, accept them and incorporate the experience into your speech. The more direct knowledge you obtain, the more meaningful the speech will be.

The key to a successful interview is planning. Without it, establishing rapport, moving beyond surface formalities, and getting useful information are extremely difficult.

A man's study should be everywhere, — in the house, in the street, in the fields, and in the busy haunts of men.

— HENRY WARD BEECHER

PREPARING THE SPEECH. Once the interview and the observation are completed, write a detailed analysis of what you have learned. Combine it with your previous experience and follow the steps in preparation suggested in Chapter 2. Give special attention to the purpose question, "Why am I speaking on this subject to this audience?" Why is the subject important to your listeners? Have you discovered some information they could get only by duplicating your interview? Is your information entirely outside their normal experience — is it genuine "news"? Do you have a new viewpoint on an old idea? If you can give good answers to some of these questions, your talk will not be a mere mechanical report but a serious effort to interest your hearers in your subject.

In the actual presentation of the speech, your audience must feel your personal identification with the ideas you present. Particularly in the introduction, avoid such statements as, "To get ready for this speech, I interviewed Mr. Sam Jones, the president of the bus company." Say rather, "If you are in hopes of lower bus fares to the college, you are certain to be disappointed. Unless some radical changes are made soon, fares will be higher, not lower." Introduce the interview as support for a point of view, rather than making it the focus of your speech.

When you have completed the organization of your talk, deliver it with the same qualities of directness, physical alertness, and physical freedom you used in presenting personal speeches. If your preparation has been careful, this speech will be as vital to you as the most personal subject you have spoken on, and your audience should share your interest.

A Speech Based on Limited Reading

In Chapter 2 we observed that the beginning speaker is sometimes tempted to read a single magazine article, to outline but not absorb its content, and to parrot back the words he has read. The futility of such speeches is not the fault of the author of the article, whose ideas are usually well stated and at least broadly suitable for a speech to a college audience. Usually the trouble lies in the failure of the speaker to assimilate the new facts and ideas to what he already thinks and knows and adapt all this to the specific needs and interests of his hearers. If new ideas are to be effective, the speaker must make them so vital that the members of the audience think of them as having become the speaker's own, though he of course fully acknowledges their source.

To help you develop facility in dealing with ideas acquired by reading, we now suggest that you make a speech combining materials derived from limited reading with facts drawn from personal observation and interview as well as information you already possess. This is no cut and dried assignment, for the selection and editing of details from both printed and personal sources demand skill of a high order. Yet if you do it well you will have less difficulty hereafter in making new ideas come alive for your audience.

Choosing a Subject. There are two requirements for your choice of a subject for this assignment: (1) You should know something about the subject before you begin, or should be able to inform yourself quickly by personal investigation; (2) you should be able to find a thoughtful, well-written magazine article which you can use as a major source.

Your subject should be chosen in consultation with your instructor, who will probably wish to see your source material before you begin preparation. We suggest that you choose a nonfiction magazine article of at least two thousand words. Avoid the easy convenience of "digest" magazines, whose editing of an article may be inappropriate for your purpose. Part of the value of the assignment lies in making your own selection of content from a source too long for your speech.

Some typical subjects. Here are a number of areas in which you may find suitable subjects, together with bibliographical references suggesting the types of article which may prove useful. By consulting the *Readers' Guide to Periodical Literature* (see page 72) you will discover similar articles written more recently. On many subjects, however, articles are relatively timeless, and older materials may be as valuable as recent ones.

    1. *Education.*

> Oscar Handlin, "Are the Colleges Killing Education?" *Atlantic Monthly,* May 1962, page 41.
> H. G. Rickover, "Democracy: The Subject Our Schools Don't Teach," *McCall's,* March 1962, page 98.

2. *Languages.*
Mario Pei, "Ending the Language Traffic Jam," *Saturday Review,* September 9, 1961, page 14.
3. *Science.*
Michael P. Walsh, "The Promise of Science," *Vital Speeches,* May 1, 1962, page 443.
4. *Health.*
Kenneth N. Anderson, "The Coming Struggle for Pure Water," *Today's Health,* August 1961, page 44.
5. *Travel; Literature.*
William Golding, "Shakespeare's Birthplace," *Holiday,* May 1962, page 82.
6. *Automobiles.*
A. W. Baum, "Where Are Those Dream Cars?" *Saturday Evening Post,* March 31, 1962, page 34.

Preparing the Speech. When you have chosen a subject which interests you and a well-written article as a base from which to develop your speech, we suggest that you use the following method of preparation.

1. Read the article and make an outline or a summary of the ideas advanced by the author. If the article is long and contains several different ideas, select the one which stimulates your thinking the most.

2. Write out a statement of your own views on the same subject.

   a. If it differs from that of the author, state your reasons for preferring your own view.

   b. If your views correspond with those of the author, give additional support for the position, drawn from facts you already know.

   c. If you agree with the author, but think he has not gone far enough in his proposals, develop the case further and support your position.

3. Beyond this, follow the advice given in Chapter 2 to put the materials in suitable form for a speech. (See pages 25–26).

You might reasonably expect that a speech prepared in this way would be approximately equally divided between reporting the ideas of your source and developing your own comment, criticism, and support, based on what you already know or can learn through personal investigation.

Woe be to him who reads but one book.
— GEORGE HERBERT

That book is good
Which puts me in a working mood.
— RALPH WALDO EMERSON

Major Research Speeches

The two kinds of speeches described so far in this chapter, like those discussed earlier, are based on a limited portion of the resources available to the speaker. Like the tennis player who must master the fundamentals before he is ready for tournament play, you have so far worked on the preliminaries. Now that you have tested your skill in a limited area, you are ready to plan speeches built on whatever materials best serve your purpose, regardless of their origin. You will be most effective as a speaker when you are able to draw freely upon your own experience, on personal investigation, and on the limitless resources of printed materials — newspapers, pamphlets, magazines, and books.

Sources of Materials

Even in major research speeches, the library is never a complete substitute for personal investigation. Your prestige as a speaker is enhanced when your audience feels that you have personal knowledge of your subject, either through long experience or because you have gone to the trouble of securing first-hand data for your speech. For this reason we strongly recommend that whenever your subject permits, you draw at least part of your development from your own experience or from observation or interviews conducted specifically for your talk.

In many speaking situations, however, it is difficult if not impossible to get all the facts you need by personal investigation. And even if you have enough facts from personal sources to make a speech, it is probable that better materials are available in the vast wealth of human experience recorded in print. Wise use of printed material may both broaden your understanding of the subject and provide specific ideas and facts with which to develop it. Indeed, you are not really well prepared to speak until you know far more about your subject than you will say to your audience. You will be most effective when you have several points in reserve for each one you actually use. Such an abundance of material will give you confidence and provide flexibility if something in the audience situation makes you decide to change your development as you speak.

To make your research reading efficient, you need to be familiar with general reference works, bibliographical aids, and specific sources for a given field of study. Since we cannot list all such sources here, let us begin by calling attention to the people who will help you locate printed materials. In the first place, consult the reference librarian in both college and public libraries. Tell him the problem you are working on and ask him to help you locate suitable general reference works and bibliographies which will lead you to more specific sources. Also talk with your instructors in fields related to the subject of your choice. Some of your best leads may come from faculty members in political science, economics, physical science, or any field into which you venture for speech materials.

REFERENCE WORKS. Aside from leads furnished by librarians and instructors, there are standard reference works which are generally helpful. Every library has several good encyclopedias, including such familiar ones as *The Encyclopedia Americana, The Encyclopaedia Britannica,* and *The New International Encyclopaedia.* Articles in these will give you a broad understanding of your subject and suggest books and articles you may consult for more specific materials. More specialized treatment of narrower areas is provided by such works as *The Encyclopaedia of the Social Sciences,* Larned's *History for Ready Reference,* and Langer's *An Encyclopedia of World History.* Some other subject matter fields also provide specialized reference works, which may be identified by asking your reference librarian or subject matter specialist.

Many books provide biographical data. *The Dictionary of American Biography* and *The Dictionary of National Biography* (British) provide concise but informative biographies of deceased persons of note. Usually sources of further information about these people are specified at the end of the article. *Who's Who* (British) and *Who's Who in America* give brief biographies of persons living at the time the book was compiled. Many specialized books of this type deal with smaller geographical areas or particular professions, such as *Who's Who in the West* and *The Directory of American Scholars.*

A number of books compiled each year contain facts and statistics on innumerable topics. *The Statesman's Yearbook, Information*

Please Almanac, World Almanac, The Statistical Abstract of the United States, and numerous state yearbooks are publications of this kind. Most of these are well-indexed and are handy reference sources for factual data of all kinds.

Three publications found in most libraries provide information on both sides of current controversial issues. *The Congressional Digest,* in magazine format, and the *Reference Shelf,* in book form, are clearly organized around debatable propositions. If you have the time and patience to dig through the *Congressional Record,* you will also find facts and opinions on both sides of every national question in the pages of this official publication of the Senate and House of Representatives.

BOOKS AND MAGAZINES. Libraries index their holdings in card catalogues, according to subject, author, and title in a single alphabetical listing. It is comparatively easy, therefore, to discover books dealing with any theme by looking under two or three possible subject headings.

Magazine articles have been indexed since 1900 by subject, author, and title in the *Readers' Guide to Periodical Literature.* To locate a news story about a specific event, the *New York Times Index* is helpful. Although this is designed for use with the *Times,* a press service story can be located in almost any newspaper by the date specified in the *Index.* Your instructors and your reference librarian can help you find indexes to specialized publications. For example, for information about public speaking, we would refer you to the *Bibliography of Speech Education* and its *Supplement.*

SPECIAL SOURCES. Many organizations interested in the outcome of public issues prepare pamphlets or even books which they will send free or at nominal cost upon request. Such materials have been published from time to time by the National Association of Manufacturers, the Edison Electric Institute, the American Medical Association, the American Federation of Labor and its constituent unions, and many other groups. A letter or telephone call to the local headquarters of such interested organizations will often be enough to discover what is available. Of course such materials are published for the sole purpose of influencing public opinion in one direction or the other. You must remember this as you read and balance your research by investigating the opposite point of view as well. Then make up your own mind on the issue and speak accordingly.

Most government agencies issue periodic reports on matters under their jurisdiction. If your library maintains a section devoted exclusively to government publications, your librarian will direct you to those dealing with the question you are studying. If not, ask to see the *Catalogue of the Public Documents,* and the *Monthly Catalogue of the United States Public Documents.* From these you can decide what government publications would be helpful to you. Most of them are obtainable at nominal cost from the Government Printing Office, Washington, D.C.

A Plan for Preparing Major Research Speeches

Whenever you prepare and deliver a speech containing information and opinions new to you, take time to absorb the new material and to make it a part of your pattern of thought. This means that you ought to select as soon as you can the subjects for all the research speeches you will give during the term, for long-range planning makes efficient preparation easier. In making your selection, take care that you choose subjects worthy of the time you will spend on them. There are too many topics of consequence to use your energy and research hours on trivia. Unless you make sure quickly that you will find enough material for a significant major speech, you may find yourself in the speaking situation equivalent to arriving at a picnic with plenty of relishes but no fried chicken.

Let us suppose you have become interested in *consumer cooperatives* and decide to talk about them if you can get the necessary information. Is there a cooperative store in your community? If not, do you know anyone who has been active in cooperative stores? Are you acquainted with a person who owns a privately operated food store, or who manages a store belonging to a grocery chain? If you can answer yes to any or all of these questions, your chance of getting personal interviews and observations is good. To check on published materials, discover what books on cooperatives are listed in your library card catalogue. Are there pertinent magazine articles listed in the *Readers' Guide to Periodical Literature?* Does your local cooperative store have any publications about cooperative methods and principles? Is there an article on consumer cooperatives in the *Encyclopaedia of the Social Sciences* which might lead you to otherwise unnoticed sources? The answers to these and similar questions will tell you whether it is probable that you can find enough material to make a good speech. You will no doubt discover other useful leads as you examine bibliographies and reference books and consult your librarian and your instructors in economics and sociology.

TYPICAL SUBJECTS. Perhaps the nature of this preliminary analysis will be more meaningful if you consider what sources are available on three additional subjects for speeches:

1. *Civil Liberties.* Inquiry into sources should suggest interviews or correspondence with officers of the American Civil Liberties Union, the American Heritage Project of the American Library Association, and the National Association for the Advancement of Colored People. You may wish to discuss the subject with faculty members in the departments of history, political science, and sociology. Textbooks in these fields will also be useful references. The *Encyclopaedia of the Social Sciences* has interesting and definitive articles on both the British and the American Bills of Rights, with cross references to other sources. Additional materials may be located by looking in your card catalogue and the *Readers' Guide* under such headings as civil liberties, civil rights, minority groups, bill of rights, freedom of speech, and freedom of press.

2. *Juvenile Delinquency.* Interview a juvenile court judge or police officers on a juvenile detail. If at all possible, talk to juvenile delinquents. Discuss the subject with faculty members in sociology, and consult textbooks in social problems and criminology. Call your local newspaper office to see whether the paper has run a recent series on the problem. Check the card catalogue and *Readers' Guide* under juvenile delinquency, gangs, narcotics, and similar headings.

3. *General Education versus Professional Training.* Possible interviews might include college deans, chairmen of faculty committees on educational policy, personnel directors in business and industry. Read *General Education in a Free Society,* Report of the Harvard Committee (Cambridge, Massachusetts, 1945). Check the card catalogue and *Readers' Guide* under such headings as education, general education, technical education, college, liberal arts college, and so on.

Other Subjects — An Exercise

Since you should not choose a subject for a research speech without investigating several alternatives, we now ask you to explore at least three possible subjects for speeches. Use those listed below, or take any other you think might prove profitable. Hand in to your instructor a preliminary analysis of the idea, including the following:

1. Title
2. A possible purpose for the speech
3. Sources of interviews (or personal observations)
4. Available printed sources: books, magazines, pamphlets, and newspapers

Suggested subjects:

1. *Education.* Federal aid to education; the honor system; student marriages; general education or professional education
2. *Social Issues.* Race relations; civil liberties; juvenile delinquency; prison reform; medical insurance; public housing; marriage and divorce
3. *Political Issues.* A candidate for President (governor, congressman, mayor); labor legislation; farm policy; reciprocal trade; universal military training
4. *Local Problems.* Smog; public recreation facilities; slum clearance; revision of the city charter; public transportation
5. *International Problems.* The United Nations; American policy in Asia; Germany and European peace; new nationalism in Africa; the Communization of Cuba
6. *Other Subjects.* Women in modern life; jazz; advertising; unity of religious denominations; do-it-yourself; modern art

Your instructor may tire of hearing speeches on such well-worn subjects as capital punishment, socialized medicine, and federal aid to education, yet he and your classmates will respect you if you take one of these hardy perennials and give it a vital, new, and insightful treatment. Until these problems are settled to the satisfaction of everyone — and it is most unlikely that they ever will be — there will be new materials on them available every year. In every speech class old subjects are talked about as well as new ones. If the old are made good, they compete well with the new. And if the new are good, they will someday become old.

READING AND NOTE TAKING. Locating material related to your subject is an important part of good preparation, but it taxes your patience more than your mind. The real test of ability comes when you begin to read and sift the data you have discovered. Perhaps the best way to start is to scan an article or book to determine what pertinent material it contains. With a book, this is simplified by the table of contents and the index. Usually a few minutes spent in looking over these aids will tell you whether any sections of the book are likely to be helpful. In other ways your examination of books, pamphlets, and magazine articles will be about the same. Scan the entire article or book section by reading topic sentences. Make a brief notation of any part which may contain material important to your subject. If only the general point of view expressed in the article seems of value, summarize it briefly on a card or a page in a notebook, and file it for future reference. If some parts seem to need further analysis, return to them and read them more carefully.

In addition to summaries of long passages, two methods of note-taking are useful to speakers. One is to outline a section which seems to offer valuable suggestions. The other is to make copies of statements which contain ideas, facts, or statistics of direct value in the form in which they appear in the article. Work out your own system of taking notes and filing them. There are, however, two essentials to any good system.

1. *Be sure you have an adequate citation of the source.* You probably will not use the full citation in your speech, but it is wise to have it ready in case the question is raised. Moreover, during your preparation you may wish to return to the original material to add to what you already have in your notes. You will waste a great deal of time in relocating the material if your citation is incomplete. The tortures of the damned are hardly greater than the distress of the student who remembers reading something of value in a book that had a blue cover, or maybe it was green. For magazines, cite author, his qualifications, title of article, issue of the magazine, and page. For propaganda or public-relations pamphlets you should also include the sponsoring organization.

2. *Devise a system which makes classifications and rearrangement of materials easy.* Looseleaf notebooks are acceptable for this purpose if only one item is placed on a page. Most instructors prefer 5 x 8 inch cards which can be filed as your outline develops and your store of material grows. Title each card to identify the subject it deals with. Follow with the summary, outline, or verbatim quotations — the body of the note. In quotations, indicate omitted material by dots and enclose added phrases of your own in brackets. Place the citation of source at the bottom. These cards can be arranged and rearranged as your speech develops. Some may even prove useful in another speech on a different subject. Here is a

sample card, containing a direct quotation, an identifying phrase at the top, a bracketed phrase of the author's to summarize the meaning of words left out (note the dots), and finally the source.

> *Preparation of Franklin D. Roosevelt Speeches*
> "The preparation of some of the speeches ... took as many as ten days and very few took less than three. That does not mean actual writing time. But there were long memoranda and proposed drafts to be read, and information and statistics to be gathered. Irrelevant data had to be separated from relevant data. Many people had to be interviewed, sometimes a dozen or more for a single message .... Sometimes a speech went through as many as twelve or thirteen drafts before the President was finally satisfied ... [It although many people worked on every speech] the speeches were always Roosevelt's. They all expressed the personality, the convictions, the spirit, the mood of Roosevelt. No matter who worked with him in the preparation, the finished product was always the same -- it was Roosevelt himself."
> Samuel I. Rosenman, *Working with Roosevelt* (1952) pp. 11-12

Here is another note card, combining the techniques of summary and outline.

> *Value of Speech Training* (summary)
> The fact that some men use speech skill to do harm is not a valid argument against acquiring such skill.
>   1. Properly presented through speech, truth and justice will prevail.
>   2. Speech skill helps explain technical information to uninformed audiences.
>   3. Speech skill makes a speaker understand both sides of an issue.
>   4. Speech skill allows a speaker to defend himself.
> Those who defend just causes are obligated to become effective speakers.
> Jane Cooper, *The Rhetoric of Aristotle* (New York: 1932) pp. 5-6.

It is easy to write a check if you have money in the bank, and writing comes more easily if you have something to say.

— SHOLEM ASCH

The notes you take as you read are the raw material of your speech, to be digested later and used as you plan and outline what you will say. Except for an occasional quotation, they are not to be used as speaking notes.

MAKING THE MATERIALS YOUR OWN. Once you have selected your subject for a research speech in consultation with your instructor, start your preparation as soon as you can. Begin at once to gather material, and continue the process until it is time for you to speak. Use the advice of later chapters to help you select details, organize the speech, and plan the wording and delivery. Try to add something to your knowledge of the subject every day until you speak.

Whenever you rely upon printed materials for the major portion of a speech, there is danger that you may become impersonal and distant, losing the sense of dealing with subject matter which is vital both to you and to your audience. This is a danger faced not only by students in speech classes, but by business executives, lawyers, professors, and indeed by all speakers. If you learn to avoid this danger now, you will always find it easier to make new materials vital to audiences. Here are four suggestions which we believe will help. Some of them have already been discussed under other headings. We think them important enough to repeat.

1. *Make printed materials your own by constant conversation with anyone who will listen.* The more often you discuss a new idea, and the more you modify it in response to the opinions of others, the more fully you become identified with it. It becomes not just something you have read, but something you have thought. When you put this thought into a speech, you will not need to remember the words or ideas of others; they will have become your ideas, and you will need only to rethink them.

2. *Identify yourself with printed materials by blending them with personal materials.* Draw upon your own background and personal investigation. Audiences are entitled to know the source of your facts, and you may often strengthen your position by citing your authority. But the basic ideas of the speech should be compounded of materials derived from personal investigation, reading, and full-time

thinking. If you succeed in blending all of these fully, your audience may be aware of the source of your facts but feel that all the thoughts you express are your own regardless of their origin.

3. *Identify printed materials with your audience by rephrasing and reorienting examples and other materials to relate them directly to your hearers.* Some of the methods for achieving this are suggested in Chapter 5.

4. *Maintain the same standards of communicative delivery you found useful for personal speeches.* Remember that speaking involves personal relationships between speaker and audience, and that the communication process operates in both directions. Nothing is changed when the subject matter consists of new ideas. The ideal for your speech is still animated conversation enlarged to suit the needs of an audience situation.

SUMMARY: STEPS IN PREPARING MAJOR RESEARCH SPEECHES.

In summary, then, here are the steps to follow in the preparation of a major research speech for any audience.

1. After preliminary reading, observation, and discussion with others, select a subject area that interests you.
2. Make a list of available printed sources and sources for observation and interview.
3. Read several general articles about the subject, keeping careful notes.
4. Determine and write out the purpose of the speech.
5. Evaluate material in terms of purpose and audience and make a preliminary plan.
6. Discuss ideas informally with friends. Note the weak spots and gaps in your information.
7. Read to fill those gaps and to amass a wider selection of details. Conduct observations and interviews to personalize materials. Select supporting materials which meet the requirements laid down in Chapter 5.
8. Prepare a final outline following the suggestions in Chapter 6.
9. Plan the delivery and the wording of the speech to free and strengthen ideas as recommended in Chapters 7 and 8.

Criticizing Speeches For Substance

As preparation for criticizing speeches based on new ideas and new materials, carefully review the four suggestions for making new materials your own, given on pages 78–79 and the summary immediately above. Remember that in both delivery and organization the net effect of the speech on the audience should be the same for personal speeches and those based on new ideas. Therefore, review the questions for criticism on pages 43–44 at the end of Chapter 2. Then add these two new questions:

1. Did the speaker make a contribution to audience knowledge — did he bring "news" or did most of his listeners know as much as he did? Was he thoroughly at home with his subject? Did he seem to know more than he had time to develop in his speech? Did his selection of details seem to be the best he could have made?

2. Did he successfully combine personal materials, direct observation and interviews, and printed material where it was appropriate to do so? Did he avoid being detached and impersonal in handling printed sources? In short, did he acquire and present new ideas which were vital to himself and stimulating to his audience?

5 SUPPORT:

Making Ideas Communicable

Henry Ward Beecher's preaching demonstrated great skill in using examples drawn from the experience of his listeners.

IN CHAPTER 1 we defined ideas as information, opinions, and attitudes, and communication as the process of establishing such ideas in the thinking of other people. Later we explored ways of using the idea resources your life has provided up to now; also, we took up ways of increasing the number and depth of your ideas through research and reading. Now we come to the entirely practical business of studying the means of making these ideas communicable.

In an earlier analogy we suggested that a quarterback's signal call in a closed huddle approached perfect communication. He held attention, his meaning was understood; and he was believed. This was possible only because the speaker (the quarterback) and his audience (the team) possessed identical knowledge and opinions. Of course this ideal communication is almost never reached by a platform speaker. Normally the ideas which you present to an audience need to be supported. You must learn to find in yourself and your audience, as well as by investigation and research into the values inherent in your idea, those factors which will make your speech interesting, clear, and believable. As this chapter shows, your ideas will become communicable when you can *state them clearly, develop and support them within the interests, understanding, and beliefs of your audience,* and learn how to *reinforce* them so they will be remembered, accepted, or acted upon.

Stating Ideas

An idea is merely a hazy impression in your mind until you can state it clearly — preferably in a simple, declarative sentence. Until you can get the main idea and the sub-ideas of a speech into a form specific enough for analysis, you will not know what has to be done with them in order to make them interesting, clear, and believable. Many speakers fail just here: they do not analyze and phrase their ideas carefully enough before they speak. Such a speaker does not know what he means until he has heard himself say it. Often the untrained speaker stands up merely to say something about football, love, or taxes, and fails to communicate a single clear idea. He has not isolated his ideas or clarified them in his own mind, and hence is unable to frame a simple, declarative sentence expressing an attitude or a fact. Indeed, he has not sensed the difference between an idea and a subject for a speech. "Love" is a subject; "Love makes the world go round" is an idea.

Make your subjects become ideas. Rework vague impressions into explicit idea statements. These statements may be phrased to include the content of an entire speech or any section or paragraph of it. In any event, idea statements are only partial representations of your thought processes. Sometimes they summarize your opinion, as in "Flying is fun," or "George Walker should be elected mayor." Other idea statements lay out an area of information or fact you plan to cover in a speech or section of a speech, as, for example, "Current flows through a vacuum tube from cathode to plate," or, "The single wing in football delivers maximum power at the point of attack."

Idea statements are more than convenient methods of systematizing your thinking. Clearly-worded statements of judgment or information in your speech also serve the simple but necessary function of letting your audience know what the speech is all about. When such statements are put together in logical order, and are frequently repeated, they provide your audience with a basis for memory. In this pattern your idea statements form the framework of your speech, often corresponding to the main points of your outline.

Until you can put an attitude clearly into words, or explicitly phrase a factual statement, you cannot properly consider your audience as you set about achieving interest, clarity, and believability. Therefore, word your ideas in brief and specific sentences. This done, you may find some of them so immediately clear and acceptable that communication can occur without development. Others must be improved in clarity, interest, or believability. These you must develop.

Exercises

1. Formulate a clear-cut statement of attitude or opinion about each of the following subjects. Also, make for each a clear-cut statement of information without expressing an attitude.

   a. football   *f.* traffic problems
   b. student government   *g.* books
   c. hobbies   *h.* typing
   d. my chosen profession   *i.* final examinations
   e. my home town   *j.* required courses

2. For each of two statements you have just written (on two different subjects) analyze the probable knowledge and beliefs of your classmates. How might they influence your development of the subject? What questions would your statement raise in the minds of your listeners?

Developing Ideas: Forms of Support

The purpose of developing ideas is to clarify meaning, create interest, and gain acceptability. Since it is easier to comprehend and accept specific and concrete materials than general and abstract ones, the best method of development is to make general statements more

---

ON HAVING IDEAS

What could be more pathetic than an empty speaker pouring himself forth to a full house?

— JOHN ANDREW HOLMES

specific, abstract ones more concrete, and complex ones more simple.

A few ideas are simple enough and direct enough to be immediately understood. It is fairly easy to communicate more complex ideas to audiences which have background, knowledge, and beliefs similar to those of the speaker, whereas the same statements may be meaningless to other audiences with different backgrounds.

Suppose you make the statement that "Insurance is the foundation of credit selling." This is a broad generalization, but it will be understood at once by an insurance man. From his own background he can fill in substantially the same facts which caused you to make the statement. But for those who know little about insurance, this idea is too abstract to communicate readily. You will make your point clearer to a general audience if you go on to narrow the range of the idea covered by your generalization. You might then say: "Without insurance it would be difficult to persuade banks to lend money to buy property which might be destroyed by fire or other disaster." Since this statement is more specific than the first, it conveys more information to the audience; yet it may fail to hold interest because it seems to apply only to merchants and bankers. Suppose, however, that you direct your idea specifically to the listener: "The First National Bank would not lend you a nickel to buy your new convertible if it did not know your purchase was fully insured by a reliable casualty company." In the light of this more interesting and easily understood statement, the original generalization is finally made clear to almost any listener. Note that this meaning was conveyed in three steps, increasingly concrete and specific.

One of the best ways of heightening concreteness in speaking or writing is to go beyond even the most specific type of generalization into material which is often identified by the term *forms of support.* Included in this term are three main types of materials:

1. Explanation
   a. Definition
   b. Division
   c. Details

2. Exemplification
   a. Examples (real or hypothetical)
      (1) Developed (illustration)
      (2) Undeveloped (instances)

   b. Analogies (compared examples)
   c. Statistics (codified and classified examples)

  3. Accentuation
     a. Repetition
     b. Restatement
     c. Quotation

Our purpose in studying forms of support, however, is not so much to learn to identify them, or even to insure that a certain number of them appear in the speeches you make in class. Rather, you need to know specifically which kind of support will be of most value in communicating a particular idea to a particular audience. With this in mind, let us see how supporting materials make ideas communicable by sharpening clarity, promoting believability, and holding attention and interest. Later we will see how other forms of support accentuate and reinforce ideas which have been communicated to the audience.

Gaining Clarity

If your audience fails to understand you, it is easy to blame the stupidity of your hearers. The fault, however, is probably as much yours as theirs, for you must always assume the responsibility of gauging the level of audience understanding and adjusting to it. Do terms which have meaning for you mean the same thing to your listeners — or, indeed, anything at all? Are some of your concepts too broad and general to have any real meaning to the members of your audience? Have your hearers had an opportunity to examine the facts on which your present ideas and beliefs are based? Your answers to these questions will show whether you need to employ definition, division, specific details, and examples to make your ideas clear.

DEFINITION. If you are to communicate your thoughts to the audience, key words in the statement of your idea must have the same meaning to your hearers as they do to you. The need to define technical terms is so obvious that it hardly needs mention. Other words may need to be defined when their exact meaning is not clear from the context in which you use them. Most English words in general use have more than one possible meaning. Moreover, each person associates special meanings with some words as a result of his own experiences, and these meanings are not necessarily shared by other people.

Your first impulse in defining words should be to consult your dictionary. But while a dictionary definition will clarify your thinking, it is seldom the best one for you to present in a speech. A formal definition is often too complex for your listeners to grasp easily, because they do not have time to analyze it as they hear it. Moreover, the dictionary statement may not carry the added values you intend. It has been purposely stripped of connotations and is nearly always colorless and lacking in warmth and interest.

Suppose you have been asked by the principal of your high school to talk to seniors on "A College Education." If you try to define your terms, the dictionary will be of little help. *Webster's Collegiate Dictionary* defines a college as "A society of scholars incorporated for study and instruction," a definition unlikely to create enthusiasm among high school students. The definition of "education" is equally unpromising: "Discipline of mind or character through study or instruction." If you are to use either of these definitions, it had better be well along in the speech, after you have won attention by other means. Moreover, either definition will be more acceptable if it is introduced informally, for example: "A college is, after all, a place where students go for study and instruction." Simplified and informal definitions were used in the statement about insurance (page 84). There the concept of "credit selling" was spelled out in these words: "banks to lend money to buy property." "Insurance" was defined as protection against "fire or other disaster."

There are other ways besides dictionary definitions to make the meaning of terms clear. General concepts like justice, liberalism, freedom, and many others which are used in widely different senses by different people can often be made more precise by *negative definition,* in which the speaker tells what the thing is not, and eliminates in turn those definitions which do not suit his purpose. Terms may also be made clear by example (see pages 89–91), by the use of synonyms, or by dividing into parts in order to simplify understanding. Whatever your method, ask yourself two questions about every definition you plan to use: (1) Does it really make the concept clear? (2) Will the audience listen attentively enough to hear the definition? If it meets these tests, your definition is a good one.

DIVISION. Sometimes an idea stated in general terms may be unclear, not because it contains undefined terms, but because it is too broad in scope to be readily understood. Such a statement may often be made more meaningful if divided into smaller concepts. A preacher may believe that the verse of the Bible he uses as a text contains a profound truth which needs only to be heard to be accepted. If he speaks on the theme, "Faith without works is dead," he may divide his speech into sections dealing with the questions: (1) What is faith? (2) What are works? (3) What is the relationship between them? The politician may have as his basic theme, "The opposition party has no solutions for the problems before us." He will find it easier to talk, however, if he limits his charges to farm policy in his speech in Kansas City, reclamation and public power in Portland, Oregon, and labor in Detroit.

Even these divisions may prove too broad, and the candidate may eventually narrow his generalizations still further to fit the specific problems of each local area. Thus in Portland he might concentrate on the theme, "The Northwest cannot develop properly except under full freedom for private enterprise," or "Public resources like water power should remain under the control of the public." Each of these in turn would be divided within the speech. Thus the public power advocate might deal with each of these themes: (1) The natural resources of America belong to all the people, not to a favored few; (2) The Tennessee Valley Authority has shown that large scale development of the resources of an area by a public body results in benefits to all the people and to private industry as well; (3) Developments similar to TVA are essential to the proper growth of the West. Each of these subdivisions might be divided further and made still more specific.

The nature of the subject usually determines the most favorable ways to divide it. In the foregoing example, the theme was divided according to *logical* causes, and each subdivision was intended as a section of proof of the major generalization that water power should remain under public control. In the sermon, the division was based on the obvious need to develop clear meaning for two words in the Biblical text: "faith" and "works." In other instances, a speaker may make a purely arbitrary separation for convenience in handling the idea. For example, "The campus of this college has three sections," or "There are two kinds of students: those who want an education, and those who are looking for a four-year loaf on the old man's dough." Breaking an idea down into simpler and more easily understood parts is always an important process of development. If this process is carried far enough, the speaker will finally be dealing with basic factual materials: specific details and examples.

USING DETAILS. In many speeches or parts of speeches, after suitable divisions of the central theme have been made, the basic method of development is the selection and arranging of *specific details.* Selecting and arranging should depend on the subject matter *and the interests of the audience.* A sergeant explaining the care of a rifle to a group of recruits would select specific details showing how parts should be removed, cleaned, and reassembled in the proper order. The tennis instructor starting a class of beginners would select details based on the fundamentals of the game and the specific needs of his pupils. Senator George Norris, speaking to his colleagues on the appearance of Hetch-Hetchy Valley, chose and arranged his details on the basis of a comparison of the layout of the valley with that of the floor of the Senate chamber. (See page 174 for the text of this analogy developed by details.) Thus time factors, space factors, and interest value factors inherent in the subject determine the choice of details and the order in which they are presented. It is less important, however, to label the method you use than to make sure your development is clear and interesting to your hearers. Determine exactly what details are essential to clear understanding, and highlight these in your presentation. If you wish to use others, make sure that they add to the clarity and interest of what you say.

The sergeant, like all effective speakers, knows that he must select details essential to understanding and point them out clearly and logically.

USING EXAMPLES FOR CLARITY. Let us define an "example" as *a cross section of experience which the speaker offers as typical of the general knowledge on a subject.* Later you will see that examples add to the believability of ideas, but at this stage we are necessarily focusing on clarity. Thus while examples may be used to establish the truth of assertions, they may also be used to make statements clear. Moreover, examples are potentially the most interesting of all methods of development. Hence an example used as part of an explanation can be more valuable than either definition or division.

Here is an example told as a story by a student speaker explaining the nature of Little League Baseball:

> One evening early last summer I was driving past the city playground and noticed a crowd watching a baseball game. I like baseball; so I pulled up and parked as near the field as I could get. While I was elbowing my way through the crowd, I could see players in uniform on the field, and I assumed that the game would be a softball contest between two teams in the industrial league. I knew I was wrong when I heard the unmistakable crack of a bat against a hard ball. I got my first full look at the players and the field just as the ball was disappearing over a four foot fence near a sign indicating 180 feet from home plate. A twelve year old boy was rounding second base with the easy trot of a home run hitter. It was then that I realized that the bats, the bases, the fences and the players were all cut from the same pattern. It was hard ball all right, but played in dimensions that suited the physical development of ten, eleven, and twelve year old players. This was my introduction to Little League Baseball.

There is nothing in this example that could not have been said more quickly in a formal definition: "Little League Baseball is regulation hard ball, with the dimensions of the field and the weight of the equipment scaled down to suit the physical development of ten, eleven, and twelve year old players." If you were giving a speech explaining Little League to fathers of young boys preparing to organize a new league, the shorter form would probably be preferable. With such an audience there would be no problem of interest, and you would want to get directly to the point. But the general audience of this student speaker knew little about the Leagues, and only a few of his listeners had any advance interest in them. Thus the speaker not only had to clarify the meaning of Little League but to arouse interest as well. He used what we call a *developed example,* and it served both his purposes.

If a man's sermon is like a boiled ham, and the illustrations are like cloves stuck in it afterwards to make it look better, or like a bit of celery . . . laid around the edge for the mere delectation of the eye, it is contemptible. But if you have a . . . use for the illustration, that has a direct relation to the end you are seeking, then it may be ornamental, and no fault should be found with it for that.

— HENRY WARD BEECHER

Sometimes clarity is best achieved by a series of short *undeveloped examples.* Such explanations are more interesting, and often clearer in the impression they make on the audience, than any amount of formal definition. Consider William Jennings Bryan's definition of a "business man":

> We say to you that you have made the definition of a business man too limited in its application. The man who is employed for wages is as much a business man as his employer, the attorney in a country town is as much a business man as the corporation counsel in a great metropolis; the merchant at the cross-roads store is as much a business man as the merchant of New York; the farmer who goes forth in the morning and toils all day — who begins in the spring and toils all summer — and who by the application of brain and muscle to the natural resources of the country creates wealth, is as much a business man as the man who goes upon the board of trade and bets upon the price of grain. . . . We come to speak for this broader class of business men.

Bryan's vivid use of a series of undeveloped examples in this selection gave a new meaning to the term "business man" and made it possible for the speaker to reinterpret the relationship between government and business. In the Appendix, page 279, you will find a speech by John Jay Chapman in which undeveloped examples are used skillfully in many places. Read the speech and see whether you can pick out those examples.

The *hypothetical example* is a fictional example. It is malleable and can be designed to fit the special needs of the speech. To be effective, it must be obvious that the fiction parallels life. The first day on campus of the typical freshman may be captured in a hypothetical example, because the experience is a universal one and nearly all of your fellow students will recognize themselves in one or more of the situations you invent and describe. In some respects the hypothetical example may be superior to a real one in a descriptive speech, since it can be planned specifically for the purposes you intend. Although hypothetical examples have little value as proof, they can be made fully acceptable to an audience by careful selection of lifelike details. Their principal function, however, is to make the idea clear and interesting.

Exercises

1. Here are some typical explanations which might be made by a developed example, either true or hypothetical. Try your skill at the use of this kind of material by writing one or two paragraphs about several of these topics or similar ones. Ask your instructor to comment on your paper.

   a. Explain the forehand drive in tennis by describing the way you saw it used by a leading player in a tournament match.

   b. Explain the way the student council guides, supervises, or controls student activities on campus by describing what happened on one occasion in one activity.

   c. Explain the operation of the primary election system by telling what a particular candidate did between the time he decided to run and the time he was nominated in the primary.

   d. Explain the registration system for freshmen in your college by outlining relevant activities of a typical freshman from the time he graduated from high school until he attended his first college class.

   e. Explain the law of supply and demand in terms of a pound of coffee or butter, or a suit of clothes.

   f. Explain a method of getting an unwilling child to go to bed by describing your own experience as a baby sitter.

   g. Explain any activity or concept about which you have personal knowledge by a developed example of a single case illustrating your concept.

2. Use negative definition blended with positive examples to clarify the meaning of one or more of the following terms: truth, justice, democracy, school spirit, Americanism, faith. Read your definition to the class and ask for comments.

3. Define one or more of the following terms by a series of undeveloped examples: conservation of natural resources, statesmanship, the ideal all-American halfback, values of scientific research, skill in speech.

Believability — Gaining Acceptance

If you are to communicate to others, your ideas must be not only clear but acceptable. The members of the audience must believe that the statements you make are true. In a speech to inform, the discovery of one error of fact will tend to discredit the accuracy of other parts of it. In a speech to persuade, of course, the acceptance by the audience of the truth of your statements is paramount. To some extent, acceptance of your ideas is a result of your personal prestige. If your hearers believe you are an authority on the subject, they will be less critical of what you say. Beyond this, acceptance depends on the extent to which your statements fit into established patterns of belief and prejudice. If your speech runs counter to these patterns, you must support your generalizations by converting them into simpler and more readily acceptable terms. At the most elemental level, you will present examples and group them into the relationships which caused you to arrive at your present beliefs. You may thus lead your hearers into new channels of thought.

USING EXAMPLES FOR PROOF. When you are puzzled about the accuracy or truth of an idea, your natural tendency is to ask for an example. "I can think of a million good reasons why I shouldn't study tonight," your roommate declares. "Name one," is your skeptical reply. The bantering mood of this exchange does not invalidate the point. One good example, clearly stated, would be far more convincing than the sweeping generalization. The interest, clarity, and acceptability of every statement of judgment or information depend upon the belief of the audience that it is based upon experience. As we have said, *the example is a cross section of experience which the speaker offers as typical of the general knowledge on a subject.* Because examples are specific, concrete, and simple, they are easily understood and accepted. Because they are close to the listener's experience, they maintain interest.

In the last political campaign in your state, it is certain that the party out of power (whether Republican or Democratic) charged the incumbent governor and legislature with extravagance, and asserted that when the "rascals had been turned out" economy would prevail. No amount of counter-assertion would destroy the impression created by the charge, but a specific example could do much to develop the facts.

Note how Adlai Stevenson used a *developed example* to support his assertion that economy and extravagance were not identifiable with either political party:

> In the last session of my legislature in Illinois I presented a very tight budget that called for no tax increases, in spite of all the cost increases in the previous two years. And, I called upon the legislature not to add to that budget without subtracting from it in order to keep it in balance. What do you think they did? They subtracted $300,000 and added $50,000,000. I hope it isn't indelicate to advise you that it was an overwhelmingly Republican legislature in both Houses.
>
> The Republican leader, in that session, sponsored and passed a bill to increase all old-age pension allotments 10 per cent automatically, although we have a system of automatic adjustments in accordance with living costs. The cost of that measure we estimated at roughly fourteen millions, but he made no effort whatever to provide any of the money with which to pay for it. . . .
>
> I could entertain you at length with the difficulty I had to get one Republican vote to cut a large appropriation and thereby balance the budget at all, in the previous session. Indeed, if I recounted all my experiences of this kind I am afraid you might get the impression that I am slightly partisan. But I am sure you will forgive me if I say that from where I sit the carefully cultivated impression that Democrats are all extravagant and Republicans are all provident is a fairy tale and part of the phony folklore that a careful citizen will examine carefully.[1]

If Stevenson had made a blanket assertion that the Republicans were the party of extravagance and the Democrats the party of economy, this example would be completely inadequate support. But his generalization was carefully qualified. He simply asked his hearers to examine a glaring exception to a generalization offered by his opponents. The case was so clearly stated by the example that it was hardly necessary to give further support.

But a single example is seldom adequate proof for a generalization. Sometimes a speaker will begin with a developed example like Stevenson's, and then add shorter examples, statistics, or other

[1] Adlai E. Stevenson, *Major Campaign Speeches of Adlai E. Stevenson* (New York: Random House, Inc., 1953), pp. 106–107.

UNDEVELOPED EXAMPLES . . .

In a speech on the functions of government, each of the following, briefly mentioned, could be an undeveloped example.

The police

U.S. Highways

National defense

The postal service

The judiciary

Any one of the undeveloped examples of government functions shown on the opposite page could be expanded by further detail. Thus the police not only

Direct traffic, but

Take evidence from ballistics

Communicate by radio

Keep files of fingerprints . . . and so on.

kinds of material to support the idea further. Perhaps a more common method is to cite a series of short examples without elaboration. Note how Henry George in his lecture, *The Crime of Poverty,* moves from a generalization to more specific general statements, to two specific undeveloped examples in support of his thesis that poverty is contrary to nature.

> . . . There is nothing in nature like this poverty which today curses us. We see rapine in nature; we see one species destroying another; but as a general thing animals do not feed on their own kind; and, wherever we see one kind enjoying plenty, all individuals of that kind share it. No man, I think, ever saw a herd of buffalo, of which a few were fat and the great majority lean. No man ever saw a flock of birds, of which two or three were swimming in grease, and the others were all skin and bone. Nor in savage life is there anything like the poverty that festers in our civilization.

When such *undeveloped examples* are used, the speaker must assume that members of his audience are able to supply the required details or will understand and accept the examples without them. Perhaps the details are common knowledge and the listeners need merely to be reminded of them to make the example complete. Members of the United States Senate did not need developed examples in order to follow Senator Robert A. Taft's argument that constructive criticism was essential to the development of a wise foreign policy:

> Whatever the value of unity, it is also true that unity carried to unreasonable extremes can destroy a country. The Kaiser achieved unity in Germany. Hitler again achieved the same unity at the cost of freedom many years later. Mussolini achieved unity in Italy. The leaders of Japan through a method of so-called thought control achieved unity in Japan. In every case, policies adopted by these enforcers of unity led to the destruction of their own country. . . .

ON INACCURACY

Napoleon III acquired such skill in the art of lying that the journals complained you could not depend on the exact contrary of that which he stated.

— RALPH WALDO EMERSON

Today it is just as easy for us to adopt a false foreign policy leading to the destruction of our people as for any other nation to do so. The best safeguard against fatal error lies in continuous criticism and discussion to bring out the truth and develop the best program.[1]

ANALOGIES. *Analogies* are considered by some writers to be a special method of development. Actually, however, an analogy is a method of reasoning based on *compared examples*. You might argue that the city manager form of government would improve civic conditions in city A because it had done so in city B. To validate your analogy you would *develop the two examples simultaneously* and in detail, showing that the two cities were alike in all relevant ways except their form of government. You would try to demonstrate that the evils still existing in city A had been removed from city B after the adoption of the city manager plan.

Analogies may also be used for explanation rather than for proof. Only approximate similarities are then needed. Thus you might explain the operation of the transmission in an automobile by using the example of a kitchen egg beater in which the gears can be plainly seen. Such *figurative analogies* should not be judged by standards of proof. Their sole purpose is to make an idea clear and interesting. Like other forms of the example, analogies also appear in undeveloped form, such as the humorous analogy used by Franklin D. Roosevelt in his address at the Jackson Day Dinner, January 8, 1938. After noting that the owners of only four per cent of the securities of electric utilities were able to control the management of the companies, he rounded out his argument with these three sentences:

> There, my friends, is the case of a ninety-six inch dog being wagged by a four inch tail. If you work it out in feet and inches it is an amazing dog. But think of the power of that four inches.

Both developed and undeveloped analogies give your listener two chances to grasp an idea instead of one. If the comparison is valid, interest, clarity, and acceptability are all enhanced. All of these factors are well illustrated in the following explanation by Sir James Jeans of why the sky looks blue. Note that his analogy is based on

[1] A. Craig Baird, *Representative American Speeches: 1950–1951* (New York: H. W. Wilson Company), p. 67.

*An illustration is a window in an argument, and lets in light.
You may reason without an illustration; but where you are employ-
ing a process of pure reasoning and have arrived at a conclusion,
if you can then by an illustration flash light upon what you have
said, you will bring into the minds of your audience a realization
of your argument that they cannot get in any other way.*

— HENRY WARD BEECHER

---

the comparison of two examples, the "experience" of sunlight in the
air and that of waves striking a pier.

Imagine that we stand on any ordinary seaside pier, and watch
the waves rolling in and striking against the iron columns of the pier.
Large waves pay little attention to the columns — they divide right
and left and re-unite after passing each column, much as a regiment of
soldiers would if a tree stood in their road; it is almost as though the
columns had not been there. But the short waves and ripples find the
columns of the pier a much more formidable obstacle. When the short
waves impinge on the columns, they are reflected back and spread as
new ripples in all directions. To use the technical term, they are
"scattered." The obstacle provided by the iron columns hardly affects
the long waves at all, but scatters the short ripples.

We have been watching a sort of working model of the way in
which sunlight struggles through the earth's atmosphere. Between us
on earth and outer space the atmosphere interposes innumerable obstacles in the form of molecules of air, tiny droplets of water, and
small particles of dust. These are represented by the columns of the
pier.

The waves of the sea represent the sunlight. We know that sunlight
is a blend of lights of many colours — as we can prove for ourselves
by passing it through a prism, or even through a jug of water, or as
Nature demonstrates to us when she passes it through the raindrops
of a summer shower and produces a rainbow. We also know that
light consists of waves, and that the different colours of light are produced by waves of different lengths, red light by long waves and blue
light by short waves. The mixture of waves which constitutes sunlight
has to struggle through the obstacles it meets in the atmosphere, just
as the mixture of waves at the seaside has to struggle past the columns
of the pier. And these obstacles treat the light-waves much as the
columns of the pier treat the sea-waves. The long waves which constitute the red light are hardly affected, but the short waves which
constitute blue light are scattered in all directions.

98

Thus, the different constituents of sunlight are treated in different ways as they struggle through the earth's atmosphere. A wave of blue light may be scattered by a dust particle, and turned out of its course. After a time a second dust particle again turns it out of its course, and so on, until finally it enters our eyes by a path as zigzag as that of a flash of lightning. Consequently the blue waves of sunlight enter our eyes from all directions. And that is why the sky looks blue.[1]

Exercises

To test your ability to use both developed and undeveloped examples, take one or more of the following generalized ideas and develop it as suggested:

1. Our college should have a good football team next year.
    a. Developed example — tell the story of the exploits of the best player who will return from this year's squad.
    b. Undeveloped examples — supplement the story of the star with sentences and phrases describing other promising members of the team.
2. The Republican (or Democratic) party has the best available candidates for President (Governor, Congressman, Senator, etc.).
    a. Developed example — tell in detail the qualifications of the person you believe to be the best candidate.
    b. Undeveloped examples — supplement with sentences and phrases describing other promising candidates.
3. A college education is an aid to a young man in getting his first job.
    a. Developed example — tell in detail the experience of one job candidate whose college education was helpful to him.
    b. Undeveloped examples — supplement with sentences and phrases describing the experiences of others confirming the developed example.
4. The state of _____ has the most beautiful scenery in the United States.
    a. Developed example — describe in detail the beauty of one outstanding spot in the state.

[1] Sir James Jeans, *The Stars in Their Courses* (New York: Cambridge University Press, 1931), pp. 25–27.

      b. Undeveloped examples — supplement with the names of other beauty spots and one sentence or phrase identifying an outstanding feature of each.

   5. The United Nations has been more successful than is often supposed.
      a. Developed example — tell in detail how the UN settled Iran's dispute with Soviet Russia.
      b. Undeveloped examples — cite progress made in Israeli-Arab, Pakistani-Indian, and other disputes.
      c. Undeveloped examples — cite agreements reached in non-political commissions of the UN.

   6. The honor system should be adopted in our college.
      a. Developed analogy — cite relevant similarities between your college and an institution where the honor system has worked well.
      b. Undeveloped analogies — list other colleges where the system has also worked.
      c. Developed analogy — show why the conditions which caused the failure of the honor system in one college do not apply in yours.

Read your supported generalization to the class and ask for comments on clarity, believability, and interest.

STATISTICS: CODIFIED AND CLASSIFIED EXAMPLES. Statistics often seem cold, impersonal, and remote from experience. If they give this impression to an audience, however, it is because the speaker has failed to realize that the raw material of statistics is the example. Statistics are simply codified and classified examples expressed in numbers. Consider the origin of the statistics compiled each decade by the United States Census Bureau. The census taker assigned to your neighborhood covers his district with painstaking thoroughness. He calls at every house in the area, asking the number of occupants, their ages and occupations, and sometimes much more personal questions. Every family is to him an example of American life, and the answers to his questions are examples of income, marital status, age, and so forth. These examples have to him a substance which is no less real because it will not appear on his reports. He will recall the number of dogs who dislike strangers, the small boys who show off before visitors, and the embarrassment he felt when a troubled wife insisted on telling him about an errant husband.

Stripped of these interesting human details, the census taker's report is forwarded through the proper channels to the Census Bureau, where the individual examples known to the interviewer are converted into statistics by combination into various meaningful categories. The results of these tabulations and those of other surveys conducted by the Census Bureau are compiled in the reports of the Bureau, and the more widely useful ones are incorporated into the *Statistical Abstract of the United States*. Statistics compiled by other government agencies, such as the Departments of Commerce, Labor, and Agriculture, are derived in much the same way. In fact, whether statistics are gathered by government agencies, by endowed foundations, by university and college research, or by private groups, the raw material is always individual examples — segments of experience. Yet because statistical data cover a wider range of experience than the individual example, they serve a function which more limited materials cannot match.

Values and Limitations of Statistics. Even though your hearers may accept your examples as true, they may feel that the examples are not conclusive proof of your generalization. Are the examples typical or exceptional? Have you studied enough examples so that you can be sure the general statement is correct? Suppose you assert that the major cause of strikes in the United States is not wages and hours but union jurisdiction. You support the statement by describing a serious jurisdictional strike about which you have some knowledge, developing the example in detail. Your *developed example* is impressive because it is vivid and personal. Yet your audience may doubt that it is typical. To broaden the scope of your statement, you cite six similar cases, without giving details. These *undeveloped examples* serve to strengthen the first case by covering a larger area. Yet your hearers will reject your entire argument when someone presents the statistical analysis of the cause of strikes published by the U.S. Bureau of Labor Statistics, showing that approximately half of all strikes are caused by disputes over wages and hours, while controversies within or between unions cause less than five per cent of all strikes. Thus the statistics argue convincingly that your original assertion is untrue.

Statistics are not infallible, however. There is an old saying that "Figures don't lie, but liars will figure." Statistics are no more reliable than the source from which they are derived. Moreover, it is perfectly possible to confuse or deceive an audience with statistics — to give an illusion of authenticity to contemptible clap-trap. This is a device used by modern demagogues, in marked contrast to the shouting rabble-rousers of the nineteenth century who simply substituted noise and abuse for all forms of support. Moreover, statistics can be, and often are, dull. If they are used as the only means of support, speeches lose in interest, and often even in clarity, more than they gain in proof value. But there is no reason why this need happen. A skillful speaker can learn to handle figures without losing either interest or clarity. Following are some practical suggestions on how to use statistics.

1. Do not give your audience statistical details that they cannot possibly remember. Reduce figures to round numbers, as Senator Taft did in a campaign speech in Ohio in 1950.

> Already our government is spending more money than we have ever spent in peacetime and yet the President wants the Brannan Plan which might cost $5 billion, socialized medicine that will cost another $6 billion, and his program has made huge spending necessary for the armed forces. In fact, your own freedom has been limited by this huge taxation. Just add up the money deducted from your pay over this year, and then remember besides that when you buy food or clothing or shoes or anything else, the price includes about 20 per cent of taxes paid along the way by the farmer, the railroad, the manufacturer, the retailer and all the rest of them. Altogether the government takes more than 25 per cent of the national income in taxes. You work one day in four for the government, and only three for yourself. Most of those taxes are passed on to the poor old consumer.

2. Remember that statistics are derived in the first place from human experience. Once, the facts of which they are composed had life and interest value. If they become dull in the hands of a speaker, it is because he lacks the imagination to put them back into human terms. Note how Senator Taft related taxes to deductions from the worker's pay check, to the cost of objects to the consumer, and to unpaid labor one day out of four. These are vital images to the listener and carry far more weight than listing items in the budget down to the last thirty-two cents. If you are an inventive speaker, you will translate a table on the cost of electricity per kilowatt hour into the cost of operating the family toaster for Sunday morning breakfast. You will analyze the budget of your college in terms of professors' salaries or student tuition. It was this type of imaginative treatment of economic data that enabled John Bright to marshal British opinion in the nineteenth century against the Corn Laws which were shutting off food imports while the population was constantly rising. See how he combined statistics with a vivid analogy to sharpen his attack.

> Since we first came to London two million human beings have been added to the population. . . . The table is here as before, the food is spread out in the same quantity as before; but two millions of fresh guests have arrived. . . . These two millions are so many arguments for the Anti-Corn Law League.

If you can learn to treat statistics with imagination and a sense of human values, they will not be dull but will add to the impact of your speech.

3. *Represent statistics visually for your audience.* Statistical data are much easier to comprehend in graphic form than in spoken form. Study the charts and graphs shown on pages 104–105. Note that a "pie" graph is ideal for representing percentages, as in the amount of the national income taken in taxes or as in the distribution of the budget expenditures. A line graph is best for representing fluctuations such as those in production, employment, or stock market averages. A pictograph is best for representing comparative sizes, as of the armed forces relative to the labor force, or the production of steel compared to the production of coal. A bar graph sometimes has less attention value than a pictograph, but it is likely to be more accurate. In any case, when you wish to represent statistics visually, study the figures and determine which method will give the most accurate and vivid portrayal of the idea you wish the audience to accept.

ON USING FACTS

Facts mean nothing unless they are rightly understood, rightly related and rightly interpreted.

— R. L. Long

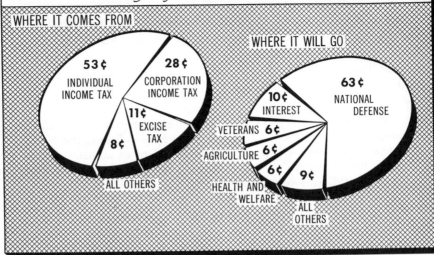

A Dollar Breakdown of President Kennedy's Budget for Fiscal 1962-1963

WHERE IT COMES FROM

53¢ INDIVIDUAL INCOME TAX

28¢ CORPORATION INCOME TAX

11¢ EXCISE TAX

8¢

ALL OTHERS

WHERE IT WILL GO

10¢ INTEREST

63¢ NATIONAL DEFENSE

VETERANS 6¢

AGRICULTURE 6¢

HEALTH AND WELFARE 6¢

9¢

ALL OTHERS

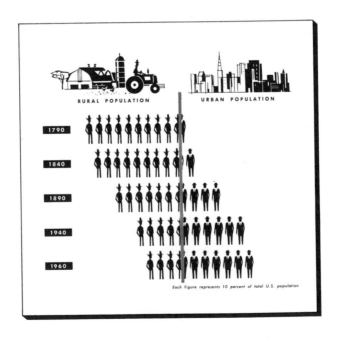

RURAL POPULATION   URBAN POPULATION

1790

1840

1890

1940

1960

Each figure represents 10 percent of total U.S. population

CHARTS AND GRAPHS . . .

Visual representations of statistics can help a speech but must be large and clear enough to be seen and grasped readily. The pictogram (see bottom of opposite page) is usually memorable but may be inexact. The line graph (steel production) is clear at a glance. The "pie" chart is a good device, but this one is perhaps too complex for use in a speech. The bar graph to the right is better.

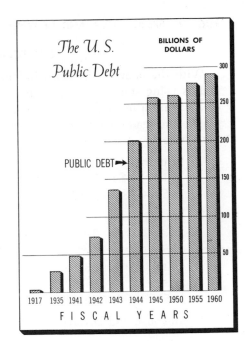

The U. S. Public Debt

BILLIONS OF DOLLARS

PUBLIC DEBT ➤

1917 1935 1941 1942 1943 1944 1945 1950 1955 1960

F I S C A L   Y E A R S

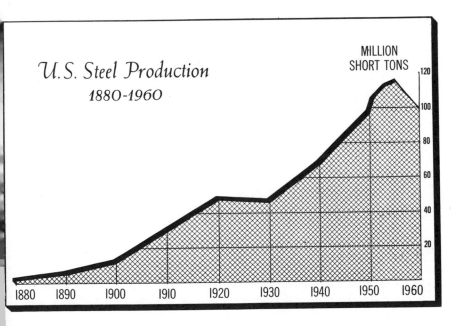

U.S. Steel Production
1880-1960

MILLION SHORT TONS

1880 1890 1900 1910 1920 1930 1940 1950 1960

Exercises

With the above suggestions in mind, develop one or more paragraphs using statistical data. The figures given below may suggest an idea and a method of development. Write out one or more paragraphs and read them to the class for comment and criticism. Utilize the advice about statistics given above.

1. Insurance — Life insurance in force in the United States: 1910 — $14,772,000,000; 1950 — $234,168,000,000; 1960 — $586,448,000,000

2. Immigration —

Year	Aliens Entering	Aliens Departing	Excess of Entrants
1921	978,163	426,031	552,132
1932	174,871	287,657	—112,786
1950	676,024	456,689	219,335

3. Marriage and Divorce — rate per 1000 population.

Year	Marriage Rate	Divorce Rate
1890	9.0	0.5
1900	9.3	0.7
1910	10.3	0.9
1920	12.0	1.6
1930	9.2	1.6
1935	10.4	1.7
1940	12.1	2.0
1946	16.4	4.3
1950	11.0	2.5
1960	8.5	2.2

4. In the current issue of the *World Almanac,* study the figures on per capita consumption of major food commodities.

5. In the current issue of any statistical book in the reference room of your library, select a table about which you can write an appropriate paragraph or two.

Maintaining Interest

In the foregoing pages, we frequently observed that the value of a given method of development lies not merely in its clarity and acceptability, but also in the degree to which it holds attention and creates interest. This concept is so important in public speaking theory that several textbooks have insisted that "what holds attention determines action." This is probably an over-simplification; yet it is certainly true that action is never determined by speeches which do not hold attention, unless it be action contrary to what the speaker wishes. Because attention and interest are essential to communication, there has been a great deal of experiment and practical observation on how to achieve them. Here are some good rules.

1. *Keep the speech moving.* Nothing destroys interest more quickly than the feeling that a speech is not going anywhere. If there is not a sense of movement and change, even the most favorably disposed audience will find it hard to listen attentively. The difficulty may be lessened by skillful delivery. Changes in voice pattern, platform movement, and gesture may all contribute to the sense of movement. But skill in delivery cannot long disguise dullness of material. A speech should not dwell too long on one point, and effective transitions between points should make the hearer aware of the change in emphasis. When possible, examples should be chosen for the sense of movement they convey. Frequent use should be made of contrast and comparison, and examples involving conflict should be used when they fit the theme. Thus in the example given on page 89, the action of the Little League players contributed to the sense of change; Bryan's definition of a "business man" on page 90 profited by quick movement from one short example to another; Taft's discussion of thought control on pages 96–97 contained an implication of conflict. In each of these passages, a sense of movement and change helped to maintain interest.

2. *Draw upon the experience of your audience.* This precept is equally important to interest, clarity, and acceptability. Of course you do not need to draw your examples exclusively from audience experience, but your examples should be compatible with what the audience knows and believes. The speaker needs to seek common ground between himself and his hearers. This is comparatively easy if the speaker and his listeners belong to the same cultural, economic, religious, or political groups, and more difficult if they do not. Yet it is hardly possible to live in the same community, state, or nation with your hearers without discovering some common

ground. If you wish to speak on a technical engineering subject, you may make up for their lack of scientific knowledge by dwelling on their daily use of the products of engineering skill. If you think your audience disagrees violently with the political views you wish to defend, you still have a common interest in the welfare of your community or your country. When you speak, therefore, look for the interests and knowledge you and your hearers have and use this common ground in developing parts of your speech.

3. *Appeal to basic human needs and desires.* When the development of your speech can touch upon universal and elemental needs — such as food and drink, health and personal comfort, life and death, sex, home and family — you can be sure of a high level of attention. It was appeals to such basic needs that gave life to the statistics cited by Senator Taft in the development on page 102. Five minutes spent leafing through the advertising section of a national magazine will convince you that business firms believe in the power of appealing to these basic needs. You may want to use them with more subtlety than some advertisers do, but you cannot afford to ignore them.

4. *Blend less interesting materials with more interesting ones.* Because they are close to human experience, examples frequently touch the natural or acquired interests and desires of your audience. This usually makes them more interesting to hear than statistics, testimony, definition, or explanation by use of details. Since these other methods are often essential to clarity and acceptability, interest may be increased by blending them with examples. In a speech on traffic safety, you might arouse interest by telling in detail the story of a major accident resulting in death, then give some figures: "In New York State alone in 1960 there were 2,046 such deaths, most of them preventable with greater foresight and courtesy on the part of the people involved; in California there were 3,723. In the United States as a whole in the same year there were over 38,000 traffic fatalities. More than twice as many Americans died in traffic accidents in 1951 as were killed in the same year in the Korean war." Used this way, the statistics take on vividness and interest from the example, while the proof value of the example is multiplied by 38,000. The comparison with the deaths in Korea highlights the uselessness of highway slaughter. Meanwhile the listener is rested by the change in pattern from one type of support to another. Blending the kinds of material enhances clarity and believability as well as interest.

USING VISUAL AIDS . . .

Visual aids — maps, models, pictures, and the like — give variety to the speech and provide a double sensory impression to increase the impact of ideas.

5. Use visual materials wherever appropriate. We have already discussed the desirability of representing statistics visually. In addition, there are many opportunities to use models, maps, pictures, and photographic slides to illustrate your speeches. Visual aids give variety to the speech, and they provide a double sensory impression to increase the impact of ideas. In Chapter 2 (pages 40–41) we offered some advice about the use of such aids. We would add a word of caution. Do not use visual aids to impress on an audience ideas which are perfectly clear from the spoken word. A map or a model can tell a story which language alone cannot project. But a list of the points in the speaker's outline suggests the schoolroom or the sales manager's pep talk. A competent speaker should not need such an aid to impress his ideas on his listeners.

Reinforcing Ideas

After an idea has been clearly stated and developed, the speaker still needs to clinch it in the minds of his hearers. Except in speeches whose only purpose is to amuse and entertain, success depends on how much the audience remembers, thinks about, and acts on the suggestions voiced by the speaker. Ideas thus need to be reinforced and emphasized as well as stated and developed. Some of the techniques for reinforcing ideas are matters of language and will be explained in a later chapter. Others are designed to fix ideas in mind by repeating or restating them, or by lending them the weight of authority.

Repetition

Speeches permit far more repetition of words, phrases, and ideas than written discourse. If a reader misses the import of an idea and is confused when he passes to the next section, he can always go back and reread the part he missed. The listener has no such opportunity. Hence a speaker not only may, but often must, repeat words and phrases to give them the emphasis they deserve in the development of his idea. The preacher repeats his text or portions of it many times during a sermon in the hope that his hearers will memorize it and retain it as the nucleus of a half-hour discourse. The politician may use a slogan which he will repeat frequently throughout a series of speeches to impress it upon his hearers. In 1948 President Truman sold the voters on his slogan about the

"Do-nothing Eightieth Congress." In 1952, Dwight D. Eisenhower promised several times in nearly every speech to "clean up the mess in Washington." Campaign slogans in the twentieth century have presented an interesting variation on a few key words: Theodore Roosevelt's "Square Deal" and Woodrow Wilson's "New Freedom" were combined in Franklin Roosevelt's "New Deal," perhaps a symbolic union of the earlier progressive movements. Harry Truman offered the variation of "Fair Deal," and John F. Kennedy campaigned on the slogan, "New Frontier." These phrases were not without content, for each of them was developed and supported in campaign speeches, but their mere repetition served a function beyond their actual meaning. In a speech in the Senate in 1856, Charles Sumner used the word "swindle" eleven times in one paragraph of less than three hundred words. When he had finished, his attitude toward the Kansas-Nebraska Act was unmistakable. We do not advocate the violence and intemperance which characterized this speech, but the technique of repetition is effective. Do not be afraid to use it.

Restatement

Sometimes it is better to restate an idea in different words than to repeat it in exactly the same form. Such restatements should be used in summaries and transitions within the speech as well as in the conclusion of the speech as a whole. If you are tempted, like many beginning speakers, to assume that your point is clear without restatement, you must remember again that your audience is composed of listeners, not readers. Restatement is insurance against a momentary wandering of attention. It protects you against the passing truck and the blonde across the aisle, as well as against the normal fatigue of listeners sitting in uncomfortable seats in a stuffy room.

Restatement is not necessarily formal and easily recognizable. Often it is interwoven into the fabric of a sentence or a paragraph in order to emphasize and reinforce the central idea. In the following segment of a speech from the Lincoln-Douglas debates, note how Lincoln repeats and restates his charge that Douglas sticks to the Dred Scott Decision "not because he says it is right in itself, . . . but because it has been decided by the court."

This man sticks to a decision which forbids the people of a Territory to exclude slavery, and he does so not because he says it is right in itself, . . . but because it has been decided by the court; and, being decided by the court, he is, and you are, bound to take it in your political action as law, — not that he judges at all of its merits, but because a decision of the court is to him a "Thus saith the Lord." He places it on that ground alone, and you will bear in mind that thus committing himself unreservedly to this decision commits him to the next one just as firmly as to this. He did not commit himself on account of the merit or demerit of the decision, but it is a "Thus saith the Lord." The next decision, as much as this, will be a "Thus saith the Lord." There is nothing that can divert or turn him away from this decision.

Both repetition and restatement were used here. In print it seems redundant, but if you will read it aloud, you will see that to the ear it serves to point up and give weight to Lincoln's central idea.

In 1879, when William E. Gladstone, leader of England's Liberal party, wished to refute a charge made by the Tories who held possession of the government, he used restatement to make sure that the nature of the charge could not be misunderstood. The entire content of the paragraph is given in the first sentence. The second and third merely restate the ideas expressed in the first.

We are told, we are incessantly told, that there is no fault in the Government, that this is all a spirit of faction on the part of the Liberal party. I need not quote what you know very well; that that is the stock and standing material of invective against us — it is all our faction. The Government is perfectly innocent, but we are determined to blacken them because of the selfish and unjust motives by which we are prompted.

Again, the writer would no doubt express this thought more briefly, but the speaker needs the emphasis of restatement. Moreover, material of this kind lends itself well to changes in delivery, which add to the emphasis achieved by restatement.

Quotations

One of the most effective ways to reinforce an idea is to use a quotation. Quoted material may be used to add color or literary freshness to an idea, thus making it easier to remember. Good quotations may serve to bring the prestige of the author to bear on the side of the speaker and to summarize and restate a generalization with force and clarity. But quoted material should be used sparingly and should be a supplement to, rather than a substitute for, other developmental materials.

QUOTATIONS AS PROOF — TESTIMONY. In persuasive speaking, quotations from authority are commonly used as testimony on behalf of the generalizations the speaker is supporting. So used, quotations may be regarded as a method of developing rather than reinforcing ideas. We have chosen to treat quotations as reinforcement because we do not believe that speeches are effective when they rely too heavily upon the opinions of others as a basis for belief in ideas advanced by the speaker. The debater who measures the height of the stack of books from which he is prepared to quote, and talks slightingly of the smaller pile cited by his opponent, is making no contribution to understanding, interest, or belief. Testimony is most effective in a speech when it is combined with examples and statistics and used as a summary and confirmation of the speaker's own conclusions. This way, it may often serve as the clinching support for the ideas presented in a speech.

There is in some advertisements a great deal of nonsense which passes for evidence. Testimonials from movie stars, sports figures, and other celebrities are freely used in support of claims which these "authorities" have no logical right to make. Yet the very fact that advertisers find it worth-while to use this sort of testimony indicates that it has some influence on the judgment of those to whom it is directed. In your speaking, you should not be content with the flimsy connection which often appears in such advertising.

Legitimate testimony, however, is often of great value. To test the validity and persuasiveness of testimony, ask these questions:

1. Does the person quoted have the necessary training and experience to make his opinion of value on this question?
2. Has he had specific opportunity to óbserve the facts about which his opinion is expressed?
3. Is he well enough known by the audience to make his opinion impressive? If not, can his authority be quickly established?

Thus on a question of organizing a college curriculum in general education, the presidents of Carroll College and of Northwestern University might be equally well qualified to speak by test (1) and test (2); but except in the immediate vicinity of Carroll College, it would be easier to validate the opinion of Northwestern's president simply because his institution is better known. On the same question, the opinion of a movie beauty would fail completely to meet tests (1) and (2), and would qualify for test (3) only in the minds of those who could not discriminate between wide popularity and the possession of authoritative knowledge. Yet on a subject dealing with acting in motion pictures, the movie star, if not the best authority, would be better than either of the two college presidents, and by all three tests.

QUOTATIONS FOR VIVIDNESS AND EMPHASIS. In speeches to stimulate audiences or to inspire new ways of thinking, quotations may be used to give vividness to an idea or even to enhance the prestige of the speaker. Quotations from the Bible or Shakespeare and epigrams coined by distinguished literary, philosophical, and political figures are often used effectively in this kind of speaking. You will find thousands of apt statements in such works as Bartlett's *Familiar Quotations,* and Edwards' *New Dictionary of Thoughts,* although it is much better to familiarize yourself with the original sources by wider reading. Such epigrammatic quotations are not subject to the limitations you must impose on testimony intended for proof. It is the vividness with which the idea is expressed that is primarily important. Does it stimulate the thoughts and feelings of your hearers?

How might you use each of the following quotations in a speech? Write out one or two paragraphs about some of these epigrams to show possible uses for them.

1. Speeches cannot be made long enough for the speakers nor short enough for the hearers. — James Perry, English political writer and editor, 1756–1821.

2. As a vessel is known by the sound, whether it be cracked or not, so men are proved by their speeches whether they be wise or foolish. — Demosthenes, Greek statesman and orator, 384–322 B.C.

3. There are three things to aim at in public speaking; first to get into your subject, then to get your subject into yourself, and lastly, to get your subject into your hearers. — Alexander Gregg, American Episcopal bishop, 1819–1867.

4. Any man may make a mistake, but none but a fool will continue in it. — Cicero, Roman statesman and orator, 106–43 B.C.

5. Few minds wear out; more rust out. — Christian Bovee, American author and editor, 1820–1904.

6. An egotist is a man who talks so much about himself that he gives me no time to talk about myself. — H. L. Wayland, American clergyman, 1830–1898.

7. No man is free who is not master of himself. — Epictetus, Roman Stoic philosopher, 60 A.D.–120 A.D.

Epigrams like these are usually most effective when they are combined with examples illustrating the kind of behavior they praise or lampoon. Quotations may also be used as summaries of ideas developed in other ways.

Exercises

1. Build a speech on a subject of your own choice, working for maximum clarity, believability, and interest. Follow the plan of preparation suggested in Chapter 4, page 67.
2. By marginal notes on your outline, indicate to your instructor what techniques you have used to insure clarity, believability, and interest.
3. Some of the subjects suggested in exercises within Chapter 5 might be used for full speeches. You may also use subjects from Chapters 2 and 4 which have not been spoken about.
   Here are some additional suggestions:
   a. *Campus:* fraternities and sororities; subsidized athletics; student government; student transportation.
   b. *Local Problems:* running the public schools; the city manager plan; mass transportation; air pollution; adequate recreation facilities.
   c. *National Problems:* party responsibility; the next President; Congressional demagoguery; national defense; public housing; civil rights.
   d. *International Problems:* reciprocal trade agreements; world Communism; alliances and national security.
   Most of these subjects are too broad to be treated in a speech of ordinary length, and need to be divided or made more specific in terms of issues which are current at the time you speak. If none of these suits your interests, consult your instructor.

Criticizing the Communicability of Ideas

You may recall a clear statement of opinion cited early in this chapter that "flying is fun." Suppose this is the "idea" which some speaker would like to communicate to an audience of college students. He might say:

Flying *is* fun. When I fly I often like to do a series of stalls. In a stall the airfoil, that is to say, the wing, is moving through the air too slowly to provide lift. Without "lift," gravity takes over. At this moment the plane ceases to be a wonderful "flying machine," and begins to behave like a lead brick. In the instant between flying and falling there is an exciting sensation of weightlessness. If you have ever ridden in a rollercoaster, or rapidly driven a car over a sharp hill summit, you have experienced a similar sensation. If you like it you may find that flying, too, would be fun for you.

Other pilots have preferences of a different kind. Some enjoy the feeling of quick power and acceleration on the take-off run. In fact, each of the 140,000 private pilots in this country doubtlessly has his own personal pleasure in some particular maneuver. And all of them think it is fun to fly.

Now before you head for the nearest airport, suppose you glance back at the paragraphs above. What communicative devices and methods can you identify in this passage? Is there a statement of an idea in a simple sentence? An example was defined as a cross-section of experience. Is the paragraph on the stall an example? Do you find two undeveloped examples compared in order to present an analogy? Do you find definition, or division, or repetition? In short, do you see the simple progression in which the speaker first stated an idea, then developed it, and then restated it in order to reinforce it? And, in particular, did his method of development give you a chance to be interested, to understand, and to accept or believe?

The short speech on flying was purposely loaded with several of the techniques discussed in this chapter. Perhaps you will use fewer devices in a passage of similar length in a speech of your own. Nevertheless you and your classmates must depend upon these methods to make your ideas communicable. With this in mind, test the content of speeches by your fellow students by asking these questions:

1. Did the speaker make his ideas clear?

a. Were the central idea and the major subdivisions clearly stated? Could you as critic remember them when the speech was finished? If not, was it because they were not well-stated or because your interest lagged?

b. Were terms defined where necessary? Were the definitions clear? Would other means of definition have been preferable to those used?

c. Were any parts explained too fully, continuing after the audience clearly understood?

2. Did the speaker make his ideas believable?

a. Had he correctly judged the beliefs and attitudes of the audience about his subject? Did he use those attitudes to full advantage?

b. Did he develop controversial ideas sufficiently to make them acceptable? Did he use enough supporting examples? Would other kinds of developmental material have been more advantageous than those he used? Were any parts developed too fully?

3. Did the speaker make his ideas interesting?

a. Did he make adequate use of the experience of the audience?

b. Did he make adequate use of basic human desires and interests?

c. Would the use of other kinds of materials for development have given higher interest value?

Remember as you prepare your speech that you too will be judged by these standards. There will be less cause for negative criticism from your classmates if you check your speech against these questions before you deliver it.

6 STRUCTURE:

Giving Ideas Form

A carefully planned, orderly progression of ideas characterizes television documentary programs like David Brinkley's Journal.

CLE AROR *gani zati onisessen tialtound erst and ing.* Does this sentence make sense to you? It is not written in Esperanto or some obscure Indian tongue. In fact, its letters are in their right sequence for clear English. It is the lack of an orderly grouping which defeats your normal impulse to seek meaning in the symbol impressions you receive. Yet just a slight re-arrangement of the letters tells you that *clear organization is essential to understanding.*

Similarly, a speech may carry useful information and still fail to reach the audience because confused organization obscures meaning. As a result the listeners' attention wanders and they do not accept the speaker's ideas. Clarity, believability, and interest are all impaired.

Clear speech organization makes communication easier for both speaker and listener. Coherently arranged materials are easier to remember when you stand before an audience. Indeed, if your ideas

made sense when you prepared your outline, you have only to rethink them as you speak rather than labor to recall a miscellaneous
collection of unrelated details. Moreover, arranging ideas so that
they make good sense to the speaker surely improves the listener's
ability to follow and remember. Conversely, if you ended preparation with a welter of half-formed ideas and disorderly thoughts, the
effort to speak will compound your difficulty and perhaps force your
listeners to wonder why you made the attempt. Clear organization
helps the speaker remember what he wants to say and the listener
understand and retain what he has heard.

Much of the advice on speech preparation in the earlier chapters
dealt more or less indirectly with the skills of organization. When
you first began to think of a speech subject you related your ideas to
a central theme or purpose. As you selected materials, you determined whether they advanced this purpose. You chose examples,
statistics, or other supporting material because you thought it would
make the central idea or a sub-point more understandable, believable, or interesting. In each stage of preparation, you weighed and
evaluated ideas, tested their relevancy to your purpose, and determined their relationship to each other. In short, you organized your
thoughts. In the speeches you have already given, therefore, you
have learned a great deal about organizing ideas. We now ask you
to evaluate this information and to supplement it with a more extensive and practical study of clearly structured thought.

The Basic Organizational Plan

No two good speeches are ever exactly alike in their arrangement.
A well-planned speech derives its organization in part from its content, in part from the knowledge and beliefs of the audience, and
in part from the personality and prestige of the speaker. The structure of speeches by John F. Kennedy and Richard Nixon on the same
political subjects differed because they believed different things,
addressed themselves to different groups of people, and had markedly
different personality assets. No textbook, therefore, can properly
prescribe for you a rigid formula for speech organization which can
be tortured to fit any and every subject, speaker, occasion, and
audience. Perhaps this is why writers who have recommended an
exact structure differ so widely on what it should be. The Greek and
Roman rhetoricians proposed from four to six specific sections in a

speech. One modern writer suggests a neat five-step arrangement called the "motivated sequence," while another proposes a four-step "formula." There are obvious advantages to the beginner in such rigid patterns, but they can hardly be tailored to fit every subject and occasion with the same grace and ease. The maturing speaker soon discovers their inadequacies.

Yet you should not feel that, in the matter of organizing materials, we are casting you adrift in an open boat. Fortunately, there are three minimum essentials in speech organization about which there is general agreement. The speaker needs, first of all, to get started. Next, he must organize the bulk of his speech content into a logically developing pattern which makes his ideas clear, believable, and interesting. Last, he must bring the speech to an effective end. These three essential parts are generally called by the unimaginative but accurate names, *introduction, body,* and *conclusion.* The minimum content of each was clearly stated by the country preacher who described his method of organizing a sermon as follows: "First I tells 'em what I'm gonna tell 'em; then I tells 'em; and then I tells 'em what I told 'em." More sophisticated speakers could plan worse — and sometimes do.

It is true, of course, that many speaking situations are too complex to be covered fully by the country preacher's simple formula. Thus we need to study the aims and techniques of introduction and conclusion and to examine the structure of clear outlines for the speech as a whole. We shall then have the tools with which to tackle the basic problem: how to discover the shape your thought should take, and the most suitable pattern of organization for any particular speech.

The Introduction

Some years ago a public prosecutor cleaning up racketeering in a large city reported his progress to the people in a series of fifteen-minute radio broadcasts. In one of them he began with these words: "Tonight I want· to talk to you about murder — murder in the bakery racket." With this one sentence, he achieved the three principal purposes of a good introduction. By using personal pronouns, he established contact with his audience; by blunt and forthright terms — "murder" — "racket" — he caught the attention of listeners absorbed in their evening newspapers or twirling the dial in search of music; by a direct statement of his theme, he announced the subject of his talk. There was no point in a longer introduction when this was enough to achieve these three ends. A good introduction thus seeks to (1) *establish contact* (rapport, good will) *between the speaker and his audience;* (2) *catch attention and arouse interest;* (3) *state the subject of the speech and establish the speaker's point of view.*

Whether it takes ten seconds or ten minutes to gain these ends depends on the time available, the nature of the subject, the relationship between speaker and audience before the speech begins, and the attitude of the audience toward the subject. Do not consider these three aims as separate steps in your introduction. All may be achieved by a single device, or you may use several different methods.

Examine carefully the opening techniques described below. They are only suggestions, and you need not be limited by them if you have another idea which will serve the purposes of a good introduction. Whatever your method, if you succeed in establishing contact, getting attention, and making the theme of your speech clear in the minimum time consistent with your speech purpose, you will have begun well.

TECHNIQUES FOR THE INTRODUCTION

1. The Occasion and the Audience. Even though the members of the audience have assembled for the specific purpose of hearing you speak, they will at the beginning be thinking about everything else under the sun. One is pondering a business deal; another is mentally cursing the erratic driver who nearly forced him off the road ten minutes before; and a third is anticipating a pleasant

Like an applicant for a job, a speaker must make a good first impression. His appearance, his attitude, and his approach to his subject vitally affect both his style and his delivery.

Wit has truth in it; wisecracking is simply calisthenics with words.

— DOROTHY PARKER

---

evening at the Homecoming Dance. Yet your hearers also have much in common. They may belong to a club and so have a mutual interest in its aims. They may be celebrating a special occasion. Or they may be members of the same speech class. Whatever their background, they have gathered to hear a speech, and probably have at least a passing curiosity about the subject. They are all in the same room and are able to see approximately the same things. They probably live in the same town and experienced the same weather coming to hear the speech. In a classroom audience, college events are common ground. Thus you have a wide range of facts and events to which you may allude to establish this kind of contact with your audience and to shift their attention from their own affairs to you and your subject.

TYPICAL EXAMPLES

a. A student referred to the color scheme of the room at the beginning of a talk on "Color and Conduct."

b. Theodore Roosevelt began a speech on "The Strenuous Life" by describing the bustling character of Chicago, the city in which he was speaking.

c. Winston Churchill opened an address to Congress by referring to his American ancestry.

2. Narrative and Descriptive Material. At no point in the speech is a developed example more effective than at the beginning. A carefully chosen story may not only gain attention, but may also suggest the theme of the speech more vividly than any other opening. Often it can make your audience instantly aware of the seriousness of the problem you intend to discuss. For maximum effect, choose details that lead directly into the body of the speech.

Occasionally you may select an example or a narrative because it is humorous or whimsical. If so, it may also amuse your audience and establish good will. We must, however, offer two warnings about the use of humor. First, nothing is more demoralizing to the sensitive speaker than to tell what he thinks is a hilarious story only to find himself a minority of one. So do not try too hard and lose your dignity. Second, if you succeed with humor, do not go on using it until you have no time left for the meat of your speech. No matter how effective your introduction is, the body of the speech is more important and must not be long postponed.

Typical Examples

a. A student began his discussion of Little League Baseball with a description of a game he had seen. (See page 89).

b. To lead into his main theme, Booker T. Washington told a story of a ship becalmed at sea. (See page 128).

3. *Curiosity and Surprise.* Striking facts often whet the curiosity of an audience and thus help to arouse interest and gain attention. Perhaps you have an unusual set of statistics with surprising or frightening implications. Or you may use a little-known fact such as, "The Colonies did not first declare their independence on July 4, 1776." If you had planned to use such facts later in the development of your speech, it is often wise to lift them out of context and place them first. Their strong attention value enables you to lead into your central idea with interest already at a high pitch.

A startling or shocking opening statement may also bring the audience to sharp attention and give the speaker a chance to state his theme while everyone is listening. But he usually qualifies his opening statement quickly to dispel any apprehension it has created. Dr. Melvin Wheatley, a prominent Los Angeles minister, opened his sermon, "Better Dead than Red — But," with these words:

> G. K. Chesterton once commented on the sentiment of the super-patriot, "My country, right or wrong." Said he, "My country, right or wrong, is a statement no patriot would think of making except in a desperate case. It is like saying, 'My mother, drunk or sober!'" What Mr. Chesterton strenuously objects to in this popular slogan is the fact that it carries the implication that there is no strong preference between my country right *or* wrong, between my mother, drunk *or* sober. I have a similar objection to that new slippery slogan of the super-patriot, "Better dead than Red." Only in this case my objection is to arbitrary elimination of all but the two options — dead or Red, neither of which, I am convinced, is the honest preference of any of us.

Obviously, it is important in introductions of this kind that the speaker startle his audience into listening without alienating them. Used wisely, such an introduction can be arresting — even electrifying. It can also be ill-timed, in poor taste, or offensive.

TYPICAL EXAMPLE

Robert G. Ingersoll began a lecture on "Liberty" with these words: "The history of man is simply the history of slavery, of injustice and brutality, together with the means by which he has, through the dead and desolate years, slowly and painfully advanced."

4. Questions. Another way to gain attention quickly is to open with a question or a series of questions. Often such a direct challenge will stimulate thought along the line the speaker wishes to develop. Thus you may pose a set of questions in your introduction which later become the main topics in the body of your speech. On the other hand, a question is often of value simply for the immediate curiosity it stirs up about the speaker's aims, without being closely connected to the subheadings of the speech. But such· questions must not be very far off the theme.

TYPICAL EXAMPLES

a. Bernard Baruch opened a statement before the Senate Committee on Banking and Currency with a series of questions. (See page 129.)

b. A student began a speech on "The Case for Democracy in Africa" with the question, "What do you think of when I say the word 'colony'?" She then followed with a series of questions offering different definitions from the one she intended and concluded the series with her own definition.

5. Quotations. An apt quotation often serves the double purpose of getting attention and disclosing the subject of the speech. A sentence quoted from Thomas Jefferson, Shakespeare, or the Bible has high prestige value and will help to gain an instant hearing for your idea. The main value of a quotation, however, lies in the effectiveness with which it is phrased. Does it actually state your theme better than you could state it yourself? Or do the circumstances under which it was uttered give it a special significance for your speech? Perhaps that is why preachers begin with texts from the Bible, politicians with statements from party platforms, and Fourth of July orators with words from the Founding Fathers. As we shall see later in the chapter, such a quotation can be used as the framework for an entire speech.

The danger of literary quotations is that they may set too formal a tone for a speech and erect a barrier between the speaker and the audience. Often it is better to begin the speech on a lighter note and introduce the quotation after rapport with the audience has been established.

Typical Examples

a. A student began a speech on "Interdependency" with John Donne's "No man is an island."

b. Abraham Lincoln began an address at Cooper Union in 1860 with a quotation from his lifelong opponent, Stephen Douglas. (See pages 150–151.)

6. *Statement of Central Idea.* The statement of the central idea is usually the self-evident product of other opening techniques. A quotation is frequently a direct statement of theme. An opening narrative, if well conceived, will usually convey the central idea even before the speaker states it. Other methods of opening a speech can also lead naturally into the theme. Once in a while a speaker needs no introduction other than the statement of his central idea. If a crowd gathers to hear a talk on a specific subject, initial interest may be so high that no attention-getting devices are needed. Or the theme itself may be so vividly worded that it gains attention on its own, as does Ingersoll's opening sentence quoted above in the section on *Curiosity and Surprise.*

Any direct statement of the central idea will do much to get a speech off to a good start. Such a statement should first of all be clearly worded. If it can also stimulate curiosity, or please by incisiveness or novelty, so much the better. Above all, avoid the hackneyed and limping words, "My speech today is about. . . ."

Typical Examples

a. A speaker used a two-edged statement to begin a speech on "Diet": "What you eat becomes *you,* but what you eat does not necessarily *become* you."

b. Erwin D. Canham of the *Christian Science Monitor* opened a commencement address with these words: "Let me tell you my thesis at the outset. It is that the struggle for the salvation of free society in our time will be lost unless we in the West — and particularly we in the United States — awaken to and project the fact that we are the great revolutionaries in world history, and that our revolution is basically a spiritual one which we have already proved in action."

These, then, are a few of the ways you may begin a speech. With a little ingenuity, you may find in each new speaking situation additional means of establishing contact, gaining attention, and stating your theme.

DELIVERY IN THE INTRODUCTION. At the outset of a speech, most audiences are favorably disposed toward the speaker. Your delivery can help consolidate this good will or can dispel it. If you are fidgety and seem uncertain, most of your listeners will think, "What can a person so unsure of himself offer that is worth the time I give to hear him?" If you are brash or belligerent, they will resent your tone and resist your ideas. A friendly and communicative manner is particularly important at the beginning. If you begin with informal and offhand remarks, be sure to blend them into the main portion of your prepared speech so that your hearers are unaware when one part ends and the other begins. Try to convey the impression that you are fully informed and competent to speak, but that you want to think through your idea with your audience rather than stuff it down their throats. If you can establish this feeling in the first few minutes of your speech, you will usually be able to sustain it. As a result, you will greatly increase the possibility of having your ideas favorably accepted.

SOME GOOD INTRODUCTIONS. In the introductions given below, we have identified some of the techniques the speakers used. Examine them carefully, and try to determine the effectiveness of the methods under the conditions which the speaker faced. Would you have preferred some other techniques? Remember that these are introductions to longer speeches than the ones you usually give in class.

Booker T. Washington's Atlanta Speech. In 1895 the directors of the Atlanta Exposition invited the great Negro leader, Booker T. Washington, to speak before an assembly of Negroes, white southerners, and northerners. Thus Washington, the first Negro invited to address a mixed audience following the Civil War, faced a difficult and complex situation. Much of the success of the speech lay in his skillful use of his introduction to establish common ground with his audience and set forth the basic theme of the speech.

Occasion and audience

Statement of central idea

Mr. President and Gentlemen of the Board of Directors and Citizens: One third of the population of the South is of the Negro race. No enterprise seeking the material, civil, or moral welfare of this section can disregard this element of our population and reach the highest success. I but convey to you, Mr. President and Directors, the sentiment of the masses of my race when I say that in no way have the value and manhood of the American Negro been more fittingly and generously recognized than by the managers of this magnificent exposition at every stage of its progress. It is a recognition that will do more to cement the friendship of the two races than any occurrence since the dawn of freedom.

Occasion and audience

Surprising statement

Not only this, but the opportunity here afforded will awaken among us a new era of industrial progress. Ignorant and inexperienced, it is not strange that in the first years of our new life we began at the top instead of at the bottom; that a seat in Congress or the State Legislature was more sought than real estate or industrial skill; that the political convention or stump speaking had more attraction than starting a dairy farm or truck garden.

Narrative example leading to statement of central idea

A ship lost at sea for many days suddenly sighted a friendly vessel. From the mast of the unfortunate vessel was seen a signal: "Water, water; we die of thirst!" The answer from the friendly vessel at once came back: "Cast down your bucket where you are." A second time the signal, "Water, water; send us water!" ran up from the distressed vessel and was answered: "Cast down your bucket where you are." And a third and fourth signal for water was answered: "Cast down your bucket where you are." The captain of the distressed vessel, at last heeding the injunction, cast down his bucket, and it came up full of fresh, sparkling water from the mouth of the Amazon River.

[Washington then applied the example to both
the Negroes and the whites of the South, developing
the theme in the rest of his speech.]

Bernard Baruch on National Mobilization. Bernard Baruch was
an advisor of presidents and other political leaders from Wilson to
Eisenhower. In 1950, shortly after the outbreak of the Korean War,
he appeared before the Senate Banking and Currency Committee
and advocated a vigorous program of total mobilization. His introduction was a challenge to the committee and the nation.

Audience and occasion	It is an honor to be asked to appear before this Committee. Events have left us no choice. We have to mobilize. Already our young men are being called.
Striking fact	Casualty lists are coming in. The issue before us — before this Committee — is how *quickly* and how
Statement of theme in question form	*well* is the job of mobilization to be carried out? Shall we do *now* what we know will have to be done later — and thus hasten the victory of peace? Or shall we fumble and falter and invite defeat?[1]

A Sermon by Edward D. Gates. Here is the introduction to a
sermon by Edward D. Gates, then a Presbyterian minister of Peoria,
Illinois. The sermon won $1500 from the Freedoms Foundation
Awards in 1950. Do you see any suggestion of its prize-winning
quality in the portion presented here? Do you recognize any of the
introductory techniques we have discussed?

I want to tell you about a sermon which I prepared but never
delivered. In this sermon I wanted to point out that the crisis the
world is now facing is nothing new, that surely things are not as bad
as they seem. In my reading I found what I thought to be clever
quotations to illustrate my point. For instance, on a recently discovered
Syrian tablet nearly 3000 years old were written words to this effect:
"Prices and taxes are too high. Parents are neglecting their children
and everyone wants to write a book. The world is in a sad state."
Or here was Disraeli commenting on conditions of his day: "In industry, commerce, and agriculture there is little hope." Or the Duke
of Wellington in 1851, shortly before he died: "I thank God that I

[1] A. Craig Baird, *Representative American Speeches: 1950–1951* (New
York: H. W. Wilson Company, 1951), p. 84.

may be spared seeing the consummation of the ruin that is gathering about us. . . ."

Here were statements, I believed, that proved my thesis: By its very nature the world must progress. The prophets of yesterday's doom have been proven false. The prophets of today who bring us messages fraught with disturbing news cannot be right. Things are not as bad as they seem.

But I am glad now that I never preached such a sermon. Any minister who preaches a "God's in his heaven, all's right with the world" type of message to his congregation, who thinks that the necessary equipment of a Christian is a set of rose-colored glasses, is doing a great injustice to the people whom he serves. He is certainly neglecting his high office as a spokesman for the church when he refuses to face the cold hard facts of reality. . . .

Does this excerpt arouse your curiosity enough to make you glad to learn that the rest of the sermon may be found in Harold F. Harding's *The Age of Danger* (Random House, 1952)?

The Conclusion

Perhaps you have observed the acute distress of a fumbling speaker who has finished his speech but has no way to conclude. In despair, he shuffles off the platform mumbling, "I guess that's about all," and

---

ON ENDING SPEECHES

The hostility of most audiences to long-winded speakers has found its way into American folklore. Consider this list of epigrams, some of them anonymous:

1. *The longer the* spoke, *the bigger the* tire.
2. *The best test of a sermon is depth, not length.*
3. *When all is said and done, too many people just keep on talking.*
4. *When a sermon at length comes to an end, people rise and praise God, and they feel the same way after many other speeches.*
    — JOHN ANDREW HOLMES
5. *Second wind: what a public speaker acquires when he says, "In conclusion."*
    — CINCINNATI INQUIRER

takes his seat. You listen in silence and suffer with him. On the other hand you probably felt no such sympathy for the insufferable bore who had finished his speech but would not admit it. Neither speaker, whether he aroused sympathy or vexation, attained his purpose. Yet both might have been effective with a well-planned conclusion.

Beyond the obvious aim of providing the speaker with an effective way to end his speech, a good conclusion will serve any or all of three purposes: (1) *help the audience remember the main points of the speech;* (2) *suggest specific action;* (3) *make the audience wish to respond to the speaker's suggestions.* As with introductions, these are not necessarily separate steps. One device may accomplish all three ends, or three separate methods may be needed. The important thing is to determine what must be done to achieve your purpose, and to select those methods which do so best.

TECHNIQUES FOR CONCLUSIONS. Unlike introductions, conclusions seldom can be judged except in relation to the speech as a whole. So instead of giving capsule examples of good conclusions, we ask you to examine the longer examples given on pages 134–137, and to note how concluding techniques are used by speakers you hear.

1. Formal Summary. Since one purpose of the conclusion is to help the audience remember the content of the speech, most speeches require a summarizing device. The simplest is the formal summary, which merely lists the points made in the order in which they appeared in the speech. Usually this is followed by a general statement covering the theme of the speech as a whole. This may be either a modified restatement or an exact repetition of a sentence used earlier in the talk. The method is direct and to the point, and is particularly well suited to short informative speeches, although it is by no means limited to such talks. But the formal summary is unimaginative, and other endings are more interesting and stimulating.

2. Narrative Summary. In longer speeches, a summary can be made more interesting by narrative examples. In your conclusion, tell a story which focuses attention on the central idea advanced in the speech. If you used an opening narrative, you may restate portions of it, changing details, or applying them, to sharpen the significance of your central theme. In narrative summaries, the details must be carefully chosen to draw together the ideas of the speech. Properly used, they are more vivid and interesting than formal summaries and leave the audience with attention strongly fixed on the central ideas of the speech.

3. *Quotation.* Quotations used merely to dress up a speech and display literary or historical knowledge may leave the audience feeling that the speaker has a new copy of Bartlett's *Familiar Quotations* and is determined to use it. But a quotation which expresses your theme more vividly than you can state it in your own words is an effective summary, and its prestige value is an added dividend. Thus a student ended a talk on germ warfare with a quotation from T. S. Eliot: "This is the way the world ends, Not with a bang, but a whimper." If you began with a quotation, you may wish to repeat it or a part of it at the end. Avoid long poems, particularly of the popular newspaper variety, unless you are convinced that a poem best expresses your idea and unless you can read it with more interpretative skill than most speakers.

4. *Questions.* Questions may be used to introduce a summary or to challenge and stimulate thought. If you began with a question, you may wish to repeat it in your summary, and then to state the answer you developed in the speech. When new questions are introduced, they often grow out of the general query, "What are we going to do?" If you can phrase specific, thought-provoking questions of this kind, you may be able to arouse the audience from passive indifference to active searching for the answers you want them to find.

5. *Specific Procedures.* Sometimes questions are not enough. Your listeners may need specific suggestions for action. Such suggestions may be combined with questions or they may be presented independently, but they should be as specific as possible. Vague and general appeals may make your listeners feel good, but they seldom produce action. Tell your audience exactly what you want done and how it may be accomplished.

6. *Creating the Desire to Act.* Listeners often have a great deal of inertia which must be overcome, and suggestions for action may not be enough. You must make the audience *wish* to act on your proposals. Since people are complex, you may find it wise to use more than one appeal. Everyone acts more readily when his own interests are affected, so if you wish people to follow your suggestions, show that the proposal will benefit them, their families, or the community in which they live. But in civilized society, people feel more self-respect when they believe they do not act for purely selfish

reasons. Hence you may show that action is also justified by altruistic motives: the public interest, "the greatest good for the greatest number," or patriotism. If these motives appear to conflict, you may not have evaluated the interests of your hearers correctly, or you may be speaking for a bad cause. Appeals of this kind must be solidly grounded on facts developed in the body of the speech. Without such a foundation, they will sound — and often are — insincere, sordid, or maudlin.

7. *Repeating the Theme of the Introduction.* Several of the methods above suggest repeating some of the introductory materials in the conclusion. This is often a good technique in any kind of conclusion, since it gives unity to the entire speech. Moreover, attention is highest at the opening and the close, and by tying these together to emphasize your central theme, you may succeed in fixing the idea in the minds of your hearers. They will certainly remember and act upon it more readily than if the speech fails to give a unified impression. This does not mean, of course, that every effective conclusion must echo the introduction.

Conclusions grow out of the content of the speech. Perhaps your material will suggest a device different from any we have listed. In any event, conclude in a way which summarizes your ideas and fixes them in the minds of your listeners.

DELIVERY IN THE CONCLUSION. In classical rhetoric the conclusion was called the *peroration,* and was thought to carry the greatest emotional impact. Among nineteenth and early twentieth century orators, this tradition often produced purple passages delivered in a dramatic and elevated manner. Thus Daniel Webster concluded his debate with Hayne with words once memorized by every schoolboy: "Liberty and Union, now and forever, one and inseparable." And William Jennings Bryan told his audience of believers in free silver: "You shall not press down upon the brow of labor ˌhis crown of thorns; you shall not crucify mankind upon a cross of gold." Conclusions of this kind would be empty and meaningless unless they were delivered with the power and conviction of intense feeling.

Today, such highly charged passages are out of fashion, and probably for most of the subjects you will speak on would have been in bad taste even a hundred years ago. Yet the conclusion can properly be more intense than other portions of the speech. Your audience will judge your estimate of the importance of what you say by the earnestness and force with which you speak. Since the conclusion draws together all your most important points, your delivery here should be the strongest and most vital in the speech. This need not imply loudness, dramatic gestures, or wide ranges in pitch, though all these may be effective in moderation. Perhaps your material is best presented by intense and simple directness, which makes the audience feel that you are asking a personal response from each individual present. Whatever the technique, you must feel the importance of what you say and convey this feeling to your hearers. Unless you leave this final impression by your delivery of the conclusion, your chance of success in the speech is materially diminished.

A GOOD CONCLUSION. On page 129 we quoted the introduction to Bernard Baruch's testimony before the Senate Committee on Banking and Currency. Baruch challenged the committee with the provocative question: "Shall we do *now* what we know will have to be done later — and thus hasten the victory of peace? Or shall we fumble and falter and invite defeat?" In the body of this speech, Baruch argued for a vigorous program of mobilization, including austerity if necessary. His testimony was given in a period which was neither peace nor war — a "police action" it was called. There was much apathy and considerable doubt about the wisdom of adopting the measures of total war. In his conclusion Baruch tried to overcome these feelings by using many of the techniques we have described. Study them carefully and decide whether they were the best he could have used.

Formal summary

To sum up my recommendations: —

Specific procedures

Creating a desire to act: appeals to general welfare

1. Organize America for all-out mobilization, with a general ceiling over the entire economy to prevent further inflation and an all-embracing system of priorities to strengthen our defenses and minimize dislocations.

Creating a desire to act

2. The very least that must be done is to amend this priorities legislation to provide for effective price and wage control and rationing authority. To do less is to invite cruel suffering and possible disaster. [Baruch then listed six more specific recommendations which he had made in the body of his speech. Since his remarks were available to the committee

in stenographic report, this was perhaps unduly repetitious. He then continued as follows:]

Narrative summary

Nearly three years ago I clipped an item from a newspaper which seems ominously prophetic today. It told of a boast made by a Soviet general. This general boasted that the Western democracies were bound to be defeated by the Soviet Union because they would not make the sacrifices necessary to arm themselves. They prized their standards of living too highly. They would not be willing to accept the discipline to put "guns" over "butter." In Russia, though, this general boasted, the people were inured to hardship. The Soviet government would force the sacrifices to mobilize. A lean and hungry, but mobilized Russia would overrun a Western world which couldn't bring itself to mobilize — in time.

Restatement of ideas of introduction and central theme in terms of the narrative summary

That is the test which confronts us — not only this country but all of the free peoples of the world. It is the choice of "peace" or "butter," of mobilizing our strength now, while peace can still be saved, or of clinging to petty wants and petty profits, imperilling our freedom and our civilization.

Creating a desire to act: appeal to pride and fear; challenging question

No outside enemy can defeat us. We *can* defeat ourselves. Gentlemen, yours is the decision. Which shall it be — discomfort or defeat?[1]

Exercises

1. Addressing a predominantly (but not exclusively) white student audience, William Paterson spoke bluntly of the failures of education in underprivileged Negro areas in Los Angeles. He placed part of the blame on the educational and social system, part on Negro leaders themselves. In his conclusion he used a loose formal summary, an analogy, questions, and appeals for action. Can you identify these devices? In addition he used a number of statements not wholly acceptable to all members of his audience, and he phrased some of them in colloquial, almost crude language. What is your own reaction to these statements? Would

[1] A. Craig Baird, *Representative American Speeches: 1950–1951* (New York: H. W. Wilson Company, 1951), pp. 92–93.

they have stimulated you to think about the problem, or would they have offended you and turned you against his ideas? Would the conclusion have been better with different language?

There is another job to be done, perhaps not as sensational as the civil rights struggle, but every bit as important. That is the Negro leader's role in the upgrading of his own people. For although the Negro is theoretically and biologically the equal of any race, the plain fact is that in many behavioral aspects, he ranks considerably lower than other groups in the population. True enough, this is really not his fault. But no matter how logically we can make a case for him, the fact still remains that until he pulls himself up by his bootstraps, many whites are going to continue to look down on him. This may be grossly unfair, but I think it is a fairly accurate reflection of reality.

We here in this room today are enlightened college students, most of us have Negro friends here on campus, and all of us have a completely different view of the Negro than the general population, who still hold to the stereotype of the gaudy illiterate. It is this image that the Negro is going to have to correct, and only the educated Negro leaders can do so. A new type of Freedom Ride is needed, not to Mississippi, but to Watts and Harlem; for what the poverty-stricken urban Negro desperately needs is a generation of Negro missionaries, a black Peace Corps, if you like. This Peace Corps needs to bring with it the tools of learning, for with these tools the Negro can construct a way out of the slum; without them he is trapped. By cooperation the white community, the Negro community, and the school system can, I think, furnish the urban Negro with the equipment for first-class citizenship.

Yet if the Negro can achieve this goal, as I believe he can, and we in the white community still refuse to accept him, the job has been for naught, and his road to first-class citizenship has been a dead end. We whites must restructure our attitudes toward the colored man. It doesn't take anything in the way of guts to stand in a Northern city and rant against the White Citizens' Councils. It doesn't take much integrity to mouth the platitudes of brotherhood. It does take guts to stand up to intolerance when you find it in your own back yard. Does your community enforce segregation by refusing to allow Negroes to buy within the city limits? What are you going to do about it? Does your club, church or fraternity practice segregation? Can you justify your membership? Does a Negro move next door to you? Are you the first to greet him in your neighborhood, or do you excuse your prejudice by mumbling something about property values? It is not easy to stand against intolerance when it counts. Some will think you are a nut, others will call you a half-baked crusader, and others will tell you to go easy, but in your heart you will know why you are doing it.

There is just no other way.

2. Analyze the conclusions of your last two speeches before this class. Did you use any of the devices described in this chapter? If you were to repeat those speeches, how would you change your conclusions? Write out a new conclusion for each of them and submit it to your instructor for comment.

The Body of The Speech: Outlining

The core of the speech, which determines whether you really communicate your ideas to your listeners, lies in the main portion of your talk, generally called the *body*. Earlier chapters dealt with the *substance* of the speech: discovering ideas, the sources of materials, and the kinds of materials which make ideas clear, interesting, and believable. Here we are more interested in *structure*: the way materials can be combined, and their relationships to each other. Much that we shall say here has been implied earlier. Nevertheless, you will profit by systematizing your ideas about organization. To do this, let us examine outlining as a technique for sorting out the logical relationships between statements made in a speech and then turn to the pattern of the speech as a whole.

Logical Relationships

In Chapter 5 we pointed out that speeches composed exclusively of broad general statements usually lack clarity, believability, and interest unless the audience already knows and accepts virtually everything the speaker wants to say. It is equally true that speeches composed exclusively of specific statements and examples, without

---

ON UNDERSTANDING

The improvement of the understanding is for two ends; first, our own increase of knowledge; secondly, to enable us to deliver that knowledge to others.

— JOHN LOCKE

the conclusions and summaries of general statements, are not likely
to be very thoughtful. Effective speaking needs both the general
and the specific. But it is not enough that general and specific statements merely be present in a speech. The speaker must make the
relationships between them clear by the way he arranges them.
Consider, for example, the following list of statements:

1. Your experience shows that you recall
   well-organized talks, forget confusing
   ones.

2. Outlining calls speaker's attention
   to gaps in logical structure of a
   speech.

3. Joyce Brown had only a hazy notion
   what she wanted to say until she wrote
   carefully-worded sentences outlining
   her idea.

4. A good outline helps listeners remember
   what is said.

5. Good outlining improves communication
   in speeches.

6. Experiments by Prof. Raymond Wheeler
   show impressions received in a pattern
   are more readily understood and
   recalled.

7. Bill Cox did not see how little
   evidence he had for main idea until
   he wrote outline.

8. Outlining helps speaker clarify his
   own thoughts.

9. Outlining helps speaker develop ideas
   intelligently.

When you have read these statements, you will probably draw
two conclusions: (1) Their author claims to believe in careful outlining. (2) He does not practice what he preaches. As presented,
the statements are not clear. They make no coherent impact, but

create only a hazy impression. Yet there is nothing wrong with this material except that the order of the sentences does not show how the ideas are related. Note how easily these relationships can be shown.

1. Your experience shows that you recall *—Blunder II* well-organized talks, forget confusing ones.

I B 2. Outlining calls speaker's attention to gaps in logical structure of a speech.

I A 1. 3. Joyce Brown had only a hazy notion *—Example of clarification* what she wanted to say until she wrote carefully-worded sentences outlining her idea.

II 4. <u>A good outline helps listeners remember what is said.</u>

Central idea → 5. Good outlining improves communication in speeches.

6. Experiments by Prof. Raymond Wheeler show impressions received in a pattern are more readily understood and recalled. *Blunder II*

I B 7. Bill Cox did not see how little evidence he had for main idea until he wrote outline. *—Example of showing gaps in thought.*

I A 8. Outlining helps speaker clarify his own thoughts.

I 9. <u>Outlining helps speaker develop ideas intelligently.</u>

At first glance making such a rearrangement may seem more difficult than it really is. Begin by searching for a Central Idea: one statement among the nine which is the most general and inclusive. It should summarize everything which is implied in the other eight sentences, each of which in turn either directly or indirectly explains or proves the central idea. The rest of the statements fall naturally into two broad categories. The most general and inclusive statement in each group becomes point I or II. The other statements fall into place under these and show their relationships to each other and to the main points they support.

Rewritten to show these relationships, the outline would then look like this:

CENTRAL IDEA: Good outlining improves communication in speaking.

I. Careful outlining helps the speaker develop his ideas intelligently.

    A. The process of outlining helps the speaker clarify his thoughts.

        1. Joyce Brown had only a hazy notion of what she wanted to say until she wrote a series of carefully worded sentences outlining her idea.

    B. The process of outlining calls the speaker's attention to gaps in the logical structure of his speech.

        1. Bill Cox failed to see how little evidence he had to prove his main argument until he put his points down on paper.

II. A good outline helps listeners remember what is said.

    A. Experiments conducted by Professor Raymond Wheeler show that impressions perceived in a pattern are more readily understood and recalled than unpatterned stimuli.

    B. Your own experience shows that you recall well organized talks and forget confusing ones.

This outline is easy to understand and could readily be developed into a complete speech. Incidentally, do you not find it easier to remember the nine statements cast in this form than in the random series first presented?

The revised organization shows several principles of outlining:

1. THE CENTRAL IDEA. In all short speeches, and in most longer ones, the central idea can be condensed into a general statement phrased in one declarative sentence. In an explanatory speech on a

harvester combine, your central idea might read: "A harvester combine converts standing wheat to grain in sacks in one operation, eliminating binding, shocking, and hauling to the thresher." In a persuasive defense of a losing football coach, the theme of your speech might be: "Our coach is not getting fair treatment by the alumni and the newspaper sports writers." Thus in any speech, the "central idea" is simply a summary of the content or point of view to be developed. Until you can phrase the central idea, you do not know precisely what you want to say.

2. DIVISION. The major subheadings of a speech are divisions of the central idea. Sometimes these divisions show the natural distinctions within a body of material, and sometimes in an argumentative speech they mark the logical progression, as from cause to effect. In the outline above the natural distinction between speaker and audience suggested the two main divisions. In a typical argumentative speech, the central idea, a plea for a change in policy, may be urged under two main headings: (1) the present system is harmful, and (2) the new policy would work. But the major divisions of any outline are still general statements.

3. PROGRESS TOWARD THE SPECIFIC. In a good outline, each step down from the major headings is a move toward a more specific concept. Under point I in our outline on outlining, A and B are more specific than I, but are still general statements. The sub-points under these, however, represent highly specific examples. Under point II, on the other hand, A and B are specific examples. Sometimes, where the reasoning is complex, the example may not be reached until more and narrower generalizations have been given. Occasionally the knowledge and beliefs of the audience may make the highly specific example unnecessary. And statistics, testimony, or analogy take the place of examples in the development of some topics. But either the speaker or the audience must furnish specific materials if the speech is to be meaningful and convincing.

4. EQUALITY OF SYMBOLS. In a well-organized outline, parallel symbols indicate materials similarly related to the point just above them. In our sample outline, I and II jointly and equally support the central idea, and A and B equally establish the validity of I. Thus sentences represented by parallel symbols should make sense when joined by "and" or another coordinating connective. Sentences represented by subordinate symbols should make sense when connected to the sen-

tence they support by "because" or "for example." In many speeches to inform, only the "for example" relationship will be needed. Check by inserting such connectives:

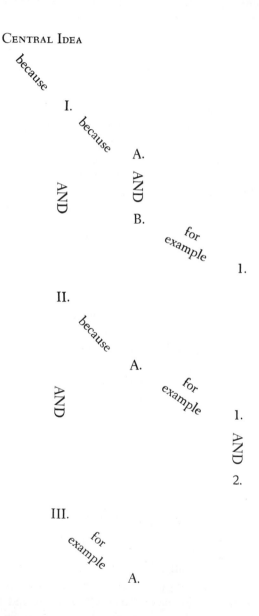

CENTRAL IDEA

because

I. *because*

A.

AND

AND

B.

for example

1.

II.

because

A.

for example

AND

1.

AND

2.

III.

for example

A.

5. OUTLINE FORM. There are some conventions about outlining which are worth observing for the sake of clarity. Use a complete sentence whenever you are making a general statement. Specific headings may be represented by phrases or key words. Use a consistent set of symbols, and indent each subordinate level of heading deeper than the one preceding it. If a topic takes more than one line, indent the lines equally. Here is a typical block plan for a complete outline.

TITLE OF SPEECH

PURPOSE: . . . .
(See Chapter 2, pages 26–29.)

INTRODUCTION
    I. Statement to establish contact with the audience
    II. Opening narrative, leading to
    III. Statement of central idea of speech

BODY
    I. Complete sentence stating first main idea of speech
        A. Complete sentence stating subdivision of first main idea
            1. Topical heading developing A
                a. Example
                b. Statistics
                c. Testimony
        B. Complete sentence stating second subdivision of I
            1. Topical heading developing B
                a. Example
            2. Another phase of B
                a. Statistics
                b. Testimony
                c. Analogy
    II. Complete sentence stating second main idea of speech, followed by development similar to that of I
    III. Complete sentence stating third main idea, etc.

CONCLUSION
    I. Summary of main ideas
    II. Narrative example to draw together all threads of speech
    III. Appeal to action

Note that in this scheme introduction, body, and conclusion each has its separate series of Roman numerals. One advantage of this system of numbering is that, as the outline continues to grow, it is not necessary to re-number it throughout for each addition or deletion. Moreover, this mode of numbering lets you see at a glance the steps in the building up of each part of the speech — introduction and conclusion as well as body.

When your outline is complete, test its consistency by inserting coordinating words between headings of equal value, and subordinating words to show subordinate relationships. If these connectives make sense, the chances are good that the structure of your outline is reasonably clear and logical. You may, to be sure, not always unfold your materials in the exact sequence of your outline. In the above pattern you might, for example, wish to open point I of the body of your speech by taking up A-l-b first. This could be done if there were special interest value in that item; yet even if used first, the item is logically placed as I-A-l-b in the outline.

Patterns of Thought and Development

In discussing the outline on outlining, we said that once the central idea had been discovered, the rest of the statements fell "naturally" into two broad categories. This was another way of saying that the thought of the speech had a natural shape or pattern. In that case the pattern was division, and the speech had two main parts, value to the speaker and value to the audience. That pattern happened to be quite obvious, indeed almost inevitable for that body of material. It is not always so easy to discover the best form a speech should take. But by its very nature thought has form, and you should soon come to see that ideas of certain kinds take on predictable shapes and follow certain general patterns. Thus a story tends to fall in the

---

ON PATTERNS

Themistocles replied that a man's discourse was like to a rich Persian carpet, the beautiful figures and patterns of which can be shown only by spreading and extending it out; when it is contracted and folded up, they are obscure and lost.

— PLUTARCH

order of time, so that you tell events one after another as they happened. An explanation seeks causes or results, or in some other way tries to point out the how and the why of a thing. An attempt to persuade looks for reasons and tries to make a desired action or belief seem good, attractive, or compellingly necessary. Because people are much alike in thought habits, ideas are more readily accepted when they are presented in a form which reflects these typical ways of thinking.

But there is another element in formulating speech patterns. Just as an architect seeks to create the plan of a house to fit both the characteristics of the site and the needs of the occupants, so must a speaker select a pattern to suit both the characteristics of his materials and the needs of his listeners. Thus an effective pattern requires not only a broad grasp and a clear analysis of the subject matter, but a lively imagination capable of adapting the pattern to the audience and the occasion. A good pattern contributes to the communicability of ideas by making them more easily remembered, more acceptable, and more stimulating. This is a genuinely creative process requiring all the resources of a hard-working, thoughtful, and imaginative speaker. It is, in fact, another aspect of full-time thinking.

To suggest how these things can be done, we shall in the rest of this chapter analyze five thought patterns widely applicable in speeches. This is not to suggest that you limit yourself always to one of these. There are others. And there are infinite variations on the ones we shall discuss. But every idea fits into some pattern, and you cannot outline a speech or formulate an introduction or a conclusion without using one. It is therefore good to know something about the shapes a thought can take, and how to recognize which one is most appropriate to your needs.

Time and Space Patterns

Often in speeches to explain or inform — and in explanatory sections of other speeches — the arrangement of details for presentation to an audience can best follow a time or a space order, Anecdotes and other narrative materials are obviously organized on a *time* principle. On pages 25–26 we suggested four steps in the preparation of a speech. If you used these steps as an outline for a speech of your own, you would use a time order. Such a pattern is ideally suited to most speeches explaining a process — any process, from tying a bow tie to building a model catapult. The steps are presented in the order in which they actually occur. The relative amount of time given to each one will be determined by the difficulty of explaining the step rather than the time consumed in the process itself. For complex processes, you may combine time and division patterns, discussing, for example, materials first, then procedures.

Space order for a speech is also dictated by the nature of your material. You might describe your campus in terms of its geographical features — the upper and lower campuses, the residence and instruction areas, or areas devoted to science and those devoted to liberal studies. Within these areas the relative position of buildings may be used as a further guide to the arrangement of details.

INTRODUCTIONS AND CONCLUSIONS. Speeches built on time and space patterns usually do not require long introductions and conclusions. Such talks are ordinarily given to audiences which are already motivated to listen. Air Force recruits in training for survival in enemy country do not need attention-getting devices to insure their interest in survival procedures. Nor do freshmen in a speech on the steps in registration procedure. Hence most time and space order speeches start with a direct statement of the theme and end with a simple summary. But you may use any of the techniques for introductions and conclusions suggested earlier in this chapter as the needs of your audience dictate.

TYPICAL TIME AND SPACE ORDER SUBJECTS

Time	*Space*
The battle of Guadalcanal	How Washington, D. C., is laid out
Building your own home	The master plan for our freeways
Fertilizing crops	Where to find uranium ore
A parachute jump	Contour farming

Cause and Effect Pattern

Sometimes a speech to inform may try to explain why certain events occurred as they did. A chemical experiment may be analyzed from *effect to cause* or *cause to effect,* the details of the speech being selected not so much in terms of the progress of the experiment (time order) as the reasons why the reaction described takes place. Sometimes a cause and effect pattern may be concerned more with belief than clarity, and may be more nearly a speech to convince than to inform. A speech on the subject, "How Munich made World War II inevitable," might have a cause-effect pattern as it seeks to discourage any present appeasement policies. A cause and effect speech before a political club might deal with the theme, "Why our candidate lost the last election," a matter on which club members might differ widely. Any of these speeches could begin with either the effect or the cause and work toward the other.

The success of the cause-effect pattern depends upon how clearly the audience understands the causal relationships and accepts their validity. It is not enough to give a list of "before" and "after" conditions. You must show that a given cause certainly produced a specific effect. Ask yourself whether any necessary steps in the cause-effect relationship are missing, whether some other cause might have produced or contributed to these effects, or whether the cause might have produced other equally significant effects. Exploring these factors and developing them with suitable details may well provide the organizational pattern of your entire speech.

INTRODUCTIONS AND CONCLUSIONS. Narratives and descriptions make good introductions to such speeches and may develop facts relative to either the cause or the effect. The talk on Munich as a cause of World War II might begin with a narrative of Prime Minister Neville Chamberlain's return from his conference with Adolf Hitler. The conclusion might then describe the British evacuation of Dunkirk or the bombing of London to typify the results of the Munich conference.

Occasionally you might open with a blunt statement of a cause and effect relationship probably unacceptable to the audience. The political club might not wish to hear, "Our candidate lost because members of this club did not do enough precinct work." Yet this might be a good opening if the speaker could support his statement, and if his listeners really wanted the candidate elected. The conclusion might predict the result of the next election if a different attitude motivated the club members at that time.

TYPICAL CAUSE AND EFFECT SUBJECTS

Natural selection in the theory of evolution
Why we had a losing season in football
Why there is unrest in the Middle East
Why Communism seeks to expand
Why demagogues are sometimes elected

Disease-Remedy Pattern

When you wish to persuade your listeners to adopt a new policy, one of the best methods of organization is the disease-remedy pattern, the basic structure of which is suggested by its title. There are existing evils which suggest a "disease." The proposal you advocate is the "remedy." Normally this pattern is used for argumentative speeches in which you advocate a change in the present policies of an organized group. This group may be as limited as your club or as comprehensive as the United Nations. In either case you will need to answer successively some or all of these questions.

DISEASE

    I. What is wrong with the present system?
      A. What are the symptoms?
      B. What are the probable causes?

REMEDY

    I. What solution would cure the disease?
      A. What are the component parts of this solution?

    II. Is this the best solution?
      A. Does it remedy the symptoms?
      B. Does it remove the causes?
      C. Is it better than other solutions?
      D. Is it free from other evils?

    III. How may this solution be put into effect?
      A. What are the general means?
      B. How may this audience help?

INTRODUCTIONS AND CONCLUSIONS. When you use the disease-remedy pattern, a vivid example answering the question "What are the symptoms?" may make an effective introduction, serving to get attention and prepare the way for a statement of your central idea. You may then proceed to describe the disease and remedy in greater detail. Thus a speech on slum clearance might begin with a description of a particularly noxious slum, or the story of a teen-age delinquent brought up in a slum environment. Material for your conclusion may be suggested by the question "How may this audience help?" Or you might return to the opening example and show how the adoption of your proposal would change the conditions you described at the beginning. Of course, any of the other suggested techniques for introductions or conclusions may be used in addition to or in place of these. Make your speech a logical and interesting entity, using the suggestions of the pattern but not considering them a rigid format from which you may not depart. Test the consistency of your outline by the methods suggested earlier, and prepare to deliver your speech.

Typical Disease-Remedy Subjects

Our fraternity should substitute a "work week" for "hell week" during spring initiations.

Our college should abolish intercollegiate football.

This city should adopt the city manager form of government.

The United Nations Charter should be revised to eliminate the veto in the Security Council.

The United States should adopt a policy of free trade.

This state should float a large bond issue for the purpose of preserving and developing outdoor recreation facilities.

The Text Pattern

Speeches often begin with quotations in order to gain attention and introduce the central idea. Sometimes, however, a quotation provides the framework for an entire speech. Such a quotation is called a *text*. A strikingly worded text is easy to remember, and if the outline of the speech is implicit in the text, an audience is likely to keep the speaker's ideas in mind for a long time to come.

Texts are particularly useful in speeches to stimulate and speeches to convince. They are most often used in inspirational addresses, particularly sermons, in which the speaker tries to influence attitudes and feelings rather than beliefs. In sermons, texts are usually taken from the Bible, but other inspirational talks may draw texts from literature, proverbs, or even carefully worded statements formulated

---

SYNTHESIS AND ANALYSIS

Knowledge comes by taking things apart, analysis. But wisdom comes by putting things together.

— John A. Morrison

by the speaker himself. Texts from appropriate sources are also used in political speeches to convince. In 1928, Democratic Presidential candidate Al Smith used texts in six of twenty major campaign addresses. One of them was a statement made by Smith himself earlier in the campaign, one a quotation from Lincoln, one an excerpt from the Republican platform, and three were statements made by his Republican opponent, Herbert Hoover, in his campaign speeches.

Here are some questions which will help you work out a suitable plan for speeches based on texts.

I. What is my central idea?
    A. Is there a quotation which expresses it so vividly that my audience will remember it? (If no suitable text comes to mind, consult such reference sources as Bartlett's *Familiar Quotations,* Edwards' *New Dictionary of Thoughts,* or a concordance to Shakespeare or the Bible.)

II. How may the text best be developed to make my idea clear?
    A. *Key words or phrases.* Divide the text into sections, each of which contains a term or phrase which can be developed in a section of the speech. "All men are created equal," could be divided to include sections defining "all men," "creation," and "equality."
    B. *Analysis of implications.* This method is similar to that of defining key words and phrases, but it suggests a somewhat deeper analysis. Charles Spurgeon once said, "Humility is to make a right estimate of oneself." If this were used as a text, the development would hinge on a satisfactory definition of "right estimate." Divisions might be: 1. Insincere and false estimates; 2. Dangers of overestimation; 3. Folly of underestimation.
    C. *Refutation.* This method is particularly adapted to political speaking. Compare the statement made by your political opponent with his record on the same subject. Or show that the facts warrant a very different interpretation of his statement from the one he wishes his audience to accept. Lincoln used this method in his Cooper Union Address to change the meaning of an assertion by Stephen A. Douglas, "Our fathers, when they framed the Government under which we live, understood this question just as well, and even better, than we do now."

Lincoln accepted the truth of the assertion but redefined its terms. Dividing the text into two parts, he answered the questions: "Who were our fathers who framed the Government?" and "What were their views on extension of slavery into the territories?" His factual development of these two points was a devastating refutation of Douglas' intent in the original statement.

III. What examples will serve to illustrate each subdivision? Examples are usually the most effective supporting material for this type of speech, but statistics, quotations, and other support may be used, particularly in the refutation pattern.

IV. What is the significance of the central idea for members of the audience? What should they do about it?

INTRODUCTIONS AND CONCLUSIONS. Depending on the text, any of the devices suggested earlier may be used. The text itself, if it is vividly or strikingly phrased, may be used as an opening statement, and it may be repeated in the conclusion. Or you might paraphrase the text at the end of the speech, showing how the ideas you have developed have modified or strengthened its meaning. Narrative examples are also effective for both introductions and conclusions of text speeches. Sometimes the conclusion seeks to motivate the audience, as suggested in question IV above. The nature of your subject and your audience will suggest which devices will be more effective.

TYPICAL TEXTS FOR DEVELOPMENT

1. We love a joke that hands us a pat on the back while it kicks the other fellow down stairs. — C. L. Edson
2. The way to be nothing is to do nothing. — Nathaniel Howe
3. Have the courage to be ignorant of a great number of things in order to avoid the calamity of being ignorant of everything. — Sydney Smith
4. "Impossible!" That is not good French. — Napoleon
5. Malice drinks one half of its own poison. — Seneca
6. Politics is the art of taking money from the rich to win votes from the poor on the pretext of protecting each against the other. — Anonymous
7. So live, that when you die, even the undertaker will be sorry. — Anonymous

8. To reform a man, you must begin with his grandmother.
— Victor Hugo

9. The measure of a man is what it takes to make him mad. —
Anonymous

Cumulation Pattern

In speeches to stimulate, the speaker may wish to make a narrow theme overwhelmingly vivid and intense. The pattern of cumulation is ideally suited to such speeches. This pattern is based on a simple statement of a central idea which is limited enough in scope so that it requires little or no subdivision. To develop this theme, the speaker piles example upon example until the listener cannot help accepting the truth of it. This technique is best known from its use by Russell H. Conwell, nineteenth century lecturer and founder of Temple University.

Conwell's most famous lecture was called *Acres of Diamonds*.[1] He began by telling a romantic story about a man who sold his farm to get money to search for a diamond mine. A long series of misfortunes was capped by his suicide. Meanwhile, his successor on the farm discovered the richest diamond mine of his day on the very piece of land the unfortunate man had sold. At this point the speaker stated his theme: Success and riches are to be found near at hand. The rest of the speech consisted of factual examples illustrating this concept.

The pattern of cumulation, then, is based upon a single idea, developed through a series of examples, all emphasizing exactly the same principle. It derives its strength from the simplicity of its structure, from the insistent repetition of the central theme, and from the high interest value of the examples. Here are some questions to suggest the development:

I. What is the central idea you wish to develop?
II. What story, real or fictional, will illustrate vividly the truth of the central idea, so that after it is told, the audience could almost state it before the speaker does?
III. What examples from the actual experiences of people may be cited to illustrate the central idea?

---

[1] It may be found, among other places, in a collection of speeches called *Modern Eloquence*.

IV. How may the members of the audience apply this idea to themselves?

INTRODUCTIONS AND CONCLUSIONS. The pattern of cumulation is generally a complete plan in itself. The introduction logically opens with a narrative which expresses the central idea. When enough examples have been given to support the idea, it is wise to end with a motivating conclusion. Perhaps the narrative with greatest impact is kept until last, or a quotation may be used which sharply states the theme.

SOURCES OF OPENING NARRATIVES FOR THE PATTERN OF CUMULATION

1. Familiar literary examples like Jean Valjean, Lady Macbeth, Jeeter Lester, or Willie Loman
2. Fables and fairy tales
3. Biblical narratives and parables
4. Historical, semi-historical, and mythical narratives

Patterns in Speeches to Entertain

In our discussion of patterns, we have so far emphasized serious speaking. But each of the five foregoing patterns may also be used in a lighter vein. The purpose of the text pattern may be varied by selecting an absurd text, like Mark Twain's comment, "Cauliflower is nothing but cabbage with a college education." Or Artemus Ward's, "Let us all be happy and live within our means, even if we have to borrow the money to do it with." The cumulation pattern is as well suited to a light after-dinner speech on feminine foibles as to a serious lecture on the evils of procrastination. Likewise the disease-remedy pattern can be pleasantly used to magnify some bit of trivia, such as recent debate in the Oxford Union on the subject, "The American colonies should swear allegiance to the Crown."

A pattern is a framework on which the speaker can build his talk. It has two great values. It suggests the shape his thoughts can take and is thus invaluable in planning and organizing. It also helps both speaker and audience remember. Even when used mechanically a pattern gives direction and movement to a speech. Used with imagination, varied to suit the subject and the audience, it can be a powerful shaping force.

Exercises

1. Patterns are particularly helpful in impromptu speaking. If time permits, your instructor may wish to devote a class hour to this assignment. Place face downward on a table a series of speech subjects. Some may be proverbs, literary quotations, or Biblical texts; others may be statements of attitudes toward campus problems; still others may be suggestions of stories, fables, or historical incidents which might furnish a framework for a cumulative speech. The first speaker may be given five minutes preparation, and each succeeding speaker may draw a subject when his predecessor begins speaking. If you and your instructor so agree, you may take your choice of three slips. Using one of the patterns discussed in this chapter, quickly organize your ideas and speak for approximately five minutes.

2. Plan a speech for delivery to the class demonstrating your understanding of the problems of organization discussed in this chapter. Your instructor may wish to assign to you one of the patterns suggested. If he does not do so, choose or invent any pattern which suits your material. When you are ready to speak, check your plan and your method of delivery against the suggestions for criticism given below. Will your classmates criticize you favorably or adversely?

Criticizing The Organization of Speeches

In preparing to criticize speeches for their organization, review the questions on making ideas clear at the end of Chapter 5. No organization is good if it does not make ideas clear. Beyond this, evaluate speakers on the basis of these questions.

1. *Introduction.* Did the introduction serve to make contact, arouse interest, and state the subject of the speech? Was this done in the most effective fashion? Were too many devices used? Too few? Would others have been better? Did the speaker's delivery succeed in establishing contact with the audience? If not, was this a fault in delivery or in planning?

2. *Body.* Were the main ideas of the speech clearly stated? Was the relationship between main ideas brought out by summaries and transitions? Were the supporting materials clearly related to main

ideas, or were they merely an incoherent mass? Did the speaker's delivery distinguish between more and less important points? What general plan or pattern of organization did he follow? Was his pattern a conventional imitation of a standard one, or did it show originality by being suitably adapted to his material?

3. *Conclusion.* Did the conclusion draw together all the important ideas of the speech? Did it contain any application of the material to the audience, or any appeal to action? If not, should it have done so? Did the key ideas of the speech get adequate emphasis in the delivery of the conclusion?

In short, did his cle aror gani zati onle adtound erst and ing?

7 DELIVERY:

Communicating Ideas

Vigor and health radiated from every line and action of Theodore Roosevelt. Note his gesture and the set of his hand.

IN CHAPTER 3 we pointed out that it is in delivery that the process of speech preparation is put to the test. Much of what we have said thus far about speech preparation applies equally well to a written essay. In both speaking and writing there are clues to the nature and quality of the author's mind. But speech gives innumerable extra clues about the speaker as a living personality. From this greater intimacy comes greater communicability. In a sense, therefore, delivery is not merely the final stage of speaking; it *is* speaking.

To simplify your introduction to speaking before an audience, we limited our earlier discussion of delivery to fundamental and elementary matters. But now that you have learned more about the process of speech preparation and have become accustomed to the platform, you need to master more sophisticated delivery skills.

Therefore, this chapter is designed to help you achieve the objective set forth in Chapter 1: *to present ideas to audiences in a manner which helps communication by the effective use of voice and body.* Effectively and willingly used, the techniques of good delivery aid immeasurably in making ideas clear, believable, and interesting. Ineffectively or unwillingly used, they are better replaced by pen and paper.

The Levels of Skill in Delivery

The single legitimate function of delivery is to help in communicating ideas. Some ways of delivering a speech achieve this purpose; others do not. We may state, somewhat arbitrarily, that ideas get one or more of four possible treatments from the delivery to which they are subjected. Using the language of analogy, let us say that ideas, as delivered, may be (1) imprisoned, (2) gilded or burdened, (3) freed, or (4) strengthened.

Ideas are *imprisoned* if delivered weakly and hesitantly by a speaker with many "uh's," a nearly inaudible voice, and an indirect or evasive manner. If such a speaker's ideas escape at all, they limp in the general direction of the audience, arriving there only if they are exceptionally hardy and the audience exceptionally patient. If you have applied in your speaking the principles set forth in Chapter 3, you should no longer be imprisoning ideas.

Ideas are *gilded* or *burdened* by the speaker whose conscious use of exhibitory skills draws attention away from his ideas and toward melodramatic gestures and a mellifluous voice. Such a speaker so enjoys the beauties of his delivery that his ideas can never quite be seen through their ornate wrappings. Their real worth, if any, is discovered only by audiences dedicated or charitable enough to penetrate the vocal decorations. More often than not, the purpose of such gilding is to conceal the absence of ideas, as with the politician who wrote in the margin of his manuscript, "This point weak; yell like h—."

Ideas are *freed* by the speaker who masters the skills of directness, physical alertness, and physical freedom discussed in Chapter 3. Such an individual realizes that many ideas are sufficiently clear and simple to gain acceptance on their own if only the speaker will "keep out of the way." He realizes, too, that more complex ideas are successfully communicated only if the speaker has a disciplined or an intuitive sense of the true meaning of delivery. The term *delivery* comes directly from its Latin ancestor, *deliberare,* literally "to set free," a derivation so full of meaning that we have made it a basic concept of this chapter. Thus in simple talks to inform, the basic skills of delivery are enough to achieve communication if the speech is well-organized and developed. If the speaker's presentation is direct, alert, and not cluttered with distracting mannerisms, his ideas will be understood and accepted on their own merits simply because they have been *set free.*

Sometimes, because of misunderstanding, indifference, or opposition in the audience, ideas need to be *strengthened* by delivery. The speaker must then use a higher order of skill in voice and bodily action to discriminate for the audience between the more and the less important in his speech, and to give weight and force to key ideas. Cultivating the delivery skills which neither imprison nor gild ideas, but free and strengthen them, is thus basic to making speeches which are clear, interesting, and believable.

Bodily Action

Bodily action aids delivery indirectly through its effect on the voice, and directly through the impact of movement on attention. A simple experiment will show you the effect of bodily action on voice. Tap your left palm with your right fist while counting aloud to the rhythm of the tapping. Tap gently at first; then, without changing the loudness of your counting, strike forcefully with your fist. The chances are that you will be unable to keep the force of your voice constant when you begin to pound more energetically. Hard pounding automatically produces a strong voice, gentle tapping a weak voice.

This, then, is the principle: *Voice production is a physical function.* All the aspects of voice — including breathing, tone production, and articulation — are produced by the contraction and relaxation of muscles under the stimulation of nerve impulses. All the physical reactions of the body are interrelated, and strong muscular activity in one part of the body stimulates similarly strong reactions elsewhere. Thus vigorous bodily action gives strength and vitality to the voice. In a similar way, more subtle physical actions also affect the voice. Radio actors, unseen by the audience, still find gestures helpful, and a radio love scene is best acted before a single microphone, with the participants inspiringly close to one another.

You can demonstrate this principle in a slightly different context if, perchance, your roommate is not now present and so will not be frightened by the experiment you are about to perform. Imagine there is a person in the room with whom you are violently angry. Say these words, forcefully and rapidly, but without a gesture or any perceptible action: "Get out of here!" Repeat the command, but this time, point dramatically and menacingly toward the door. Are you not more persuasive the second time? Does not the gesture seem to have added meaning to the sound of your words?

The second value of bodily action in speaking lies in the attention value of movement. The mere fact that a speaker is seen as well as heard enables an audience to employ two senses instead of one in receiving his message. Change and movement hold attention. Animated neon signs, motor-driven window displays, Army "How to Do It" films, actors, magicians, and good speakers all attract and hold attention by lively and interestingly varied action. Therefore, beyond the resources of his materials, his language, and his voice, the speaker has a variety of visible aids to communication: a gesture, emphatic or descriptive; a facial expression; a shrug; a change in posture or position on the platform. Conversely, psychologists have long known that people cannot pay unvaried attention to an unvaried stimulus. You soon lose interest in a swinging pendulum. And an audience can be nearly hypnotized by a monotonous and repetitive pattern of bodily action. It is the variety and the meaningful character of action which hold attention and aid understanding. In short, what the speaker does with action affects his voice and offers the audience visible symbols of his meaning.

Some good speakers are so successfully intent upon communication, or are such free individuals by nature, that their speaking methods will not fit simple classifications of right or wrong ways to speak. Such speakers do not intentionally set out to violate "rules" or to disprove theories. Rather they have merely maintained perspective, realizing that insecure or excessive attention to detail often obscures larger values and meanings. Perhaps an analogy will make this point clearer. Mel Ott, with one of the most unconventional batting stances in baseball, compiled a lifetime average of .304, and four times led the National League in home runs. Would you have "corrected" his stance, had you been his manager? On the other hand, would you train a rookie ballplayer to use an unusual stance which had proved effective with only one man? This is the dilemma of your instructor.

You may think you are the Mel Ott of the platform and entitled to violate all the rules of good posture, platform movement, and gesture. Probably you are not. At any rate, your instructor will help you to adapt the rules to your own personality and speaking manner and to emerge a more effective speaker as a result. In doing so, he will bring to your attention certain standard or traditional concepts which are completely acceptable because experience and use have shown them to be normal and workable. For example, one acceptable speaking posture is to stand erect, with the arms and hands hanging relaxed at the sides, and with the weight planted on the balls of the feet. Yet an inexperienced speaker, or one not really intent upon the total business of communicating an idea, can assume this posture and still look like an adolescent gorilla with its feet stuck in concrete. On the other hand, directness and communicative energy, coupled with a good idea, can make almost any audience unaware of a speaker's posture, however unusual.

Posture

In a practical sense, we may say that any posture is acceptable which does not draw attention to itself or away from the idea being communicated, or suggest oddity or excessive tension in the speaker. The posture most likely to produce freedom from these negative elements calls for discipline, balance, and symmetry. Specifically, it means that your weight is evenly distributed, or nearly so, on both feet. Your knees, if flexed at all, are flexed only slightly and always evenly. Thus your hips are in line, each equidistant from the floor, successfully avoiding the "tired workhorse" posture some careless speakers assume. You may find it comfortable to place the dominant foot a little forward, with a slight angle between the feet. (For a right-handed person, "dominant" means the right foot.) A sense of eagerness to convey an idea is suggested if your weight is kept slightly but not obviously forward on the balls of the feet.

When your posture has balance and symmetry, your shoulders will be at nearly the same level. They need not be pulled stiffly backward. If they are merely kept out of an excessively forward or slouching position, they are adequately placed. There is no need to puff out your chest like a pouter pigeon.

When your shoulders are balanced and level, you have made a good start on the problem of what to do with your hands. If you are disturbed by having hands, you are exactly like other insecure and inexperienced speakers. But once again, take comfort in the knowledge that there is no absolute rule establishing the right way to use them most effectively. You may find it easiest to drop them loosely at your sides, with the elbows in moderately close to the body. Or you may sometimes place them behind your back, or clasp them loosely in front of you, or if you are a man, occasionally put one hand in a coat pocket. You may rest them easily but not desperately on a speaker's stand or lectern. Wherever you place them, keep these two important questions in mind: (1) Can you easily and frequently bring your hands into use for descriptive and emphatic action? (2) When they are not in specific use, do you avoid such distracting activity as coin jingling, ear scratching, knuckle cracking, pencil twisting, or the tactile admiration of an engagement ring? So long as you are comfortable, ready to move, and free from nervous mannerisms, your hands are well placed and well used.

To put this concept of posture in positive terms, let us return to the principles of Chapter 3. A good speaker has physical alertness and physical freedom. He seems to be, but need not literally be, "on his toes." He is free and relaxed enough to suggest naturalness and spontaneity in his movements and actions. If you achieve these goals, you may be confident that your delivery is capable of setting ideas free.

Movement

Any posture, no matter how "correct," will prove tiring to both the speaker and the audience if it is unvaried. Consequently good speakers learn to change position and, if circumstances permit, to move about on the platform. Even when a microphone or a restricting pulpit prevent completely free movement, shifting the position of the feet, turning the body, and moving about within the limits permitted by the occasion are all desirable. Like posture, platform movement must be disciplined and balanced, suggesting freedom but not giving the impression of an athlete warming up for the decathlon. Perhaps freedom of movement can be attained most quickly by speaking without a lectern or table. Your tendency then may be to move too much, but with the guidance of your instructor and the advice of your classmates you can learn to temper this action until it suits the nature of your talk and the circumstances under which you are speaking. Learn to move at times that accentuate changes in the direction of your speech, or to reflect varying moods, cultivating all the while the balance and poise that characterize the speaker at ease with his audience.

Dress

You will find it easier to develop poise in posture and platform movement if you consider each appearance before an audience as an occasion for looking your best. Most young women do not need advice on this matter. But a surprising number of undergraduate men appear on the platform uncombed, unbarbered, or unshaved — perhaps in a T-shirt battered and begrimed. We do not recommend that every student speaker wear a suit coat and a tie for each appearance before a class. On some campuses such dress would be so unusual as to be distracting in itself. You will appear to best advantage if your dress observes the customs of your campus. In talks given off campus, of course, more formal dress is usually indicated. Meet the expectations of the audience for pleasing, well-groomed appearance on the platform wherever you speak.

Exercises

Achieving good posture and freedom from distracting actions takes practice and discipline. These qualities cannot be attained in formal speaking assignments alone. To develop poise, try these exercises.

1. Practice a speech before a full-length mirror. For the moment, pretend to be both speaker and audience. Try to prevent yourself from assuming any bad posture or distracting mannerisms.
2. Station an observer at the back of the room when you are giving a speech. Ask him to imitate any bad postures or distracting mannerisms you use. Work out other signals to help you improve your bodily movement. Adapt to his suggestions as you speak.
3. Sometimes a beginning speaker can gain insight into, and control over, distracting habits by discovering that they can be overcome and eventually eliminated through excellence in another aspect of speaking. We suggest some negative practice. In the privacy of your room, or in a classroom with one or two friends present, do the best speaking you can while engaging in some deliberate distraction, such as putting both hands high over your head as if you had been commanded to "Stick 'em up." Put all the meaning you can

into your voice. If you have listeners, engage them in direct eye contact, or look at yourself in a mirror. Work with a sound idea and try to word it well. What will you prove? If you can speak well with your hands up, why not even better when they are placed in a normal position and available for use?

If you think it would help you, ask your instructor if you may try this exercise in front of the class.

Strengthening Ideas Through Gestures

Poise and good posture, coupled with disciplined platform movement and an acceptably pleasant appearance, help set ideas free; conversely, poor posture, uncoordinated platform movement, and careless or inappropriate dress become barriers which imprison ideas. In effective speaking, ideas are always freed. But beyond this, some ideas need to be strengthened through gestures. Movements of the head and shoulders, facial expressions, and hand gestures to describe or emphasize will help to give clarity, believability, and interest to the things you say.

Gestures give ideas greater clarity by illustrating or reinforcing them in a manner more direct than can be achieved through language alone. They improve believability by enhancing the impression of earnestness and sincerity made by the speaker. They increase interest by introducing variety and change in delivery. In doing this, gestures utilize the element of vision and provide an audience with the chance to "see" what cannot be seen through language or voice. Visible underlining of the non-visible, we might call it.

Good gestures, like good posture and appearance, do not draw attention to themselves, or suggest tension or oddity on the part of the speaker. Gestures should be meaningful, free, relaxed, and yet specific. If you have spoken under tension and have realized that awkward gestures are distracting, you may have fallen victim to the fallacious belief that the less you do the less you will get hurt. Imagine a timid boxer entering the ring in mortal fear of his opponent and reasoning: "Maybe if I don't do anything he won't hurt me." Such matches do not last long. Likewise, a timid speaker who uses no gestures, or only a few tentative and ineffectual ones, merely compounds his reasons for timidity. This behavior is perfectly understandable under the stress of inexperience in speaking before an

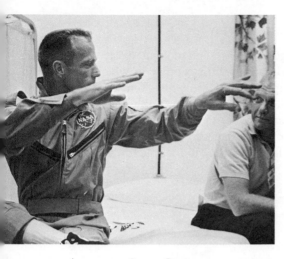

Astronaut Scott Carpenter uses gestures, the "visible underlining of the non-visible," to describe his flight into outer space.

audience, but the reasoning behind it is clearly fallacious, as you will see if you compare this kind of action with the physical behavior of any person in direct conversation.

All of us use action in animated conversation and informal discussion when we are unaware that we are "making a speech." Countless instructors have tried unsuccessfully to encourage a tense student to use action in class, only to be sought out privately by the same individual, who then without inhibition and with surprisingly effective gestures, declares, "But Sir, it just isn't natural for me to use action!"

Indeed, it is normal and human for any person to employ head movements, facial expressions, and hand gestures in direct, conversational speech with friends and associates in any informal situation. In good public speaking, these same actions are used easily and unconsciously by a competent speaker. True, they are somewhat altered or edited to fit the larger context of the speech situation, but this altering is eventually done without thought and is for the sole purpose of making the actions seem as natural within the larger context as within the smaller or more private one. If you have difficulty in achieving this transition or simple enlargement of your own natural gestures, you may look for the reason in your own fear, or in the false notion that there is a perfect and proper way for speakers to gesture.

Perfect and proper gestures as such do not exist. This is true despite the tradition of the nineteenth century in which a great deal of nonsense was urged upon hapless students about the "correct" use of gesture. For example, here is a diagram published many decades ago in a book devoted exclusively to gesturing. Study it only long enough to feel a sense of relief in today's assumption that gesture is not something to be codified, charted, and learned by rote.

The elocutionist's repertoire of gestures, from Bacon, Manual of Gesture. You will not get instruction of this type today.

Though it is impossible to say precisely what a "good" gesture is, or that a given gesture is "good" under all conditions, there are certain characteristics of effective gesturing which should be stressed. We urge you to give attention to the three listed below.

Fullness and Completeness

Good gestures are full and complete, but not melodramatic or mechanically forced. Perhaps we can best convey the concepts of fullness and completeness by redefining them as functions of total

FREEDOM IN BODILY ACTION . . .

. . . *comes slowly. These speakers wish to gesture, and are rightly trying to do so. Unfortunately, none is really succeeding. One speaker stands flat-footed. Another is restraining her gesture instead of giving it free play. Still another is forcing his gesture so much that it is at best ineffective, at worst ludicrous.*

body coordination. A simple pointing gesture with the index finger of your right hand activates not merely the muscles of the hand, or even of the whole arm. Well-executed, the gesture involves the entire body, beginning with a tensing of arm and shoulder muscles and accompanied by the preliminary motions of a slight shifting of the entire body weight forward onto the right foot, particularly at the instant of maximum reach. It is in this sense that gestures call for complete body coordination.

We may say that gestures are full when they are expansive enough to fit the size of the audience and the size of the idea. For example, the pointing gesture we have cited need not be made with the full length of arm. But whatever distance the hand is extended, it should be moved firmly and with the degree of muscle tension which implies that the speaker wishes to give precisely this much emphasis, no more and no less. If made too weakly, the gesture will look half-hearted, sloppy, or lazy. To prove the matter to yourself, point half-heartedly, using your arm alone as if it were independent of the rest of your body. What have you implied? Conversely, too much energy or amplitude can be put into a gesture. When this happens, you have *gilded* or *burdened* the idea. The gesture intrudes into the consciousness of the audience and defeats its basic purpose of strengthening the point. Like old-style melodrama in which all actions are exaggerated, an over-reached gesture is unintentionally comic, and occasionally pathetic.

Meaning and Timing

Good gestures serve meaning when they are well-timed and used for description or emphasis. Descriptive gestures generally deal with tangible concepts, such as size, shape, motion, location, and direction. Emphatic gestures generally treat of abstractions or idea values, such as urgency, inclusiveness, simplicity, and sincerity. But whether descriptive or emphatic, gestures should come at the proper instant to produce added meaning. Usually this is at the exact moment you are uttering the word or phrase for which the gesture is most meaningful and needed. You will recall that we informally defined gestures as a visible underlining of the non-visible. Working as we must at this moment only through the medium of print, we ask you to believe that in the next sentence we strongly feel that the word "try" is most important. "These are the times THAT try men's souls." What happened? What word stuck most firmly in your mind? Suppose a speaker used a gesture a split second too early. The result would be the same unfortunate distraction of attention away from the key word. Both clarity and believability would be reduced. It so happens that in the printed illustration we gave you, we "gestured" too early. The attention values or meaning of our selected word, "try," would be equally obscured in speech if this happened: "These are the times that try MEN'S souls."

The timing of a gesture is in part a product of what you do before and after the actual stroke. In a hand gesture you must anticipate the need for an action as the key word or phrase approaches, and get your hand into a position from which the gesture can be made. If you wait until the key word is upon you, you will probably make one of those weak and futile "fish flop" gestures from the hip. At best such a movement indicates that you thought something was important but were not quite sure what it was. At worst it suggests unrelieved tension accomplishing no purpose. Similarly, when a gesture is completed, you do not need to jerk your hand back as though you had touched a hot stove. Simply allow your muscles to relax naturally, and return your hand to any comfortable and inconspicuous position.

Frequency and Variety

Good gestures are frequent and varied, but not excessive, hackneyed, or repetitive. Gesturing with suitable frequency will become a natural part of your speaking style as you cease to fear gestures and begin to use in public speech all the communicative implements of informal conversation. Beyond this no law of proper frequency can be established. Some individuals are by nature more animated and active than others and will naturally gesture more often. Some will gesture less, but all will gesture some. The inexperienced speaker is the only actionless creature on earth. At the beginning, therefore, you must not hide behind the rationalization that action is not suited to your personality. It may be necessary to force it a little until the strangeness of the situation has worn off. As a matter of fact, the more quickly you become an active speaker, the sooner will speaking to an audience seem a normal type of expression for you.

When free bodily actions begin to come spontaneously, you will realize that different types of material call for varying amounts of gesture. Descriptive passages gain in interest and clarity by frequent

VARIETIES OF GESTURE . . .

Student speakers soon learn there are so many ways to gesture that monotony is inexcusable.

Experienced public speakers know that effective gestures are spontaneous and free, reflecting the whole person in the act of communication.

demonstrative gestures. Vigorous climaxes are made more believable by a succession of strong gestures to underline important words. On the other hand, there may be periods of little overt action in a speech. Hamlet's advice to the players is equally sound for speakers in other situations: "Suit the action to the word, the word to the action, with this special observance, that you o'erstep not the modesty of nature."

Once you have begun to use gestures with sufficient frequency to support your ideas, you may discover that you tend to repeat the same gesture in every situation. In a few cases this may actually impair your meaning. Perhaps you always gesture with your index finger. Thus if you declare, "There are too many Communists in high places," and through habit point dramatically toward the president of the Chamber of Commerce in the third row, your gesture will be misleading, to say the least. Most gestures, however, are not so specific. The danger is in monotony more than in confusion of meaning.

Moreover, there are so many ways to gesture that there is no excuse for monotony. One of the old elocution books noted twelve positions of the arms and fifteen positions of the hands, any of which could be executed with either hand or with both. We do not intend to encourage mechanical and artificial gestures in the nineteenth-century tradition, but surely no intelligent speaker needs to become dependent on one or two bodily actions when there are dozens available. Observe yourself and others in conversational speech. Keep it up for a few days and then make your own classification of the types of action. In addition to hand gestures, you will discover (1) head motions: shaking, nodding, tossing; (2) facial expressions: lifted eyebrows, smiles, frowns; (3) shoulder motions: shrugs, liftings, and lowerings; (4) major changes in position. With such a variety available, you need not become a single or double meat-cleaver speaker, or a right-handed semaphore. And above all, do not fall into the pattern of silent-movie stereotypes, with sweeping motions of rejection, or fist-poundings for every third word. "Suit the action to the word, the word to the action," and you will find that physical responses enhance your meaning and give strength to your ideas.

Practice and Performance

You will automatically and naturally become skilled in the use of action to the extent that you are observant and courageous. Still, some practice will have value in the learning situation. Your progress in your speech class will be directly proportional to the amount of time you spend in actual practice, in private and before friends, working aloud and intentionally using action. It is not necessary, indeed it is probably unwise, for you to plan and rehearse specific gestures for a speech you are preparing. For when the time comes to speak in class, you may spend more time in remembering gestures than in re-thinking ideas; and if so, your audience will sense it. Still, in your practice you must give yourself the chance to free your body, to become accustomed to descriptive and emphatic actions as a natural part of the speech you are working up in your mind. It matters little whether in the actual presentation of the speech you use the same actions you used in practice. What does matter is that you use spontaneous action of whatever type seems necessary at that moment in order to free and strengthen your ideas. This, we repeat, will be easier if you have practiced in an effort to develop the same freedom and spontaneity.

Perhaps an analogy will help. If you wish to become an expert at a sport like tennis, golf, diving, or baseball, you expect to devote long hours to practice, refining your technique. Form and skill must be developed through training and repetition. Yet when the actual moment comes, whether it be executing a back flip from the high board or stepping up to the batter's plate, the prime objective becomes paramount. The good batter will not consciously think of form; he will try for a hit. Similarly, a good speaker will think not of gestures but of ideas and communication.

Exercises

Practice the following exercises with the advice on practice and performance in mind. Your purpose here is to develop spontaneity and naturalness in gesture, not to memorize a specific pattern of movement.

Repeat the first two exercises on page 163, adding gesture to the suggestions given there.

2. Practice the following passages, using whatever gestures seem appropriate on whatever words seem to need emphasis. Repeat the sentences with different gestures. Find at least five ways to use action which emphasizes the key ideas. Try them out before a mirror, modifying the gestures until you are convinced they are appropriate, full, complete, and well-timed.

   a. There is only one answer to the problem of air pollution: tough, two-fisted, uncompromising enforcement against every person and every industrial concern that insists on fouling the air.

   b. Playground facilities in our city are completely inadequate. What's more, unless we act now all the vacant areas which would make good parks will be covered with tract houses filled with more children to add to the problem. Our present planned inaction will create problems of juvenile delinquency in the years ahead.

   c. Let us suppose that the Senate Chamber represents the Hetch Hetchy Valley. It will then represent an irregular floor containing between 2½ and 3 square miles, surrounded by cliffs that rise 4000 feet in the air. The floor will be the ordinary meadow land, irregular it is true, and the walls not straight, as those of the Senate Chamber are, but irregular and varying as we would naturally expect in a large canyon of that kind. The floor of the valley has some timber on it, but nothing of any value, although there are thousands of honest people who believe that the flooding of this valley is going to ruin some of the great trees of California. The trees in the valley are ordinary scrub pine.

     Away over yonder in the distance there is a waterfall, the Tuolumne River, that comes down over the cliffs, falling between the rocks; and then trickling through the outlying rocks into a stream that runs through the valley; the walls of this great chasm come almost together, so that they are at the opening less than 65 feet apart. . . . This valley in the wintertime is filled with snow. I presume there are 40 feet of snow in that valley today. . . . In the springtime when the sun comes out and reflects its heat from the surrounding cliffs the snow melts and the watershed farther back over the mountains is also denuded of its snow, which is turned into water by the sun's rays; the waterfall then commences to pour itself down over the mountains, and there is a rushing flood; it cannot get out of this opening of less than 65 feet, and the result is that the floor of the valley is covered with water. — Senator George Norris to the United States Senate, December 6, 1913.

Voice in Speech Delivery

Some speakers have the unfortunate habit of using "uh's" in their speech, filling the pauses with meaningless noise in an effort to camouflage a temporarily blank mind. Of course it does not work, but there is a significant relationship between such noises and bodily action. *Speakers with poor posture and inadequate gestures use more "uh's" and generally have duller, less expressive, less communicative voices than physically poised, alert, animated speakers.* As we said earlier, voice production is as much a function of muscle movement as walking about the platform or gesturing. Moreover, what you do with one part of the body influences muscular reactions elsewhere. Thus if you have made progress toward developing visual directness, physical alertness, and physical freedom, and if you have reinforced these skills with meaningful gestures which strengthen your ideas, you have, even without serious attention to the matter, been developing a better speaking voice.

Special attention to the use of that voice can further enlarge your communicative effectiveness. This does not require learning about the physics of sound or the anatomy of the larynx, or even analyzing the subtle changes in the voice needed for acting or the oral interpretation of poetry. These are special fields of knowledge and skill which you may wish to approach in other speech courses. Here we have neither the time nor the need to study them in great detail. We ask simply — How may you adapt the best qualities of an effective conversational voice to the larger context of public speaking? To meet these needs, you must learn to free ideas by being heard and understood, and to strengthen them by developing qualities of voice which help to hold attention and interest.

Being Heard and Understood — Freeing Ideas

An old story current among public speakers tells of the Chautauqua lecturer irritated by a loud-mouthed heckler in the back of the tent who kept shouting, "Louder!" Finally, in disgust the speaker retorted in stentorian tones, "When the last judgment comes, and Gabriel comes forth upon the battlements of Heaven to sound the final trumpet, some fool will rise and yell, 'Louder, please!' "

The irritation of this speaker is understandable, but perhaps we should also say a good word for the heckler. Is there anything more frustrating than sitting at the back of a room futilely trying to hear the timid tones of a speaker who seems unaware that there is anyone beyond the third row? The speaker may have a world-shaking message, but the world will not be shaken if his words cannot be heard. Moreover, in the normal classroom speaking situation, this failure in communication is usually completely unnecessary. Few students lack the physical equipment or technical skill to make themselves heard and understood by twenty, fifty, or even a hundred people. Any speaker who is watching his audience can see the signs of irritation, inattention, or resignation that mark the listeners who cannot hear. Good speakers respond to these signs by speaking louder and more distinctly.

LOUDNESS. Loudness, even more than other aspects of voice production, is the result of adequate physical energy. Recall the exercise suggested earlier in this chapter in which you found it difficult, if not impossible, to vary the energy of hand and arm movements without changing the loudness of your voice. Unless you are making serious errors in your method of breathing, or are "choking up" with excessive tension in your throat muscles, an increase in bodily energy should help to solve the problem of inadequate loudness.

But what about the minority who cannot develop sufficient loudness by intentional energy changes? If you are one of that group, your best recourse is a change of attitude. Search for speech subjects about which you can become genuinely enthusiastic — even excited. Then try to convey your feeling to your listeners. Once a proper attitude has been established, the energy level is easier to maintain, and loudness difficulties may be solved. A small number of speakers, however, may actually have physical deficiencies or long-established habits which make adequate loudness difficult. If you think this may be your problem, discuss it with your instructor. If necessary, he will outline a suitable series of breathing or relaxation exercises, enroll you in a special course in voice training, or refer you to the speech clinic for intensive drill in voice production.

At one time it was the goal of every successful public speaker to be heard above the din and confusion of a political convention or at an enormous outdoor convocation — all, of course, without benefit of microphone and loud speaker. A few succeeded, with little apparent strain. A slightly larger number also succeeded, but only by developing unpleasant and raucous voices which could be heard two hundred yards away — if anyone was willing to listen. If you are blessed with a powerful yet pleasant voice, you have reason to be happy, for it is still an unquestionable asset to any public speaker. But there is no longer any need for you to force your voice beyond its natural limits. Any voice adequate for an audience of a hundred without a public address system is sufficient, with electronic assistance, for a group of any size.

Unfortunately, raucous loudness is not limited to voices tuned to large audiences. There is some danger that in response to pleas from your classmates and instructor to talk louder, you may respond with driving and unpleasant tones. Such a voice has the virtue of being heard, but the misfortune of possibly arousing resentment or even antagonism toward your speech. Sometimes the problem may be simply too much loudness with never a letdown, like a group of amateur musicians trying to cover gross musical barbarities with overpowering noise. In other cases, it may be a matter of excessive tension of the throat muscles, creating harsh and strident tones which listeners interpret as an attempt to whip them into acceptance of your ideas.

Loudness and Breathing Habits. Perhaps some knowledge of the way the breath stream produces sounds will help you increase the loudness of your voice without also increasing its harshness. The force with which the vocal folds are set into vibration is proportional to the strength of the breath stream as it passes through the larynx. In many ways it is comparable to the flow of a river. The velocity of river water may be changed in three ways: by increasing the amount of water in the stream, as when the Missouri and the Mississippi converge; by increasing the angle of fall, as in a mountain stream; or by forcing the water through a narrow gorge. Any of these phenomena will increase the power of the water in the river, but only the first produces a smooth power. The others result in great turbulence.

In much the same way loudness may be increased in the voice by increasing the power of the breath stream at the larynx. This may be done by increasing the volume of exhaled breath by control of the breathing mechanism; it may be done by a sudden expulsion of the breath comparable to the increased rate of fall; or it may be achieved by tightening the muscles in and around the larynx. Only the first method produces a smooth, full tone. The second produces the loudness of a top sergeant, the third a high-pitched yell.

The problem, then, becomes one of controlling the breath stream to produce a strong, sustained flow. In the chest cavity, breathing is controlled by the raising and lowering of the ribs, and by the interaction of the muscles of the diaphragm (a broad muscle and membrane forming the floor of the chest) with the muscles of the abdominal wall. When the chest cavity is enlarged by raising the ribs and lowering the diaphragm, breath is inhaled. Breath is exhaled when muscles pull the ribs downward, the diaphragm relaxes, and the abdominal muscles contract. Control of this action is secured by gradual relaxation of the diaphragm as the pressure of the abdominal muscles increases. This interaction provides a smooth, steady, and powerful flow of air.

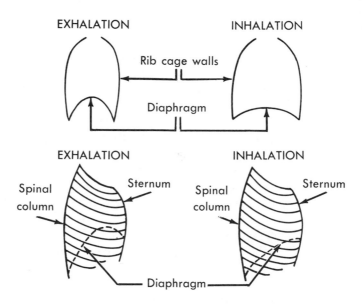

Diagram showing the changes in size and shape of the diaphragm during breathing. (From the front, above; from the right side, below.)

Speakers with inadequate loudness tend to breathe from the upper chest where the volume of stored air is less and where control is more difficult. In addition, exclusive upper chest breathing puts strain on the muscles around the larynx and causes tension in the vocal folds, producing stridency and high pitch.

When speakers with inadequate breath control try to increase loudness, they usually do it by narrowing the aperture at the larynx. This causes the vocal folds to vibrate more strongly, but also to vibrate faster and hence at a high pitch. If this continues for a prolonged period, the speaker becomes hoarse.

The following exercises may help you increase the strength of your breath stream and reduce tensions when you try to speak louder.

Exercises

1. *Controlled Breathing.*
    a. Standing in an erect position with your feet comfortably apart, place your hands above your hips so that the index fingers touch the front part of the lowest ribs, while the rest of your hand is on the abdominal wall. Your thumb should touch the ribs at the back. Take several easy but full breaths. If you are using diaphragmatic-abdominal breathing, your ribs should move up and out and your abdominal wall should bulge slightly as you inhale. On exhalation the reverse should occur.
    b. Sit in an erect position in a chair, with the base of your spine against the back of the chair. Take a firm grip on the chair with your hands in the lowest position you can reach without slumping. This will keep your shoulders from rising as you take several deep breaths. Notice the movement of the abdominal wall and the ribs as you inhale and exhale.
    c. In either of the above positions, sustain a low-pitched tone, gradually increasing in loudness as you sustain it. Do not raise the pitch. Make sure that the pressure in the breath stream comes from the abdominal-diaphragmatic area.
    d. In a standing position, count on one breath at a low level of loudness from one to five; inhale and count from one to ten; then to fifteen, adding five more until you can add no more on one breath. Repeat at a louder tone. Note how much more difficult it is to sustain the longer phrases as the loudness increases. Repeat exercises *c* and *d* until you can lengthen the phrases.
2. *Open Throat.*
    a. To relax the throat muscles, inhale through your mouth slowly. Without changing the position of your throat muscles, sound a full-toned *ah,* and sustain it. Repeat the process at a louder level, but do not raise the pitch.
    b. Keeping the same open throat, repeat the line, "Roll on, thou deep and dark blue ocean! Roll!" Sustain a full tone on all the sounds.
    c. With open throat and sustained breath, read the following sentences in a forceful tone:

    Turn it over, look at it on all sides, and it is everywhere a swindle. And if the word I now use has not the authority of classical usage, it has the indubitable authority of fitness.

d. Select a strong passage from a famous speech and read it in a loud voice with sustained tone.

DISTINCTNESS. Adequate loudness assures you that your listeners will hear your voice, but it does not guarantee that they will recognize the words you speak. Five minutes of analytical listening to the speech of your fellows will convince you that college students do not always speak distinctly. Moreover, if you could listen to yourself without being on guard, you would probably conclude that you too have moments when you condense or destroy individual sounds, syllables, words, and even whole phrases.

The habit of lazy articulation may do little damage in informal conversation with friends. After all, a listener can usually supply the missing word from the context or interrupt the conversation to demand, "Wudjuh say?" But audiences do not usually exercise this prerogative. If the speaker's articulation prevents his listeners from understanding his words, it is simpler for them to go quietly to sleep.

Moreover, it is more difficult to hear a public speaker than a conversationalist. Listeners are farther away, and the high-frequency sounds of the hissing and sputtering consonants which play such a large part in distinguishing words from each other are often obscured by distance, the rustling of papers, the creaking of uncomfortable chairs, the rumble of passing traffic, or the echoes from open beams on the ceiling. And of course, the larger the room and the greater the number of listeners, the greater the difficulty. Even a good public address system may not help much, and a poor one can make the problem worse. Unless the sounds which emanate from the speaker are clear, they may easily become completely unintelligible a short distance away.

Most of the common errors in articulation fall into two general categories and show (1) a tendency to hurry over or omit the short unaccented words and syllables, or (2) a tendency to assimilate some consonants into neighboring sounds which are formed alike or have the same auditory characteristics. Without attempting a detailed study of these problems, check your articulation of this sentence, reading it as nearly as possible in your normal conversational voice:

I wouldn't want to be President of the United States.

Probably your difficulties in articulation centered on the *d, n, t, s, z* and *th* sounds, which are produced by roughly similar positions of the tongue. When they are made in close approximation to each other, there is a tendency to absorb some of them into neighboring sounds. There is also a temptation to slur over the unaccented words *to* and *of,* perhaps to omit them entirely. Careful listening to a recording of part of one of your speeches should help you identify these or any other consistent weaknesses in your own articulation, and so help you avoid them. Usually, slowing down the rate and increasing the energy used in articulating consonants will be enough to clarify the production of sounds.

One word of caution. Just as there is no need to be raucous in order to be heard, there is no need to sound like a pseudo-Shakespearian actor in order to be understood. Some words and syllables need less emphasis than others because they represent less important ideas. Moreover, speech must not become halting and jerky because of the effort to articulate every sound. Such speaking destroys the unity of phrases and impairs both the literal meaning and the opportunity for giving proper weight to key ideas. So long as you remember that the idea is more important than the method of delivery, you should be able to avoid gross errors in loudness and articulation without loss of naturalness and communicative effectiveness.

Holding Attention and Interest — Strengthening Ideas

The enemy of attention is monotony. The constant roar of an automobile motor on a lonely road at night has put many a driver to sleep, sometimes permanently. And the monotonous drone of a dull professor's voice has encouraged more than one student to take up doodling. There are, of course, many ways to be dull, but unquestionably one of the most effective is to speak without changes in pitch, with unvaried timing, and at a constant level of intensity. Conversely, meaningful changes in these elements do much to aid the speaker in holding attention and interest. Even more, a voice intelligently varied serves to heighten meanings, to distinguish between the important and the less important, and to give strength and power to key ideas essential to the speaker's point of view.

PITCH. Speech, like song, largely depends for pleasing and meaningful variety upon changes in pitch. But the singer reflects the moods of the composer in long sustained notes, sudden and marked changes in pitch, and a carefully devised time pattern, whereas the speaker is able to reflect his own feelings in the freely chosen pitch changes which occur to him at the time of delivery. In conversation, only a speaker devoid of all physical response to ideas will talk in a monotone; yet in a platform situation some speakers "freeze" and produce an unchanging voice. You may find yourself and other speakers using an extremely limited pitch range all because of the fearful misapprehension we mentioned earlier, that the less you do the less you can be criticized. Perhaps so, but very few souls are saved this way.

In good, communicative speaking, frequent and spontaneous pitch changes are occurring all the time. Basically, there are three types: (1) *the step,* a discrete, distinct, or marked change, either up or down; (2) *the slide* or *inflection,* a change which starts gradually and continues in the direction (either up or down) in which it started; (3) *the double slide* or *circumflex,* which involves two slides with a change of direction. The relationship of these three shifts must be ever changing and always adapted to the meaning of ideas and the language being used, else a mechanical and repetitive pattern is established which leads to "sing-song" speech — or what has sometimes been called "ministerial melody," an allusion to the fixed patterns often associated with a modified speech chanting.

It is unlikely that you can simply insert these three pitch changes occasionally in your speech. Rather, discover the pitch changes which do occur in your speech, and study how they can be improved in value, and if need be, in number. Perhaps the simplest way to do this is to analyze in detail a recording of your voice made during one of your class speeches, and if possible another caught during unguarded conversation. Compare the two and note how they differ. How can you adapt the best elements of the conversational pattern to speaking before an audience? How can you strengthen ideas in the speech by introducing additional pitch changes, or by using a wider pitch range within the pattern you have established? When you have decided what changes in pitch would benefit the speech, record one section of it again and compare your delivery with the earlier recording. And of course, repeat the process until you are satisfied that this is the best use of pitch changes that you can make.

Because flexibility in pitch is so necessary to meaning and feeling in speech, it is important that you do not restrain your practice merely because you may feel that you are forcing yourself into changes which seem unnatural. In the early stages of learning they may indeed be unnatural to you, especially if your habitual speech has been lifeless and dull. But if you do "o'erstep the modesty of nature," your instructor will tell you so. Probably what seems overdone to you will not be so at all. You need merely to develop the flexibility of pitch which appears naturally in the speech of a physically alert, communicating person. As your skill grows, meaningful and colorful changes will appear easily in your speech. Your hearers will find it more pleasant to listen to you, and they will have a quickened appreciation of your meaning and feeling. You will learn not merely how to free your ideas from the bonds of monotony, but how to reinforce the ideas you most want your listeners to respond to. Meaningful changes in pitch strengthen ideas.

TIMING. To test your awareness of time values, read this sentence aloud as if it were part of a speech:

> But first of all, let me assert my firm belief that the only thing we have to fear is fear itself, nameless, unreasoning, unjustified terror.

Did you read it all at the same rate, as if you were following a metronome, or perhaps with a slight accent on alternate syllables, like the beating of a drum? Or did you vary the speed of utterance to bring out differences in meaning? Was part of the sentence read more quickly than the rest? Did you draw out some words to give time to absorb their full implication? Did you pause before or after key words to make them stand out in the minds of your listeners?

You may recognize the sentence as part of Franklin D. Roosevelt's first inaugural address. Uttered at the depth of the most disastrous economic collapse in our history, the new President's words were heard by an enormous radio audience — a panic-stricken, fear-ridden audience representing a cross section of the American people. To such listeners the new President addressed his reassuring words.

Perhaps you would like to listen to the time pattern of Roosevelt's words as he spoke them. You will find them in the Columbia record album *I Can Hear It Now*, Volume I. The changes in pitch used by the speaker were perhaps too narrow, and the time pattern was not necessarily the only one which should have been used, but there is no question that changes in timing were effective in strengthening the idea contained in the President's words. These changes consist of (1) variations in basic rate, (2) changes in duration, and (3) the use of pause.

Rate. The term *rate* means simply the speed of utterance, the number of words spoken per minute. In effective speech, rate will not, of course, be constant. A speaker whose average rate is 120 words per minute will speak sometimes at a speed of 150 words, and other times at 90. Moreover, he will have some periods of silence, or pauses, and some lengthened syllables preceded and followed by words spoken at his normal rate. In the Roosevelt excerpt, the first part of the sentence, up to the first use of the word "fear," was spoken at a moderate speed suggesting only earnest communication. Then several words were slowed by lengthening the duration of the syllables. The last part of the sentence was accelerated slightly, suggesting the intensity of feeling implied by the word "terror."

Changes in rate are perhaps the most effective means of indicating changes in mood or movement. In reading poetry, for example, the speed of utterance often conveys as much of the meaning as the words themselves. In Poe's poem, *The Bells,* what damage would you do to the meaning if you gave a markedly slow rate to "Hear the tinkling of the bells, silver bells"? Experiment with different rates on a sentence like this one of Patrick Henry: "The next gale that sweeps from the north will bring to our ears the clash of resounding arms." What rate best suits the mood? Or what rate fits this sentence from Henry W. Grady's description of the Confederate soldier after Lee's surrender: "Lifting his tear-stained and pallid face for the last time to the graves that dot the old Virginia hills, [he] pulls his gray cap over his brow and begins the slow and painful journey." In much the same way, learn to vary the rate of your own speech to fit the mood of your words.

Duration. Whether your overall rate is fast or slow, some words should be made to stand out from the context by changing their time values. Such changes are called variations in *duration.* Usually a change in duration means lengthening a syllable or a word to give the listener more time to comprehend its meaning or its mood. Roosevelt lengthened the phrase, "fear itself," by increasing the duration of "fear" and "self." Thus the value of the phrase is heightened because it stands out from other parts of the sentence. This device was characteristic of all Roosevelt's speeches — so much so that his political opponents found in it an easy means of burlesquing his delivery. Nevertheless the method was effective.

How would you treat duration in delivering this sentence from one of Winston Churchill's wartime addresses? "This wicked man

[Hitler], the repository and embodiment of many forms of soul-destroying hatred, this monstrous product of former wrongs and shame, has now resolved to try to break our famous Island race by a process of indiscriminate slaughter and destruction." In reading this passage you will probably find yourself combining pitch and intensity changes with changes in duration, and you will also wish to introduce pauses to accentuate the emphasis produced by lengthening syllables. This is normal and indeed necessary, for changes produced in isolation from other ways of expressing meaning and feeling are likely to be mechanical and forced. Respond to the mood and meaning of your thought as you speak, using variety in voice as a means to free and strengthen ideas.

Pause. Pauses are the punctuation of speech, corresponding to the marks inserted in written material. They are not, however, identical with the written marks; rather, they are dictated by the mood and emphasis intended by the speaker at the moment of utterance. Pauses not only separate phrases from each other, but they are sometimes introduced purely for emphasis in places where no written punctuation would be needed. In Roosevelt's delivery of the sentence from his first inaugural, for example, pauses corresponded to punctuation in only three places — after "all," after "itself," and a short hesitation after "nameless." There was no pause after "unreasoning," and unpunctuated pauses appeared after "belief" and "is." As you listen to the recording or read the sentence aloud with these pauses, try to determine why the speaker used them as he did. Would you do it differently?

Pauses serve three functions in speaking: (1) They are the normal places for a speaker to breathe, enabling him to avoid the breathless gasp that sometimes betrays the novice. (2) They serve to set off phrases from each other and to clarify their meaning. At the same time they give the speaker time to think through the next phrase and avoid choppiness and vocalized pauses. (3) They are a means of emphasizing and strengthening key words and phrases by concentrating the attention of the audience on words just spoken or about to be spoken.

Skilled speakers use frequent modifications of rate, changes in duration, and well-placed pauses. But a word of warning is necessary. An unskilled speaker sometimes uses pauses — even dozens of them — unintentionally. Such pauses are not so much poised controls over timing to facilitate understanding and feeling as they are harried hesitations. You must acquire and use poised pauses to avoid the intellectual pauper's pause. Try to pace the development of your ideas at a rate which fits the complexity of the material and the value of the ideas or feelings expressed. Avoid the beginner's tendency to rush headlong into a race of words, pausing only from fear or to prevent asphyxiation. Skillful variations in timing not only set ideas free, but give them strength beyond the obvious meaning of the words in which they are phrased.

INTENSITY. The term *intensity* is not easily explained. In part it involves variations in loudness; in part it is a function of the amount of pressure on the consonant sounds that may sharpen articulation. But it is also an almost indefinable quality of reserve power, such as we sense in a champion race horse held in check by his jockey just before the final surge on the home stretch. A quiet voice, when the listeners feel that every muscle of the speaker's body is alert and under control, may carry more intensity than an unrestrained bellow. When a father stops shouting at his errant son and says with awesome softness, "Junior, I think you'd better come here," Junior is likely to come.

Few modern speakers have equalled Winston Churchill in control over subdued intensity. Much of the dramatic effectiveness of his wartime speeches was created by this quality of delivery — and, of course, by his magnificent wording. If possible, listen to Churchill's use of controlled intensity in delivering this sentence, also included in the album *I Can Hear It Now:* "Let us therefore brace ourselves to our duties, and so bear ourselves that, if the British Empire and its Commonwealth last for a thousand years, men will still say, 'This was their finest hour.' "

Intensity, like all other aspects of delivery, must be varied, for unmodified intensity, whether the voice is loud or quiet, soon fails to emphasize anything. The skilled speaker learns to vary his intensity from syllable to syllable as well as from sentence to sentence or paragraph to paragraph. The unskilled speaker often fails to vary it even from semester to semester.

In a sense, variety in intensity must be felt before it is practiced. As you listen to yourself and to others in direct, unaffected conversation, try to become sensitive to the numerous and subtle changes in energy. These changes, you will find, are produced unconsciously. In public speaking, because of presumed added complications, the changes in intensity often disappear if the speaker seeks to over-control them. When, however, your speech becomes marked with poise, alertness, freedom, and directness, you will easily and automatically be using innumerable quick and subtle changes in intensity. Such flexibility is one of the speaker's best means of showing his audience the greater and lesser degrees of significance in what is being said. When you develop this skill, you appear to your hearers not as a machine, nor as a frightened robot, but as a living human being reacting to what you are saying no less than you hope they will. By this skill, then, you are freeing and strengthening your ideas for communication.

The Stages of Development in Delivery

In the study of any skill a learner may expect to go through several degrees of greater or lesser frustration and awkwardness. The same is likely to occur in your pursuit of an effective delivery. It may be of value to you and to your instructor to have a set of labels distinguishing these stages and predicting the arrival of each new one. Thus a given label can tell you where you are and what uncharted seas lie ahead. For bodily action and voice skills, you are likely to find these four stages:

1. The stage of random, excessive motion, wasted energy, repetitive language, and the excessive use of "uh."
2. The wooden-Indian stage — frozen, rigid, and riveted to the floor, with voice unvaried for fear of error.
3. The slightly stilted and mechanical stage, occurring as you seek to reach out and gain a mastery of voice and action.
4. The poised, finished, skillful stage in voice and action.

For the sake of brevity, let us call these four stages *random, frozen, mechanical,* and *poised.* It may be that your own development has not followed this order. Perhaps you started out in your speech class not afflicted by wasted motions, necktie-tugging, vocalized pauses, or verbal hash. Instead, you may have been in the frozen stage — rooted to the floor, glued to the speaker's stand, with a voice like a phonograph record designed to induce hypnotic sleep. But it matters little whether you began in the random or the frozen stage, because you have to get into the mechanical stage in order to master the new skills of speech. If you are fortunate, and energetic or dedicated in your efforts, you will not remain long in stage three. But you do need the courage to enter it. It is better for a gesture to look a bit forced and unskilled than for you to look mummified; better for your voice to sound a bit unwieldy or unsteady than monotonous. The willingness and alacrity with which you enter the mechanical stage will be a good indication of how long you remain there. The quicker you enter stage three, the sooner you will arrive at poise. We do not need to redefine this fourth stage; it arrives when the topics discussed in this chapter become second nature to you when you speak before an audience.

Criticizing The Delivery of Speeches

In earlier chapters you learned to criticize delivery in some of its aspects. Now, with a fuller analysis of the theory, you are ready to concentrate on the whole of delivery. The questions below are designed both to help you criticize your classmates intelligently and to improve your own speaking. Prepare and deliver your own speeches so that when these questions are applied to you, the answers will indicate that you are mastering the skills of spoken communication.

1. Do you think the speaker has read this chapter? Does he appear to have made improvements in his delivery which reflect a better understanding of the theory of delivery than in earlier speeches?

2. Did the speaker free and strengthen his ideas through his physical poise, through being direct, alert, and spontaneous?

3. Did the speaker use adequate action and gesture to reinforce his ideas, or to further describe them for increased clarity?

4. Was the speaker's voice loud enough and distinct enough to be easily heard and understood by everyone in the room?

5. Did the speaker have a warm, human control over variety in pitch, timing, and intensity which made it easier to listen to him attentively, to understand what he meant, and to feel that you wanted to agree with him?

6. How would you classify the speaker's present stage of development? Was he random, frozen, mechanical, or skilled? What specific exercises or practice would you suggest to advance his level of skill?

7. Did the speaker's delivery justify his making a speech, or would you have profited more from reading his remarks? Did his delivery free and strengthen his ideas?

8 STYLE:

Ideas and Language

Adlai Stevenson's skill in using words did much to make him twice the Presidential candidate of the Democratic party.

WINSTON CHURCHILL once remarked of a parliamentary colleague that he was one of those orators "who, before they get up, do not know what they are going to say; when they are speaking, do not know what they are saying; and, when they have sat down, do not know what they have said." We have been trying to teach you skills which make it impossible for anyone to say this about your speaking. We have said that the good speaker knows at every moment where he is and where he is going. He begins by selecting a subject he knows something about and can make interesting to his audience. He systematically gathers material and sharpens his thinking by formulating a statement of purpose. He shapes his material by written plans and outlines. Thus when the time comes to speak, he is ready and can concentrate on communicating his message to his audience.

Good speaking has one other element — style. Style is not easy to define. You are familiar with the word as it is applied to dress. There "style" (as distinct from mere "fashion") means verve, individuality, the expression of personality in what one wears and how he wears it. The English satirist Jonathan Swift once defined literary style as "proper words in proper places." And so it is, but that is far from the whole of it. The famous French critic, Buffon, said "style is the man himself." This broader view is perhaps nearer the truth. For style is a blend and a fusion — the product of one's interests, personality, and orderliness of mind (or the lack of it). Good style, therefore, depends upon the intelligent choice of materials and the skillful organization of ideas, and it emerges through those qualities of ethos which free and strengthen ideas in delivery. Yet the clearest expression of style lies in the *choice of words* and their *arrangement into sentences and paragraphs*.

Approaching The Study of Style

Since style is not a varnish or an ornament, it cannot be acquired separately from growth in experience and maturity. If you ask, "How can I learn to speak in the style of Winston Churchill, Daniel Webster, or William Jennings Bryan?" the answer is: perhaps you can affect a style somewhat like theirs. But *should* you, particularly at your age and in view of the subjects on which you have earned the right to speak? You cannot speak of "blood, toil, tears, and sweat," except in a crisis when these stirring words of Britain's wartime Prime Minister have meaning. The wise student will not use them to tell how he studied for his physics examination.

All this is not to say that you need be content with your present style. As you develop broader interests through investigation, reading, conversation, and reflection, you will certainly improve your style. When you demonstrate your interest in your listeners by choosing materials keyed to their knowledge and attitudes, your style benefits. And when you show a real desire to communicate

---

ON SIMPLICITY

Beauty of style and harmony and grace and good rhythm depend on simplicity.

— PLATO

ideas through direct and vigorous delivery, you add to the energy of your thinking and your style at the same time. For style *is* the man — the sum of his experience, his thinking, and his personality — expressed in his language. Conversely, no artful use of language can hide an empty mind or indifference to the needs of listeners.

Style cannot, then, be studied independently of other skills in speech. Style is the business of a lifetime; yet you can do much to improve your use of language during the preparation and delivery of speeches in the few months of this course. To clarify what you can attain immediately, let us divide the acquisition of good style into long-range and short-range goals.

Some Long-Range Goals

A Sense of Style

We have urged you to read widely, not merely to prepare for individual speeches, but to increase your stock of ideas. Reading will also help your style, for it brings you new words as well as new concepts and shows you how other people express themselves. Significant ideas, clearly and forcefully expressed by others, will influence your thoughts and your manner of expressing them. When you read your anthology of English or American literature, think about the style as well as the content of each selection. Is the idea illuminating? Is the language well chosen? Does it make the point clearly, economically, with vividness and color? Does the writer show special skills in arranging details or developing climax? Are any of his stylistic abilities transferable to speeches? Speeches are not often included in anthologies of literature, except for such occasional essay-lectures as Emerson's *The American Scholar.* This lecture is well worth detailed study for its clear statement of ideas and for the cumulative effect of well-chosen examples and analogies.

Your long-range program for improving style should also include the reading of good speeches on public affairs. Such reading should include speeches by men of widely different personalities and skills. The more you read the well-expressed ideas of others, the more ideas you will have yourself, and the better you will word them.

Several good models have been included in the Appendix to this book, pages 279–340. Baird's *Representative American Speeches* (H. W. Wilson Company) has offered an annual collection of significant address since 1937. The magazine *Vital Speeches,* the

New York *Times,* and your local newspaper print current speeches. There is also value in studying texts which have stood the test of time. Your instructor may recommend that you read speeches from such collections as *Modern Eloquence* and *World's Best Orations.* For more recent publications we recommend Parrish and Hochmuth's *American Speeches* (Longmans, Green & Company, Inc., 1954), and two books by Wrage and Baskerville: *American Forum: Speeches on Historic Issues, 1788–1900* (Harper & Row, 1960), and *Contemporary Forum: American Speeches on Twentieth Century Issues* (Harper & Row, 1962). There are, of course, other good recent collections, but we call attention to six speeches, representing a variety of good qualities of style, which you will find in these three books. Careful study of these speeches will repay you. Here are some of the qualities you may note in them:

1. Daniel Webster's "The Murder of Captain Joseph White," (Parrish and Hochmuth, pages 122–178): Vivid description, produced by careful selection of detail and use of pathetic language; strong climax through order of materials and sentence structure.

2. Abraham Lincoln's "Address at Cooper Union," (Parrish and Hochmuth, pages 284–304): Forceful and convincing; simple language and sentence structure; impressive use of details and examples.

3. Lincoln's "Second Inaugural Address," (Parrish and Hochmuth, pages 308–310): Great emotional impact in contrast to logical appeal of "Cooper Union"; simple language, but exactly the right word in the right place; strong climax produced by sentence structure in last part.

4. Henry George's "The Crime of Poverty," (*American Forum,* pages 244–255): Simple colloquial language; effective use of repetition; stimulating questions, both direct and rhetorical; vivid use of details and examples.

5. Robert G. Ingersoll's "Victory for Man," (*American Forum,* pages 301–312): Vivid but simple language; varied sentence structure in both length and form; effective questions, parallel structure, and antithesis.

6. Franklin D. Roosevelt's "Fireside Chat on the Accomplishments of the New Deal," (*Contemporary Forum,* pages 162–167): Simple, direct language; much use of first and second person pronouns; personalized examples.

Study these and other speeches not to produce a pale reflection of their style but to become aware of how words are chosen and arranged. Read portions of the speeches aloud, noting how the sound of words and the rhythm of phrases give added impact to ideas. As you grow in awareness of style, your own style will develop and improve.

Improving Your Vocabulary

You cannot use words well unless you know words well. To know them well is a lifelong challenge. You may start when ready, and we hope you started years ago. Remember, however, that words are meaningless unless they represent ideas. You profit little from the crossword puzzle type of vocabulary building. But when you enlarge your store of language with words which have specific meanings to you, and begin to use those words, you will also increase your stock of ideas.

Not all words in our personal store are of equal value to us. Some are *fringe words* which we cannot define but can interpret well enough in context to understand the import of a passage. Others are *recognition words,* which have a specific meaning to use in or out of context, but which we seldom use. Still others are *writing words,* which we use in the leisure of composition but seldom speak. Finally, the smallest group is our supply of *speaking words.* The way to increase your stock of usable words is to move them from your fringe and recognition vocabularies into your functional writing and speaking vocabularies. To achieve this, we suggest a planned program of vocabulary building.

1. Begin to make fringe words usable by giving each one a specific content. Keep a dictionary handy as you read and check the definitions of such words when you read or hear them.

ON CONFUSION OF MEANING

To me an obscurity is a reason for suspecting a fallacy.
— CHARLES KINGSLEY

The obscurity of a writer is generally in proportion to his incapacity.
— QUINTILIAN

2. Why do you think the author used a word you did not know rather than one you did? Was it more exact? More colorful? Did it have more emotional impact? *Perhaps a better-known word would have been preferable.* Decide for yourself.

3. Write a short paragraph using several new words derived from your reading. Do the new words give greater force and exactness than words you would have used before?

4. Read your paragraph aloud. Then lay it aside and speak informally about the same idea, introducing the new words. When you are certain a new word has meaning for you, use it appropriately in conversation or in speaking to audiences.

In addition to enlarging your functional vocabulary by borrowing fringe and recognition words, we suggest another method. As you write, or practice speaking extemporaneously, you may become acutely aware that you are belaboring a word, or that you are using a limping, feeble word instead of an able-bodied one. When this happens, turn to *Roget's International Thesaurus,* a book of synonyms and word groupings,which may help you strengthen your word choice. But use your dictionary and your thesaurus to find the right, the fitting word or to avoid annoying repetition, not as sources of long words and false erudition for display. If you remind yourself constantly that words are merely symbols for ideas, you are not likely to make this error.

A Short-Range Goal: Developing Style in Preparing and Delivering Speeches

If on reading this far you have decided to forget style for a few more years, your dismay is premature. You can do a great deal to improve your style by careful preparation and delivery of your speeches in this course. As delivery can imprison ideas, free them, strengthen them, or gild them, so can style. Ideas are imprisoned by a weak or illiterate style, freed by a clear style, strengthened by a vivid and imaginative style, and gilded by an exaggerated or florid style. We believe that in a first course in speech you can learn to avoid the extremes of imprisonment and gilding, develop the clarity to free ideas, and begin the slow but rewarding process of learning to strengthen ideas.

Consider how an idea can be modified by varying the language in which it is expressed. When John Mason Brown delivered the commencement address at Hofstra College a few years ago, he described the use of language in these words:

> Only those who write realize how hard it is to write anything that reads easily. And only those who have some conscience about using the language realize how wearying, heart-breaking, yet delectable is the endless challenge of trying to bend words to your will and make them say what you want them to say as you would like to have them say it.[1]

In this passage, we believe the style strengthens the idea. The choice of words, particularly in the second sentence, reinforces the thought both by its accuracy and by its figurative qualities. It is easy to conceive this idea expressed in other ways, however. Had Brown limited his objective to *freeing* ideas — making them clear — he might have done about as well with this:

> Writing well is a difficult art. No one knows this better than professional writers who work hard to make words say exactly what they intend.

But beyond the bare thought, he would have sacrificed a good deal — the warmth and the emotion, and the sense he gives of almost making the listener *feel* how hard it is to write well.

Again, if you can imagine an illiterate person trying to express the idea at all, he might say it in these ungrammatical words, weakening and *imprisoning* his thought:

> It ain't easy to write nothin' good. All the writer guys that tries it finds out it's real hard.

Finally, an intelligent but misguided high school student, seeking to impress parents attending his commencement, might have *gilded* the idea in this way:

> Only those who have put pen to paper have any realization of the difficulties which beset those who try to write with perspicuity. And only those who have some conscience about invoking the Muse understand the heartbreak and the compensating boundless joy of striving for excellence in the art of using the Mother tongue — to make words express the ineffable joys of life or describe its indescribable beauties.

[1] From the *Saturday Review*, July 3, 1954. Reprinted by permission of the publishers.

William Jennings Bryan: "Whether a man steals much or little may depend upon his opportunities, but whether he steals at all depends upon his own volition."

Woodrow Wilson: "The right is more precious than peace."

Robert Frost: "I never dared be radical when young for fear it would make me conservative when old."

Here the words are obviously bigger than the idea. If you have ever expressed yourself like this, we hope you have outgrown it.

The pages that follow suggest ways of developing a style which frees and strengthens ideas by improving clarity, believability, and interest. For the most part, we believe you can avoid imprisoning ideas through style in much the same way you avoid it through delivery. Indeed, developing direct and energetic delivery may help you rid yourself of faults in language which imprison ideas. When you want very much to communicate your thoughts, and to speak them effectively, you think faster and better. Language tends to be clearer and more direct when motive is strong. For this reason, you can profitably work jointly on style and delivery in extemporaneous practice. To achieve this, set yourself these goals: first, avoid weak and illiterate expressions; second, use pauses productively; and third, heighten language impact by skillful delivery.

Will Rogers: "I never met a man I didn't like."

Robert M. LaFollette: "The supreme issue, involving all the others, is the encroachment of the powerful few upon the rights of the many."

STYLE IS THE MAN . . .

The most distinctive speakers have a style, in words, manner, and delivery, which reflects mind, character, and personality. Note how the words of these men, and their appearance, seem to suit each other.

Avoiding Weak and Illiterate Expressions

Ideas are imprisoned by a weak or illiterate style. All of us, through carelessness, depend more or less on certain "crutch" words, clichés, or anemic phrases often used quite unconsciously: "You know what I mean," "Next I want to say," "Well, then . . . ," and so on. Most of us overwork a small band of tired adjectives and adverbs such as *very, really, just* (often pronounced *jiss*), *great, wonderful, fine.* Halfway endorsements are expressed by *sort of* (often pronounced *sorta*), or *kinda* (sometimes *kinduva*). We have no wish to remove such words as *very, just,* and *really* from your vocabulary. Sometimes they are just the words you want. But often they are little more than a cover for a mental vacuum.

With these lightweight words often appear other symptoms of non-fluency. Perhaps every other sentence will begin "Uh, 'n then, uh . . . ," with, for variety's sake, an occasional "Now, uh," or "So, uh."

Some of us, now and then, ignore the rudiments of grammar. We may use singular verbs with plural subjects: "There is three things I like." We may be troubled with a brash and impertinent "this": "While I was down town yesterday this man came up to me and . . . ." Or we use tenses carelessly: "Yesterday I come home. . . ."

If you can recognize any of these habits or similar ones in your own writing and speaking, you can eliminate them. Check your writing for crutch words, anemic adverbs, errors in syntax. If you can listen to a recording of one of your extemporaneous speeches, or better yet, transcribe it, you may spot similar faults in your speaking. But even without a recorder, you can train yourself to avoid all the stylistic flaws *which you can recognize*. In the process you should markedly improve the clarity of your ideas.

Using Pauses Productively

Many beginning speakers mistakenly feel that they must continually emit sound, meaningful or unmeaningful, or lose their audience. By habit, perhaps since childhood when they struggled for attention, such speakers vocalize their pauses in order to promise that something is coming. This is a most unproductive use of pauses. More can be promised by a brief period of poised silence. Indeed, thoughts and language do not naturally unfold in a rapid and continuous stream of sound, but rather in groupings, separated and paced by periods of silence. Recognize the necessity and value of that silence, and above all, do not fear it. A well-poised moment of silence is much less likely to drive an audience away than even the most mellifluous "uh." During that silence, learn to plan your next words without looking desperate.

For the most part, the use of productive pauses will have to be demonstrated in class activities under the guidance of your instructor. But we confidently predict that language will improve in direct ratio to the disappearance of verbal hash. The untrained speaker, for example, may first say, "This here — uh — building is — uh — awful important to — uh — our college." As he grows in skill, he may say, "This new building [pause] without doubt [pause] is critically needed by our college [pause] particularly for the physics department." Of course, developing this skill takes time. A fully poised speaker will learn to use fewer pauses, to place them well, and to vary their length. The effort to be wisely silent instead of meaninglessly noisy, coupled with the motivation of a tally keeper who notes all "uh's," will soon help you to a better style in your speeches.

Heightening Language Impact in Delivery

During speech, as you phrase each sentence anticipate the key words and give them added impact by your voice or by an appropriate gesture. You may discover that a good gesture not only stresses a word and an idea but increases your over-all physical responsiveness — which, in turn, often tends to sharpen your processes of thought. You may then come to think faster and be able to phrase the next idea more quickly and clearly. Moreover, if you are sensitive to your own meaning and intent, you will be able to highlight important words through changes in pitch, rate, and intensity. In short, you can prove to yourself that skillful delivery gives you time to think, and time to think will improve both the quality of your thinking and your style. As you grow in self-assurance, audiences will more readily accept your ideas as true.

Care about language, the use of productive pauses, and flexible delivery will do much to relieve whatever sense of desperation you may have in speaking. Unfortunately, however, desperation is not the only barrier to clear and colorful language. A major barrier, to speak bluntly of human foibles and weaknesses, is simple carelessness. For a solution to this problem we must turn to the lift-yourself-by-your-bootstraps theory. It can work. Many students have discovered that an honest oath of abstinence from weak language can work minor miracles in style.

Here, then, are three ways to improve your delivery and your language. First, learn to substitute silence for "uh"; second, discover that skilled delivery permits you to think, to select accurate language, and to be responsive to your own ideas; and third, convince yourself that what poise and freedom from desperation cannot cure, good intentions must.

An In-Class Exercise

The three suggestions given above can improve the energy and interest values of your spoken language regardless of your method of preparation. If your preparation includes writing, you can concentrate on avoiding weak words and faulty constructions. In impromptu and extemporaneous delivery (for definitions of these modes of speaking, see page 47), productive pauses and meaningful flexibility will strengthen your style. We now ask you to put these suggestions to work in a joint class project. We have chosen the format of impromptu speaking merely for purposes of illustration. The same approach may be used with extemporaneous speeches, or even speeches which have been partly or fully written out.

1. Your instructor will pick an adequate theme or themes for a series of impromptu speeches in class, such as: The spirit of a city I have visited; some other age in which I might have enjoyed living; the best book for a cold winter evening; the foods for a perfect meal.

2. Agree upon the lightweight words to be eliminated. Perhaps a good start would be *very, really, awful,* and *just.* Add others which have annoyed the class. And of course, put an absolute prohibition upon the ubiquitous *uh.*

3. Assess the group's finances and willingness to gamble both a bit of ˙cash and a bit of fun in the interest of improving impromptu style. Let each eliminated word cost its hapless user two cents. Discover how, by eliminating *uh's,* silence can truly be golden. Appoint a tally keeper and a treasurer.

4. Review briefly by discussion the elements of delivery skill, stressing their applicability to this impromptu project. Do not forget visual directness, physical poise and action, variety and emphasis in pitch, time, and intensity. But remember that a speaker can emphasize only the words he actually utters. Resolve, therefore, to make the best possible word choices, using pauses to think through the next phrase. Hunt for freshness and vitality.

5. Let the speeches begin. Your instructor, if he thinks it necessary, may interrupt to show how a sentence could be improved by rephrasing and more effective delivery. If so, repeat the idea, substituting strong for weak words, and give meaning and feeling to your language through your delivery.

Your effort to improve the vigor and literacy of your impromptu speaking can go much further than eliminating the weak words we asked you to work on in this exercise. Ask your classmates and your instructor to point out in your impromptu speaking those limping elements which you could eliminate simply by attention and firm purpose. The right mental set, coupled with disciplined delivery, can free your speaking from urgency and desperation. Good delivery will give you the confidence and the time to use good language. It can be done.

Some Devices of Style — Choice of Words

As we have said, style is not something applied to the surface of an idea. Rather, it comes from the inside. Form and content, style and idea, are inextricably interwoven. To improve style is to improve and clarify thought. Style should never be an end in itself, but it is so important to speech that it is well worth studying, and fortunately it is at least in part the product of skills which can be isolated and analyzed.

The style of most good writers and speakers is marked by the use of a good many literary devices. We shall discuss the few of these which we think most helpful to the beginning speaker. Some of them deal with economy — saying the most in the fewest words, not merely for brevity's sake, but for the sake of interest, to keep the speech moving. One device deals with figurative language, which can be vivid, exciting, and memorable. Some deal with the balance and counterbalance of ideas; some with the rhythmic movement of words and syllables; some with the creation of sound to match the sense. Powerful emotions can be invoked by cadence and euphony. All of these, and others we shall mention, are ways to make ideas clear, interesting, and believable.

Economy — Accurate and Specific Words

Those words are best which strike men with force and yet demand the least effort from them in return. This *principle of economy,* as Herbert Spencer called it, seeks short words, accurate words and specific words. If a short word must be cast out for the sake of accuracy, so be it; if one long but specific word will do the work of a whole phrase of short ones, use the long word, of course. But more often there is no clash. As Winston Churchill put it, "Short words are best, and old words, when short, are best of all."

The paragraph above contains one hundred words. Eighty-six of them are of one syllable, eight are two syllables, four are three, and two are four syllables. Of the words of more than one syllable, four are proper names, and six are technical words which could not

The common people do not accurately adapt their thoughts to objects; nor . . . do they accurately adapt their words to their thoughts; they do not mean to lie; but taking no pains to be exact, they give false accounts. A great part of their language is proverbial; if anything rocks at all, they say it rocks like a cradle; and in this way they go on.

— SAMUEL JOHNSON

be replaced. In rewriting the paragraph from our first draft, we discarded ten words of more than one syllable: *language, impact, listeners, expenditure, energy, demands, demanding, aside, interest, conflict.* None of these words is in any way unusual. Would you put them back?

It is clear that short words should not be ends in themselves. What we need is the *best* word. If, as is often the case, it is also the shortest, style benefits. Even so, it is more important to be specific. Seek words which are instantly intelligible, easy to remember — and which say exactly what you mean. Such words make it easy for your audience to understand you, and increase their interest in your ideas. The vague thinker may say "man" when he means "iceman," "building" when he means "town hall," or that he is "feeling blue" when he really means that Ethel refused him a date last night. When he says "officer," he may mean "police sergeant," "ensign in the navy," "tax collector," or "president of the senior class." Admittedly it takes effort to avoid the easy expression, "a real beautiful girl," and to say instead, "a petite, dark-eyed coed." But unless you do, your listener's imagination may transform the diminutive brunette you have in mind into a smouldering redhead. To each his own, of course, but when you speak, you are communicating an idea, not dreaming aloud.

It takes more thinking, more vigorous thinking, to find the exact and specific word or phrase than to snatch at the first ready-made and ill-fitting expression that comes to mind. The cliché, the ready-made phrase, is like the G.I. uniform, which fits a great many people passably well but very few people exactly. The accurate and specific phrase, like the tailor-made suit, costs more but fits better too.

In preparing for a speech, try to give each idea its sharpest and most accurate wording. In practicing, search for sensory words to express your idea. Can parts of your thought be vividly suggested through words of taste, sound, sight, or the feeling of motion? If so, do your best to imagine these sensations as you prepare and to find words for them. Try to respond emotionally to the ideas you wish to communicate, and it will be much easier to find the words which best carry the same feelings to your audience. Suppose you wish to describe a man's unsteady walk. By attempting to feel the event as you word the thought, you are more capable of coming up with "lurch," "stagger," or "reel" — all words you know, and all better than the colorless but easy "walked unsteadily." If you plan to tell how to prepare an outdoor meal, try to achieve some of the vividness in Mark Twain's description of "a mighty porter-house steak an inch and a half thick, hot and sputtering from the griddle; dusted with fragrant pepper; enriched with little melting bits of butter of the most unimpeachable freshness and genuineness; the precious juices of the meat trickling out and joining the gravy." Incidentally, try reading this description at a uniform rate, pitch, and intensity, and see whether you still respond to the words. Or reverse the image in your mind, picturing a thin, charred, tough, and tasteless piece of range beef, and see whether you can say Mark Twain's words with any conviction. Your attitude toward the images and feelings of your speech influences your choice of words. If you respond to the images and feel them as you speak, you will more surely find accurate and specific words which make your style economical and vivid.

What you gain in clarity, interest, and believability through specific language is partly a dividend of style. It is also the product of thinking, of molding your idea into the best form you can give it. You will remember how much color the details about the nature of insurance (Chapter 5, page 84) added to the basic idea. At that point we were discussing development, and we said that the details developed the idea. They also put it concretely, in accurate and specific words.

Consider another illustration of much the same thing. First read this sentence:

> In proportion as the manners, customs, and amusements of a nation are cruel and barbarous, the regulations of its penal code will be severe.

How quickly does the thought come through? Read it again, and see if the meaning is clearer than it was the first time. In a speech, of course, your listeners would not have a chance to "read it again."

Now read the sentence as Herbert Spencer wrote it in his *Philosophy of Style:*

> In proportion as men delight in battles, bullfights, and combat of gladiators, will they punish by hanging, burning, and the rack.

We believe there can be little doubt that in impact, interest, and clarity the second sentence is far better than the first.

To the extent that your language and ideas fall within the realm of experience and easy visualization by your auditors, you will be minimizing their effort needed to understand you. There, now, is a sentence of our own, which is far from meaningless, but might better have read: "Pick words or ideas your listeners have heard and can feel or picture, and it will be easy for them to know what you are talking about." Of course, language can be trite, too simple, or too pat to do your meaning justice. Broad and inclusive generalizations are often necessary in a speech because they are efficient, because they map out a territory or a philosophy to be explored. But as soon as you have used them for prediction or survey, begin to spell them out in detail, with language and examples which need no further development before an audience understands fully.

Figurative Language

One way to help this understanding is to use figurative language. Once past the infant stage, the human mind learns by comparing the new to what it already knows, and figurative language is a way of expressing one thing, often not well known, in terms of another, generally more familiar. How often have you heard someone say, with a pleased sense of discovery, "Why that's just like —"? We all like comparisons and have been brought up by them as well as

---

ON BOMBAST

Those of uncultivated minds . . . admire the profundity of one who is mystical and . . . obscure; mistaking the muddiness of the water for depth; and magnifying in their imaginations what is viewed through a fog; and they conclude that brilliant language must represent some brilliant ideas, without troubling themselves to inquire what those ideas are.

— RICHARD WHATELEY

on them, and comparison is the essence of figurative language. The fresher, the more imaginative the comparison, the more it is likely to stick in the minds of your listeners. Winston Churchill's famous "blood, toil, tears, and sweat" so brilliantly described the task of the British in wartime that it has become a part of our permanent vocabulary. His powerfully simple metaphor of the "iron curtain" has become a standard description of today's divided world — and has even been imitated in the good but less original and striking "bamboo curtain."

But the popularity of these phrases suggests what always happens to the most striking phrases, sooner or later. They are used until they lose their edge; people forget their figurative origin and use them without thinking what they once conveyed. It is probable that many people have already lost the original impact of the "iron curtain," and use the phrase almost as if it were a literal expression, like "diplomatic tension." The language is full of such crystallized metaphors — indeed many of our dullest clichés are phrases of this kind which must once have carried strong impact: "fresh as a daisy," "bright as a button" (a relic of the days when people wore bright metal buttons), and a host of others. It is hard to imagine a language without embedded metaphors which have lost their figurative significance. But the speech which is a tissue of them has something of the quality of a rubber stamp: no one would mistake it for genuine handwriting.

Yet many powerful metaphors are borrowed. The Bible, in particular, is a rich source of such figures of speech. Recognizing this, Lincoln highlighted the slavery controversy which was destroying the Union by borrowing a Biblical figure: " 'A house divided against itself cannot stand.' I believe that this government cannot endure permanently half slave and half free." But do not borrow worn-out figures that every one else has used — "straight as an arrow," "dead as a doornail," "pitch black," "sky blue," "crystal clear," or "sharp as a tack." Work and think to create your own. As you try them out on paper, see if some refreshing and surprising yet fitting marriage of ideas can be found. Your own good judgment, we trust, will tell you whether you have reached too far, mixed your metaphors, or made a marriage between concepts which might better have retained the innocence of singleness. Of course, you will never know unless you try, and if you never try, you may be dull. So, search out the possible value of figurative language.

Directness and Informality

Figurative language need not, of course, be literary language. Abraham Lincoln was a master of creating vivid images out of the ordinary stuff of the experience of his audiences. During the debates with Douglas, for example, he charged that the Judge had so twisted his arguments as to make it appear that a horse chestnut was a chestnut horse. His speeches were sprinkled with lively figures as diverse as corncobs and house-building. They were both entertaining and persuasive because they grew out of Lincoln's perception of audience experience and attitudes.

No matter what "devices" you may use to improve your style, never forget that you are preparing for next Friday morning's audience — three engineers, a geography major, five prospective high school teachers of English and two of history, a football star, a Phi Beta Kappa, a foreign student from India, five pre-law students, "Sleepy Joe," a redhead, and one instructor. Envision your listeners, and fix in mind, or write, references to the occasion, the place, and the people which can later be spoken as natural responses of the moment. Remember, of course, that a skillful speaker will discard or modify anything he has prepared whenever the occasion offers something better.

Direct speech comes from you as a person and goes straight to the people in your audience. If written, a speech should never sound like an essay on its hind legs. Take care that what you present has the ease and directness of talk. Since speech is generally more informal than written composition, work particularly for the suggestion of a poised informality, drawn from the use of contractions, shorter sentences, personal pronouns, occasional colloquialisms, repetition and restatement, direct and rhetorical questions, and the avoidance of both the formal rhythms and formal wording of the less personal kinds of writing.

A speech should be salted with "I," "we," "you," "I wish it were so," "Listen to this." It should be peppered with contractions: "isn't," "can't," "we'll," "I'm." It should be seasoned with personal and informal phrases: "You and I know," more likely than "It is universally believed"; "Now this is where I stand," rather than "A survey of the evidence has convinced the speaker." Do not say to an audience, "May I proceed, with your indulgence, to offer my opinion that smoking has deleterious effects upon a person's health." Say, rather, "Smoking is bad for you." Language which is too formal

*This old print lampoons the
racy, pyrotechnic speaking style
of Davy Crockett, frontiersman
and three times member
of Congress: "Pierce the heart
of the enemy as you would
a feller that spit in your face,
knocked down your wife,
burnt up your houses, and
called your dog a skunk! . . .
whar is the craven, low-lived,
chicken-bred, toad-hoppin'
red-mounted bristle-headed
mother's son of ye who will
not . . . smouse the citadel of
the aggressor, and squeeze
ahead for Liberty and Glory."
The style, in this case,
was very much the man.*

or pretentious is not usually economical. Moreover, it sounds remote, and audiences tend to sense the lack of personal contact.

Spice your speech with colloquialisms like the expressions cited above — phrases and expressions natural to the language of speech where this is different from the language of writing. But stay as clear in speech as you would in writing of the lazy thinker's clichés and of cheap or tasteless slang. Strive for the direct, natural, and regionally acceptable speech of educated people who are neither stuffed shirts nor show-offs. And be sure that what you write out ahead of time will speak well. Write by ear, for the use of the mouth, and for your particular audience. Test what you write by saying it aloud.

Some Devices of Style — Arrangement of Words

We noted earlier that stylistic devices are in part designed to improve word choice, in part to enhance meaning through skillful sentence and paragraph structure and awareness of the sound values of speech. By now it is apparent that the two are interdependent. Yet there are some aspects of style which are primarily concerned with the arrangement of words.

Internal Summaries and Transitions

Whenever you make an outline or select a bit of supporting material, you take the first step in the arrangement of words. For sentences and paragraphs can only convey intelligent ideas if the materials they describe are sensibly chosen and arranged. Since speakers cannot depend upon audiences to grasp the logic of arrangement without help, the connections between ideas must be clearly stated. In part this is achieved by making certain that each sentence within a paragraph grows out of and interconnects with the one which precedes it. Beyond the paragraph, this element of *coherence* depends upon effective use of internal summaries and transitions.

Summaries and transitions are both the glue and the sign posts of speech construction. Use them, and word them clearly. Observe other speakers. You will find that the inexperienced speaker often omits them; the less inexperienced speaker will use a few simple and often trite ones, such as "and then," or an oft-repeated "and finally." In a clear and unified speech, phrases such as the following are likely to appear:

> So much, then, from the point of view of . . . . Looking at it next from this side, we . . .
>
> On the other hand, . . .
>
> Moreover . . .
>
> Beyond this . . .
>
> In addition, there are those who . . .
>
> In short, we are forced to accept the idea that . . .
>
> And, to move ahead, . . .
>
> If, however, we re-examine the position . . .

Your summaries and transitions should grow out of your subject and your thinking. There is nothing sacred about the ones listed above, and the variety is infinite. Whenever you end one point or start a new one, be sure your audience knows it. In your preparation for extemporaneous speeches, practice inserting the necessary bits of rhetorical road information. Write out and if need be memorize even longer and more detailed transitions for the major shifts in content in longer speeches.

In delivery, indicate transitions by pauses, changes of rate, and variations in pitch. If your ideas make sense and are well-organized, good transitions and effective delivery will make them clear to your listeners.

Varied Sentence Structure

The words you choose and the images they carry can free and strengthen your ideas. Since speech is pronounced and heard, the sound of what you say also conveys moods and emotions and subtly affects the attitude of your listeners. Monotonous sentences, all of the same kind and length, can quickly put an audience to sleep. Intermix statements with questions, long sentences with short, complex with simple. Even fragments. Invert the word order now and then as Woodrow Wilson did in his first inaugural address, "With riches has come inexcusable waste," or in a more elevated mood, "Here muster, not the forces of party, but the forces of humanity." Never let your sentences be alike for too long at a time, neither an interminable series of staccato sentences nor an endless procession of literary elephants. Variety, like informality, is the spice of speech. It rests an audience and helps them keep their attention on what you have to say.

As we have noted, variety may be achieved by many methods. Certain types of sentence structure have the additional merit of sharpening the meaning of the ideas with which you deal. You will profit by learning to use rhetorical questions, direct questions, parallel structure, and antithesis.

RHETORICAL QUESTIONS. A rhetorical question is one which does not call for a voiced reply but brings a clear and predictable response if the audience is at all inclined toward your belief. A classic illustration is this passage from Patrick Henry's plea for liberty:

> They tell us, sir, that we are weak, unable to cope with so formidable an adversary. But when shall we be stronger? Will it be the next week, or the next year? Will it be when we are totally disarmed, and when a British guard shall be stationed in every house? Shall we gather strength by irresolution and inaction? Shall we acquire the means of effectual resistance by lying supinely on our backs and hugging the delusive phantom of hope until our enemies shall have bound us hand and foot?

Imagine the sledgehammer impact these sentences would have had upon you if you had been in Henry's audience. Unless you had been vehemently opposed to his ideas, each rhetorical question would have dragged a strong "NO!" from your mind, or even a loud one from your lungs. But the rhetorical question is clearly a "device," and while modern speakers use it, many use it sparingly.

DIRECT QUESTIONS. Once in a while you will also want to use a direct or "opening" question. What are such questions? How do they operate? What value do they have to an audience? When can questions suitably be used as summary or transitional devices, such as, "What, then, are the dangers of this proposal?" As distinguished from rhetorical questions, these direct questions have no immediate or clear answer, but require the development of an answer by the speaker. But they do make the audience participate in the speaker's thinking as he develops his idea. Should we ask, however, whether a speaker can use too many questions? Would you like to read this chapter if all the way through it had as many questions in it as this paragraph?

PARALLEL STRUCTURE AND ANTITHESIS. If ideas have a parallel relationship or are natural opposites, meaning is enhanced by phrasing them so that the interrelationship is clear. Note how Robert G. Ingersoll in the conclusion of his speech, "The Liberty of Man, Woman, and Child," used these twin concepts of parallelism and antithesis to strengthen his idea:

> There has never been upon the earth a generation of free men and women. It is not yet time to write a creed. Wait until the chains are broken — until dungeons are not regarded as temples. Wait until solemnity is not mistaken for wisdom — until mental cowardice ceases to be known as reverence. Wait until the living are considered the equals of the dead — until the cradle takes precedence of the coffin. Wait until what we know can be spoken without regard to what others may believe. Wait until teachers take the place of preachers — until followers become investigators. Wait until the world is free before you write a creed.
>
> In this creed there will be but one word — Liberty.

Experiment with this passage. Take out all the words which show parallelism of ideas or opposition of ideas. Note how much you have weakened the thought.

Or note how a Negro student analyzed the problem of discrimination in the North:

> I appreciate the honesty and forthrightness with which the Southern segregationists uphold their stand. Their barriers are visible. Perhaps you have seen them. After spending the first eighteen years of my

life in the South, I remember them all too well. On restrooms in bold black letters on white backgrounds, the signs read, "White" and "Colored." To the Negro, and perhaps to the whites as well, this discrimination is degrading. But nonetheless, the Southern segregationist preaches segregation and he practices segregation. His Northern counterpart preaches integration and equality, but all too often he practices segregation and inequality. The barriers of the South are visible and are loudly proclaimed; the barriers of the North are invisible and are talked about in whispers behind closed doors.

Parallelism, then, can be developed by using the same words to introduce phrases, clauses, or sentences expanding or elaborating an idea ("Wait until . . . until . . . ," in the Ingersoll passage quoted above), by intentional repeating of sentence patterns — a series of questions or a pair of declarative sentences bridging a semicolon, for example ("The barriers of the South . . . ; the barriers of the North . . ."), or by placing the same grammatical unit at the same point in a series of phrases or sentences ('With malice toward none; with charity for all; with firmness . . .'). Both parallelism and antithesis have the added advantage of marked rhythm which can be exploited in delivery to create a climactic effect.

Rhythm and Sound

The sound pattern of your words reflects your mood and makes your audience share it, whether they realize it or not. Notice how different is the sound — and mood — of these two passages from Abraham Lincoln's speeches:

> I don't want to have a fight with Judge Douglas, and I have no way of making an argument up into the consistency of a corn-cob and stopping his mouth with it.

> With malice toward none; with charity for all; with firmness in the right, as God gives us to see the right, — let us strive on to finish the work we are in: to bind up the nation's wounds; to care for him who shall have borne the battle, and for his widow and orphan; to do all which may achieve and cherish a just and lasting peace among ourselves, and with all nations.

Read these two passages aloud, or listen with the inner ear, and you will almost certainly hear two different tones. The sounds of the first are short and crisp. They suggest energy, intentness on an immediate practical purpose, and combined with the homely image of the corncob, a kind of earthy humor. Note how differently the second passage affects you. The sounds roll smoothly on, blend and combine, and help to arouse a mood of compassion, noble thought, and lofty feeling.

Within the same speech Winston Churchill often moved from a matter-of-fact passage like this:

So far the war in the west has fallen almost solely upon the Royal Navy, and upon those parts of the Royal Air Force who give the Navy invaluable help. But I think you will agree that up to date the Navy has not failed the nation.

to this more varied style:

We do not shrink from fair criticism, and that is the most dangerous of all. On the contrary, we take it earnestly to heart and seek to profit by it. Criticism in the body politic is like pain in the human body. It is not pleasant, but where would the body be without it? No health or sensibility would be possible without continued correctives and warnings of pain.

ending after additional style changes with this stirring peroration:

Come then: let us to the task, to the battle, to the toil — each to our part, each to our station. Fill the armies, rule the air, pour out the munitions, strangle the U-boats, sweep the mines, plow the land, build the ships, guard the streets, succor the wounded, uplift the downcast, and honor the brave. Let us go forward together in all parts of the Island. There is not a week, nor a day, nor an hour to lose.[1]

Notice how the urgency of the idea is reflected in the change of the rhythmic patterns as Churchill moves from his purpose to inform to his purpose to inspire. The insistent forward surge of the final passage is inescapable. The moods called up by the sounds in this speech are different from those evoked by Lincoln. But in both cases, sound is unmistakably part of the effect.

It is not, of course, the whole effect. The clipped or the lingering

[1] From *Blood, Sweat and Tears* by Winston S. Churchill. Copyright 1941 by Winston S. Churchill. Reprinted by permission of G. P. Putnam's Sons.

sound must go with appropriate ideas, words, and images, and with appropriate rhythm. Good speech brings all these things to bear at once to create a single clear impression. Contrast, for instance, the conversational rhythm in Lincoln's comment on Douglas with the measured pace of the second passage. In the latter, notice the balanced parallel phrases, beginning: "With . . . with . . . with . . . ; let us strive on to finish . . . to bind . . . to care . . . to do all . . . ." Rhythm may suggest solemnity by a regular metric beat, as it did in Ingersoll's speech at his brother's grave: "Life is a narrow vale between the cold and barren peaks of two eternities." Broken rhythms suggest unsureness; staccato rhythms, emotional intensity; smooth and flowing rhythms, confidence. Gradual lengthening of phrases in a series, with parallel grammatical structure like Lincoln's, suggests increasing importance of ideas. In long passages, rhythm adds to the effect of repetition and restatement. When your idea is clear and you are well prepared, your rhythm tends to spring naturally from your idea and your mood, and the right rhythm often suggests itself.

Cumulation and Climax

Often the impact of an idea can be heightened by piling up increasingly important concepts leading to a climax in the last of the series. Note the cumulative building in this excerpt from Montesquieu's essay on *Personal Morality:*

> If I knew something beneficial to myself but harmful to my family, I would drive it out of my mind. If I knew something advantageous to my family, but injurious to my community, I would try to forget it. If I knew something profitable to my country but detrimental to the human race, I would consider it a crime.

Incidentally, do you also observe how the parallel structure of these sentences contributes to the rhythm of the passage?

Invective and Irony

At times you may feel so deeply about an injustice that only the strongest language will express your beliefs. There is danger in such language, for you may become so lacking in objectivity as to substitute invective for evidence and anger for fact. Invective is harsh denunciation, with charged and sometimes abusive language its principal vehicle. It is a direct, frontal attack on a person or an idea. Nevertheless, properly supported, invective can have a place in effective speaking. Notice how George William Curtis used it to attack party spirit. The date is 1877, but the ideas he expressed are timeless. Would less vigorous language have served his purpose as well?

> Perfect party discipline is the most dangerous weapon of party spirit, for it is the abdication of the individual judgment. . . . It is for you to help break this withering spell. . . . There is not an American merchant who would send a ship to sea under the command of Captain Kidd, however skillful a sailor he might be. Why should he vote to send Captain Kidd to the legislature or to put him in command of the ship of state because his party directs? The party which today nominates Captain Kidd will tomorrow nominate Judas Iscariot, and tomorrow, as today, party spirit will spurn you as a traitor for refusing to sell your master.

Other occasions may call for more subtle use of language. Perhaps the most cutting of all weapons of attack is irony, a mode of speech in which what is stated is not what is intended, with the result that the literal meaning contradicts the implied one. It has been the favorite rhetorical tool of British parliamentarians from Chatham to Churchill. Though American speakers use it less skillfully, in the hands of men like Lincoln, Ingersoll, Franklin Roosevelt, and Adlai Stevenson it has been a powerful instrument. Henry George used irony to expose the fallacy of the popular economic theory of his day:

> What is the current explanation of the hard times? Over-production! There are so many clothes that men must go ragged; so much coal that in the bitter winters people have to shiver; such over-filled granaries that people actually die by starvation! Want due to over-production! Was a greater absurdity ever uttered? How can there be over-production till all have enough?

Sometimes irony and invective merge so that one can hardly determine which is being used. Wendell Phillips both angered and stimulated the Phi Beta Kappa Society at Harvard with his ironical jibes at formal education.

> What would college-graduate Seward weigh, in any scale, against Lincoln bred in affairs?

Hence, I do not think the greatest things have been done for the world by its book-men. Education is not the chips of arithmetic and grammar, — nouns, verbs, and the multiplication table; neither is it that last year's almanac of dates, or series of lies agreed upon, which we often mistake for history. Education is not Greek and Latin and the air-pump. . . . Though what we actually carry away is little enough, we do get some training of our powers, as the gymnast or the fencer does of his muscles.

Invective is a bludgeon, irony a rapier. It requires experience and skill to use irony well; yet you will never use it at all unless you are willing to try. Only remember that its primary purpose is not to be funny, but to point up and expose the irrelevant, the illogical, and the unintelligent.

Putting This Chapter to Work

At this point, you may be saying to yourself, "All these skills of style seem useful, but how do I go about fitting them into speeches?" It is a valid question and deserves a careful answer. In the exercise on pages 199–201, we suggested ways of getting rid of gross imperfections in style. We think it likely that as you worked on these problems you also improved unconsciously in other language skills. To carry the process a step further, let us see how writing and extemporaneous practice can help you toward a better style.

Writing to Improve Style

Language skills can often be improved through writing. It may be enough to write out carefully your introductions, conclusions, and transitions. Or it may be wise to write out, revise, and rewrite an entire speech. Francis Bacon once observed that "Reading maketh a full man, conference a ready man, and writing an exact man." The values of exactness are obvious, but careful writing may give your style greater strength and color as well. So long as you write for the ears of your listeners, intent on communicating ideas rather than exhibiting skill, you are not likely to gild your ideas with overblown language.

When you write in preparation for a speech, take whatever idea you have in mind and begin to give it form through the language which comes to mind as you attempt to speak it aloud. Record these words and phrases on paper, filling in until you have complete sentences. Build the sentences into paragraphs, linking each sentence to what precedes it in a continuous development of the idea. Then revise and rework what you have written, eliminating defects, and seeking the values of specific words, figurative language, rhythm, and cumulation. In all this, you will often feel that a word or a phrase fails to carry your exact meaning, or that it is lifeless. This is the practical value of writing. Strike out the dull phrase. Can you get along with nothing in its place? If so, good. If not, begin thinking aloud. If the word you know must exist does not come to mind, begin a more practical search for it. Get a dictionary or a thesaurus and hunt it down. Having captured the word, write it in and read the passage aloud. If it now seems to say what you want, with clarity, energy, and ease, lay it aside to mellow a bit and move ahead.

By feeling out your ideas, recording on paper, and testing the results, you can improve your style immensely. Your first few drafts will be far from neat, or efficient; but this is not your purpose at the moment. Your purpose is to work up a head of creative steam, and then to distill that steam into the essence of good style. For example, on the opposite page is the working copy of the first page of a speech by Adlai E. Stevenson. The full text is given in Appendix E, pages 309–340. If you compare the two you will see how many times Stevenson changed his mind and hunted for something which suited his purpose better. Proficiency in language is frequently developed by writing, testing, striking out, and rewriting.

Whether you write a paragraph or an entire speech, use the same procedure. Could you have helped your audience better understand and enjoy the speech you gave last week if you had found a hundred dull, trite, or exhibitionistic words to throw away before you spoke? Could you have found other words which, even if they did not go ringing down the corridors of time, might at least have stamped you as a skilled, creative person worth listening to because you were interesting, understandable, and believable?

Be alert to the danger that your style may burden or gild ideas. Recall from Chapter 7 that an effort to acquire skill in delivery sometimes misfires temporarily, and that skill can be used egotistically. For the alert student of speech, this is a passing danger. So, too, with style. If you are human, you will occasionally become so enamored of your own amazing virtuosity that you cannot bear to restrain it. If you must, live dangerously — and hope that your instructor and your classmates are skilled in anesthesia when they use the scalpel.

Adlai E. Stevenson
Hollywood
Oct 9, 1947

I am deeply moved by this vast gathering and the warmth of your greeting to the Democratic candidates and myself. I am grateful for your presence and for this reaffirmation of your faith in a great political party that has long endured because it has tried to serve the ~~interests~~ general welfare ~~rather than the limited welfare~~ interests of all the people rather than the special interests of some the people. ~~Wedded to that principle the Democratic party has~~ ~~and will prosper.~~ succeeded, ~~and~~ and whenever it has departed ~~divorced from that principle it has failed, and properly so.~~

That you are here in such numbers — and at a price — confirms my faith as affirmation of that idea so much as respect for ~~not our~~ these candidates and curiosity about this visitor from Illinois

I wish the world could see this meeting so it would know this democracy for what it really is — not a sordid televised struggle between the ~~officers~~ of government — not just a greedy economic giant ~~crouching~~ behind tariff walls — not just a pavaplied warrior savagely fingering his weapons — but as this — as a ~~people~~ ~~whose~~ in thousands ~~who gather together in thousands~~ to give a ~~people's~~ goal its essential vitality. Someday the world will ~~all~~ see It does not now — the vision of the real America — the vision that becomes real in a meeting such as this. And when

217

If you do undergo critical surgery, do not be discouraged. No one can learn without trial, re-trial, occasional error, and more trial. Indeed, some errors teach the most valuable lessons of all. They may never be learned unless you prepare and plan — and dare — before you speak.

Exercises

1. Test your ability to revise by strengthening the wording of the following passages. If a passage is clear but unstimulating, enliven it. If it is vague, make it specific. If it is crude, polish it. If it is gilded, remove unnecessary and meaningless ornament, or substitute vital figures for empty ones. If additional details are needed for any of these purposes, add them.

    a. A real good education had ought to include some practical experience and Jim Wallace is a pretty good case to show this because he has some brains and he went· to college like you and me are doing, but when he got out he went down to this here factory somewhere over on the other side of town and the man that hired him told him he would have to work six months as a trainee before he could have a regular job, you see what I mean.

    b. This is a very important election. I am here today because I want you to vote for a good candidate. He has a good platform. He stands right on all the important issues, such as school bonds, highway improvement, and parks. Vote for my candidate for a better community.

    c. Learning to speak well is a task of prodigious, monumental, and Gargantuan proportions. Truly it is a challenge worthy of the efforts of the heroes of antiquity. When I envision the peaks before me I tremble. I pause in trepidation at the base of Mt. Choice of Subject; I hesitate to test the heights of Organization Bluff; I quail at the prospect of climbing the twin summits of Style and Delivery. Who will help me in my hour of travail?

2. Pick a section of one of your earlier class speeches which you now believe was inadequate in style. Write 200 to 300 words developing the idea. Revise and polish until you are convinced that your choice and arrangement of words will lead to the best oral style of which you are capable.

    a. Does it have an adequate opening and clear transitions and summaries?

b. Is the language specific, accurate, and directed to the class audience?

c. Is the language vivid and colorful?

d. Do you have an interesting and varied rhythm suited to the material?

e. Have you used questions where they are appropriate?

Extemporaneous Practice to Improve Style

Writing a speech has several values, yet you would be a handicapped speaker if you went through life unable to open your mouth unless you had prepared your script. You need, therefore, to practice improving your extemporaneous as well as your written style. The theory of extemporaneous practice is that whatever you found best in preparation will come to mind automatically in the speech situation. In private, then, or with a friend who is helping you test your ideas, begin verbalizing your outline. Be on guard for errors and weak phrasing which may be eliminated in advance. Search for clear, colorful, and accurate words. They will come — if you have good ideas and have studied style. As you talk through the ideas to yourself a second time, it is probable that the better phrasings of the previous practice will come to mind. The best will stay in mind for the actual presentation of the speech. There should, of course, be no laborious effort to memorize sentences exactly; your style will improve if your purpose in practice and in actual delivery is to communicate an idea as effectively as you can.

Your style will be better if your practice is lively. Use action. Try to feel and respond to the images you are creating. Use words that arouse sense perceptions; be personal and direct in language; and be colorful and specific. Remember, the overall purpose of speech is communication. It is your job to find the ideas and the words which win attention, gain understanding, and are acceptable or believable to your audience.

THE ORATOR AND THE CRITIC

It is a thing of no great difficulty to raise objections against another man's oration, — nay, it is a very easy matter; but to produce a better in its place is a work extremely troublesome.

— PLUTARCH

Exercises

1. Narratives and anecdotes are fine vehicles for studying and improving extemporaneous delivery and style. Here is a project for your class. Let your instructor or a student tell a three- to five-minute story or anecdote, having plot, characters, suspense, and possibly a punch line. But let the telling be restrained, seeking only to establish the story and the characters. Now, send two or three students out of the room and give each one ten or fifteen minutes to make the story his own, using his own language, delivery, and action. The student who works to recreate and develop the story in his own way is truly engaged in extemporaneous preparation. He cannot have memorized the wording of the story as he heard it, yet he knows the structure of the idea and does not have to compose it as he would for an impromptu speech.

   To the extent that these speakers work earnestly and skillfully at extemporaneous preparation and style, they will bring the story back to the classroom and make it colorful, dynamic, and interesting. This exercise can be a perfect indication of how proper extemporaneous preparation can add vitality to style.

   a. If your instructor or a classmate does not have an anecdote ready for the project, here is one you may work on. Read it only *once,* then get on your feet and practice telling it aloud, with more verve and punch than this abbreviated version has.

   You've probably heard of a lot of tricks to get people out of their homes in order to make the work of a burglar easier, but have you ever heard this one? A lady received anonymously by mail two theatre tickets to a very popular show. But on the night of the performance her husband was called away on a business trip, and she gave the tickets away and stayed at home. During the evening she did some ironing. At one point she looked up to see a hand opening the kitchen door. Not knowing what else to do she reached out with the hot iron. There was the smell of singed skin, and the hand was at once withdrawn. Thoroughly shaken, and not wanting to spend the rest of the evening alone, she went (as soon as she could think what to do) to the house next door and asked her neighbor if she would come over for a while — but she did not say why. To

which the neighbor replied that she was terribly sorry she couldn't
— her husband had just burned his hand.

In your retelling, decide where you can use specific and vivid
language. To create suspense before the opening of the door? To
recreate the smell of singed skin? Can you use comparison to explain
the wife's feelings? Would questions make useful transitions anywhere in the story?

> b. Here is another condensed story, fairly well known in
> American folklore. Give it *your* delivery and *your* style.

Not long ago I was in Chicago (or any other city). There on
Sheridan Road I saw a man attempting to push a horse up the
steps of the front porch of a house. Following the impulse of
curiosity, and wishing to be helpful, I volunteered my services. He
accepted, and with much joint pushing and tugging, we got the
animal into the house. I started to leave, but the man asked me
to help him take the horse upstairs to the second floor bathroom.
There, to my surprise, the man pulled out a razor, slit the animal's
throat, and shoved him into the bathtub.

I gave some thought to a hurried departure, but in calming tones
the man told me his purpose. It seems that his wife's brother also
lived in the same house, and he was one of these "know-it-all"
characters who was never surprised by anything. Tell him that
the stock market dropped today, and he would say, "Yes, I know it,
and I could have told you last week that it would happen today."
"Why," reported my new acquaintance, "he even predicted Truman's
surprise victory in '48. But tonight, he's going to come home, go
upstairs, and soon come rushing down, screaming, 'Hey, Joe, there's
a dead horse in the bathtub.' And me, I'm going to be sitting there
on the sofa reading the evening paper. I'll nonchalantly flick the
ashes off my cigar and say, 'Yes, I know.' "

Are there any places in the story especially suited to colorful
language? Can you make the man and his horse seem more real by
detailed and specific description? How can you combine gesture and
facial expression with good word choice? Can questions vary movement and rhythm? Can some of your sentences be phrased in parallel
structure?

> c. Here are some other abbreviated anecdotes. In this form
> they are far too short to prepare your listeners for the pay-
> off line. Supply details explaining what happened before

the moment of the anecdote. Build interest by suspense through word choice and sentence rhythms. Let lively delivery aid your extemporaneous style.

1. Man to friend during robbery of transcontinental train, just before bandits arrive at their seats: "Here's the ten dollars I owe you."

2. When John Nance Garner was Vice-President, a constituent at a baseball game introduced his son to Garner, who gave the boy a ten-dollar bill. When the boy said he thought he'd frame it, Garner replied, "Then let me give you a check."

3. Explorer visiting a circus is trampled to death by elephant thirty years after saving life of young elephant in jungle. Reason: "Different elephant."

4. In a London drawing room in the late '90's, James McNeil Whistler got off a cutting remark about a figure of fashion, and Oscar Wilde complimented him: "I wish I had said that." Whereupon Whistler replied, "You will, Oscar, you will."

5. A gushing lady once came up to George Bernard Shaw at a party and said, "Oh, Mr. Shaw, I was out walking today and passed by your house." Shaw: "Thank you, ma'am."

2. Here is an exercise which combines the advantages of writing and extemporaneous practice. Prepare an extemporaneous speech of two or three minutes explaining a vivid sensory experience — something you have seen, tasted, smelled, heard, touched, or any combination of these. The mood may be exciting, calming, satisfying. Record the speech and transcribe it. Revise the transcribed version until you are sure the style is the best of which you are capable. Then, without using the script or any notes, record the speech again. How does it compare with your first recording and the revision?

Criticizing Style

The main aim of this book has been to explain and develop certain principles which will improve your extemporaneous speaking. You have, therefore, taken a series of important steps, all looking toward the moment when you stand before an audience and seek to make your ideas clear, interesting, and believable. You have examined your own ideas and searched for new ones in order to have something vital to say to a particular audience. You have worked to communicate those ideas by examples, statistics, testimony, and analogies. You have given your speech a pattern which makes your ideas easier to grasp and remember. You have worked for a flexible and natural delivery which frees and strengthens ideas. So you are ready to stand before an audience and speak extemporaneously — without a manuscript and without having written out and memorized what you will say. If you have done these things well, you will have the poise and the time to find the right language as you speak.

We have urged you to use the sections on criticism both to analyze the speeches of others and to check on your own. At this point we suggest a complete review of all previous questions on criticism. Has the speaker (or have you) learned to select good subjects, to choose suitable materials for developing ideas, to organize, and to deliver speeches? In addition, has he (have you) now begun to improve his style in these respects:

1. Did he avoid imprisoning ideas? Has he learned to substitute silence for "uh's" and to discipline himself against lightweight words and verbal hash? Did skillful delivery give him time to think, to plan his phrases and choose the best language he could?

2. How good was his language? Did he use words economically or wastefully? Was his choice of words accurate and appropriate to his ideas? Were his figures of speech vivid? inept or bizarre? Had he practiced his speech enough so that he could select at the moment of utterance words which were personal, direct, and specific?

3. Did the speaker show careful preparation of introductions, conclusions, summaries, and transitions? Did he use questions? cumulations? effective rhythm? Did he use these techniques without gilding his ideas?

4. Would the speaker have profited by writing out all or parts of his speech?

5. If the speech was delivered from manuscript or was memorized, was it direct and conversational?

6. In short, did the language used free and strengthen ideas? Did it help to make them communicable — clear, interesting, and believable?

PART THREE·

TYPES OF
SPEECH COMMUNICATION

9 PUBLIC SPEAKING

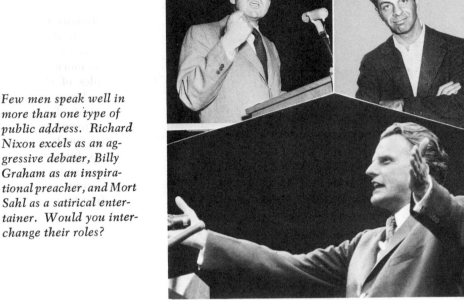

Few men speak well in more than one type of public address. Richard Nixon excels as an aggressive debater, Billy Graham as an inspirational preacher, and Mort Sahl as a satirical entertainer. Would you interchange their roles?

MANY WRITERS have tried to divide public speaking into special types according to the primary end sought by the speaker. It is true, of course, that some speeches seek primarily to inform their listeners, some to entertain, and some to persuade. It is equally true that almost every speech serves each of these ends in turn. But even though our primary purpose is to inform, the materials of a speech must still be interesting and credible; when we seek to persuade, we cannot sacrifice clarity and interest; and in a speech to entertain, laughter often comes because our hearers see clearly the incongruity of what is being said with what is actually believable.

It is evident, then, that dividing speeches into types according to "ends" is merely a convenient way of talking about primary emphasis. There would be little value in attempting to make an exhaustive classification of speeches in terms of these ends. Yet it may be useful to note a few examples of speaking situations in which the primary purpose is to inform, to persuade, or to entertain.

The Speech to Inform

If the purpose of a speech is to inform, it is obvious that the measure of its effectiveness is how much the audience is able to remember and understand. Its first goal, therefore, is clearness in structure and supporting material which will aid the memories of the listeners. Since we have already dealt with principles of clearness in organization and content, we suggest that you reread pages 85–91 and 144–153. Give particular attention to the selection of supporting materials and the development of a pattern of organization which will make it easy for your listeners to remember what you have said.

Many of the earlier assignments have dealt exclusively with speeches to inform. In Chapter 2, for example, we suggested informative speeches about places, people, objects, and processes. There are many others, of course, but here are a few typical situations in which speeches to inform might be given.

The Report

As a member of a garden club you might be called upon by your fellow members to study and report on the qualities of a new rose which has just been developed. Your primary source of information would be an interview with the nurseryman who developed the rose, supplemented by any printed material which was available. But you could not make your report without also studying the needs and desires of your fellow club members. You would need to evaluate the claims of the nurseryman in terms of what your audience wanted in a newly-developed rose: color, fragrance, lasting qualities when cut, resistance to disease. How much of one of these qualities would your listeners sacrifice in order to improve another?

It is evident, then, that a report must have a focus and not be merely a miscellaneous collection of more or less relevant material. The significant ideas must be organized within a framework determined both by research on the subject and by audience analysis. The more significant the material reported, the more necessary is the function of the speaker in organizing and focusing the speech. But whether the report be about a rose or a missile, the speaker must find the proper framework or lose the interest of his audience.

The Review

Even more than in the report, the reviewer must exercise an evaluative function. In a sense, a review is a persuasive speech rather than an informative one, since the reviewer often seeks to influence his audience to read or not to read a book, to attend or not to attend a play or musical performance. The line between persuading and informing is at best a narrow and arbitrary one. If the reviewer seeks to change the values operating in his audience, he will undoubtedly be a persuader. If the major values are the same for both speakers and listeners, the speaker's role will be primarily to inform.

But whether you seek to inform or to persuade, your role as a reviewer is always evaluative. Your focus is the intellectual, social, or emotional goal which you consider basic to the work being reviewed. This book will amuse you in odd moments, or divert your attention from a troubled world. This play will stimulate you to think about a profound social problem regardless of whether or not you agree with its philosophy. Win or lose, this basketball team is exciting to watch in action. If you do not have a focus, a set of values to be applied, your review is likely to bear an unfortunate resemblance to the annual report of the club treasurer.

The Lecture

A college classroom is a suitable place to observe both the best and the worst qualities of a lecture. If the primary faults of a lecturer are centered in dull and uninspired delivery, the lecture can be improved in the same way that delivery can be improved in any speech. But many problems in lectures are problems of inadequate analysis of ideas and inadequate attention to the structure of the lecture itself. Some lectures, in and out of college classrooms, are merely uninspired repetitions of materials available to the listeners from more interesting sources. In other lectures, new ideas may be presented, but in such disorganized form that listeners cannot grasp the thoughts which are probably there.

If you are to be an effective lecturer, you must give a great deal of attention to the form and structure in which your ideas are presented. If your lecture is a single speech, look for a pattern which your listeners can remember and which will enable them to reconstruct your line of thought after they leave the hall. If you are

The successful lecturer, whether in the classroom or on the platform, must give primary attention to the form and structure of the ideas he is presenting.

presenting new and difficult material, be sure to define your terms and relate your ideas to the experience of your audience by examples and analogies. Use clear and easily remembered statements and re-statements of the central idea; intersperse your points with well-stated internal summaries and transitions; develop a conclusion which gives unity and direction to your thoughts. If your lecture is part of a series, begin each lecture after the first with a transition from what has preceded and conclude with a preview of what is to come.

We noted above that the success of a speech to inform may be measured by what the audience is able to remember and understand. The other day we picked up the classroom notes which we took in a graduate course many years ago. The fact that the notes still made sense was a tribute to the speaking skill of the lecturer. On the other hand, a few days later we listened to a lecture by a prominent radio commentator and authority on the Far East. Although his lecture was filled with interesting and informative details about the "population explosion," his presentation was so disorganized, rambling, and unnecessarily long that for the last half hour the audience scribbled and circulated caustic notes and looked longingly toward the exits. If we remember the lecture at all, it is not for its content but for the torture inflicted on an unsuspecting audience by a speaker who should have known better.

The Speech to Persuade

When you make a speech to persuade, your purpose is to change in some way the attitudes, beliefs, or course of action of your listeners. You may wish to weaken the convictions of your opponents, to establish belief in your ideas among the uncommitted, to intensify belief and to inspire those who share your views, or to motivate them to engage in positive action to implement your proposals. In some cases you may be limited to one of these ends; in others you may attempt two or more. Your precise purpose is determined only in part by your own wishes. In larger degree you must adapt your aims to your audience. You must not expect your speech to accomplish miracles. Mark Antony's speech in Shakespeare's *Julius Caesar* is improbable, to say the least. Yet if you leave your audience with precisely the same views and attitudes they had when you began, you can hardly justify your appearance in a persuasive role.

Persuasive speeches are likely to have long sections which are indistinguishable from speeches to inform. Winston Churchill's most eloquent wartime speeches contain only a little exhortation. Mostly they are recitals of the facts, which in themselves were grim enough to persuade the people of England to unite. Explaining is one way of persuading, and the development of an argumentative generalization may be almost completely expository. It is the speaker's purpose that makes the difference. If he is merely trying to make a concept clear, the speech is informative. If he seeks to change attitudes, beliefs, or actions, the speech may be called persuasive.

Persuasive speaking occurs in many settings. We have selected three types which represent different kinds of emphasis and development. You should not regard this as a complete classification. Nevertheless it may suggest ways of applying the rhetorical advice of this book to the persuasive speaking you may do.

Policy Arguments

Argumentative speeches about policy may be individual addresses or they may be part of a debate in which both sides are represented in some kind of structured program. The President makes a speech defending a bill which Congress is reluctant to pass. The chairman of the Senate Foreign Relations Committee proposes a radical change in American relations with Communist countries. Two Presidential candidates debate the issues of the campaign. The Senate spends a week debating the merits of a civil rights measure. Four students pair off in an academic debate on the subject, "Resolved: that capital punishment should be abolished." A student in a beginning speech class makes his final speech on the subject, "The maximum Federal income tax should be fixed at fifty percent of net income."

When you make a speech proposing a change in the *status quo,* you take on the *burden of proof* — that is, you must demonstrate that what you advocate is better than what exists. To fulfill your obligation you need to give a well-supported affirmative answer to four questions, usually called the stock issues. You may wish to refine them to apply more exactly to the measure you are advocating, but you cannot escape them. (1) Is there a need for a change? (2) Would your proposal meet the need? (3) Is your proposal desirable? Is it free from worse evils than those you deplore in the *status quo?* (4) Is your proposal practical? Will it actually work if put into operation? Your answers to these questions will form the basic outline from which you will develop your speech.

If you are arguing against a change, you have greater choice. You may, of course, answer all four questions in the negative if you wish. On the other hand you may prefer to concentrate all your attack on one or two of the questions. If you can state your objections clearly and support them conclusively, affirmative answers to the others are irrelevant.

In developing speeches dealing with policy arguments, you must be sure that your speech is clear and logical in its outline. Review the suggestions in Chapter 6, pages 137–144, dealing with the logical connections of points in an outline. In addition, make sure that you have chosen supporting materials which will contribute to maximum believability. If possible, develop your points with a mixture of statistics and examples, and summarize them with quotations from recognized authorities in the area of your argument. You will profit from a review of Chapter 5, pages 81–117, as you plan your choice of supporting material.

Political Campaigning

Although many campaign speeches deal with policy and use the methods suggested above for policy debates, the central issue of any political campaign is, "Which candidate or party is best qualified to lead in the next term of office?" Events change the importance of issues, and no one can predict with certainty whether the issues of today will be relevant to the events of a year from now, to say nothing of longer periods of time. As a result, many, perhaps most, votes are cast on election day for or against the general philosophy of a party, for or against the qualities of leadership demonstrated by a candidate.

In a political campaign the candidate must use all the means of persuasion at his command — the appeal of ethos, the logic of argument, and the skill of effective delivery.

Political speeches, therefore, even when they seem to deal with specific issues are concerned with the *ethos* of a candidate or a party. You will recall that in Chapter 1 we defined ethos as a combination of integrity, intelligence, and good will. A political speech, therefore, is bound to deal with arguments which demonstrate that a candidate or a party is wise enough to lead, honest enough to be trusted with power, and committed to policies which are in the best interests of the listeners. The political campaigner will also contend, or at least imply, that these qualities are not present in sufficient degree in the opposing party and candidates.

In political campaigning the supporting material must be drawn from the platforms of the parties, the recorded votes of the candidates, their experience in executive positions, and their speeches and public statements. It is all public knowledge or can soon be made so. "Let's look at the record," Governor Al Smith was fond of telling his audiences. Campaigns are won by promises to "break foolish traditions," and furnish "bold leadership" when the party in power appears bewildered and committed to time-tested policies which do not seem to work. Or they may offer new leadership without the taint of "politics" to "clean up the mess in Washington." These were the slogans of the winning parties in 1932 and 1952. In each case, the speakers supported the slogans by citing examples of the record of the party in power.

To establish the ethos of a candidate, then, you draw upon examples chosen from his long career of public service to develop the concepts of integrity, intelligence, and good will. You point to his voting record to show that he has consistently favored measures of value to the audience, the community as a whole, or the entire

233

country. In contrast, you note the opponent's unfavorable voting record, or his tendency to be absent when any controversial measure is voted upon. You point to his reluctance to make important decisions; instead, you say, he appoints another commission to study the matter. You note inconsistencies in his career which suggest that he is not to be trusted with power.

A series of examples illustrating a single point, as in the pattern of cumulation (Chapter 6, page 152), is particularly effective in political speeches. Repetition and restatement of points you have developed with examples are also of great value. Stylistically, irony is a potent political weapon and can be used with great force to arouse enthusiasm in a partisan audience.

Inspirational Addresses

Speeches to inspire are given on such diverse occasions as college pep rallies, dedications of monuments, commencements, religious meetings, and political mass meetings, to name only a few. The purpose of inspirational addresses is not to inform, usually not to convince. Rather they seek to create a mood or attitude: a determination to win, a desire to lead a better life, a dedication to the ideals of great men. They do not argue but try to make the listener respond on the basis of deeply-rooted beliefs or loyalties. In the fifth century B.C., Pericles attributed to the fallen heroes of Athens all the virtues he hoped to develop in Athenian society. He contrasted them with the faults of Spartan society and urged his listeners to emulate the dead. In making this speech he set the pattern for nearly all memorial speeches since that time, including those of Daniel Webster at Bunker Hill and of Lincoln at Gettysburg. With the same type of appeal, evangelists like Billy Graham try to revitalize long-dormant religious beliefs of the fathers as a substitute for contemporary skepticism. And it was with an inspirational appeal that Harry Truman woke up a tired and dispirited Democratic convention in 1948 with a promise "to win this election and make those Republicans like it." Until that moment, nobody except Truman seemed to think it possible to do so.

In inspirational speeches short, vividly-worded instances and longer narrative examples are effective, and the pattern of cumulation, or the text if there is one, is a suitable framework on which to build your outline. Sometimes you may wish to conclude with a specific appeal for action. In a political speech you might outline

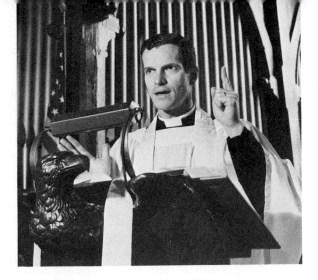

In appealing to deeply-rooted beliefs and loyalties, the inspirational speaker walks a tightrope between sentiment and high moral purpose on the one hand and maudlinism and sentimentality on the other.

aspects of the campaign in which the members of your audience may help. In a moral or religious appeal, you might ask for some physical sign of dedication, such as standing or coming to the platform. If you do not wish a specific action step, and the solemnity of the occasion is great enough to warrant it, you might echo in words appropriate to your own personality and the occasion the final appeal of Lincoln's Gettysburg Address:

— that we here highly resolve that these dead shall not have died in vain — that this nation, under God, shall have a new birth of freedom — and that government of the people, by the people, for the people, shall not perish from the earth.

One final word of caution. There are far more bad inspirational addresses than good ones. For every speech which, like Truman's, captures the imagination of a political convention, there are a dozen windy and boring ones. Evangelistic speeches sometimes insult the intelligence of listeners. Memorial addresses are often maudlin or chauvinistic. Yet an appeal to human sentiment is a legitimate function of public address, and those who do it well, like Lincoln, leave a permanent imprint upon society.

The Speech to Entertain

It is impossible to establish a clear format for a speech to entertain. If the only purpose is enjoyment, a speech to entertain may be merely a speech to inform with a novel subject and vivid supporting material — for example, that rarity, a good travelogue. The danger of such a speech lies in the tendency to substitute enthusiasm for the subject for careful planning. Interminable showing of travel slides, with no editing for photographic excellence or discernible theme, is the most obvious and painful example.

To be effective, a speech to entertain must be as carefully thought out as any other speech. You must ask, "What is there about this subject that has made *me* enthusiastic about it? How can I communicate this to my listeners and make them share my feelings? How may I use the knowledge and experience they possess and relate it to my subject?" If these questions are honestly answered, many a dim or unfocused slide will find its way to the wastebasket, while others will be kept for private showing only. Even some good ones will be omitted in order to present a unified theme within a reasonable period of time.

Some speeches to entertain are designed to make the audience laugh and relax. The after-dinner speech on a strictly social occasion is an example. If the speaker has a message at all, he usually limits it to the last few minutes of the speech. The weakest method of developing such a speech is by the use of Joe Miller, Pat and Mike humor. While a few good stories may be used, most such anecdotes have long gray beards and are received by the audience without enthusiasm. Mark Twain, whose speeches "Babies" and "New England Weather" (See Appendix C, pages 295–298) are classics, relied on gross exaggeration coupled with a whimsical poetic touch in his concluusion.

Sometimes audiences are amused by burlesques of speeches they are accustomed to hear under more serious circumstances. Some

The speech to entertain is not all on the surface. Beneath the jokes, stories, and glib asides lie careful planning and a strong sense of purpose.

speeches by political leaders at the Gridiron Club, a social organization of Washington newsmen, have been of this type. We once heard a college debater at the concluding dinner of a debating convention burlesque the techniques of tournament debaters. You will recall an earlier reference to Oxford University debaters, who are often funny even on a serious subject. They are highly entertaining on a subject like the one used in the Oxford Union: "Resolved, that this House pities its grandchildren."

But whatever form you choose for a speech to entertain, do not assume that it can be delivered without adequate preparation. Like any good work of art, such a speech must have a form and structure which can be perceived and appreciated by the listeners.

Exercises

Here are some subjects suitable for speeches of the types discussed in this chapter. Make a list of twenty other subjects divided among these seven types.

1. *Reports.* Personally investigate and report to the class.
   a. The methods used in teaching written composition, mathematics, science, or history in the public schools of your community.
   b. The master plan for super-highways in your county.
   c. The programs of basic research sponsored by industrial concerns in your area.
   d. The civil defense program for your city.

2. *Reviews.* Prepare a speech reviewing:
   a. A well-written novel of the last two years.
   b. A textbook in public speaking, other than this one.
   c. A play given in your college theater.
   d. A performance of choral or instrumental music.

3. *Lectures.*
   a. (For the Engineer's Club in your university) How to make a technical speech to a lay audience.
   b. The importance of your major subject in a general education.
   c. Presidents as historians.

4. *Policy Debates.*
   a. The United States should (should not) stop nuclear testing.

     b. The state of .... should abolish (restore) capital punishment.

     c. The President of the United States should (should not) be elected by a direct vote of the people.

     d. Our college should (should not) withdraw from all participation in intercollegiate football.

5. *Political Campaign Speeches.*

     a. .... for President of the United States.

     b. Why you should join the Republican (or Democratic) party.

     c. .... for student body president.

6. *Speeches to Inspire.*

     a. All men need a faith.

     b. The importance of freedom of speech.

     c. Jackson Day (or Lincoln Day) dinner address.

7. *Speeches to Entertain.*

     a. Why I am going back to Europe next summer.

     b. Women drivers.

     c. Men drivers.

     d. How to live by advertising slogans.

The Criticism of Public Address

In previous sections on criticism we have emphasized classroom speeches, your own and those of your fellow students. Now we suggest that you apply the principles you have learned to the analysis of speeches you hear outside academic surroundings. On the basis of the principles set forth in this book, prepare an outline to aid you in evaluating the personal appeal of a speaker, the quality of his ideas in terms of reasoning and support, and the skill with which he words and presents his thoughts.

Listen to a minimum of four speeches, including a lecture, an argumentative speech, a speech to inspire, and a speech to entertain. Evaluate the speakers and submit a written report to your instructor, or report orally to the class.

10 GROUP DISCUSSION

Problem-solving in small groups, committees, and conferences is an increasingly important part of the democratic way of life.

IN EARLIER CHAPTERS we have been primarily concerned with speaking situations in which a single speaker faces an audience for the purpose of informing, entertaining, or persuading his hearers. The reaction of the audience to the speaker, though present, is unspoken. Because there are no verbal cues to help you assess the audience response when you make a speech, you need a high degree of skill to evaluate audience reactions and to respond to them when they occur.

In group discussion, however, each participant is in turn both speaker and listener, and is therefore constantly interacting with other members of the group. Even when you act as a member of a panel in a formal discussion before a non-participating audience, you will be aware of responses from other panel members which you can only sense in the typical audience-speaker relationship attained by an individual speaker.

Discussion Defined

In this chapter we are not concerned with the sort of haphazard group talk usually called a "bull session." You engage in enough of such pleasant but purposeless activity without bringing it into the classroom. For our purposes, discussion, like public speaking, is an orderly medium for the exchange of ideas among informed people. It may be defined as *the planned sharing of ideas and facts by two or more persons acting in a cooperative framework for the purpose of discovering approximate truths or appropriate solutions to a problem about which they are mutually concerned.*

Such a concept of discussion assumes that you and your fellow participants are willing to act within a framework of informal, but none the less real, rules of procedure. Without such a framework, discussion may reveal a great deal about the character of the participants but cast little light on the subject for discussion.

This concept also assumes that approximate truths and appropriate solutions to problems, though they are not always attained, are possible in the cooperative framework. In discussion, therefore, you try to achieve general agreement, or failing that, acceptable compromises, rather than attempting to force the majority opinion upon a reluctant minority.

Discussion thus joins other forms of speaking as a valuable tool in the functioning of a democratic society. In small homogeneous groups it is perhaps the best of these tools. In large groups or in the contest for public opinion in community, state, or nation, it serves a secondary role. In our society small groups formulate solutions to social problems through discussion. Out of committees and study groups come proposals for dealing with farm surpluses, improving educational opportunity, expanding civic facilities for study of art and music, or minimizing racial tensions. These proposals are published or introduced as bills in legislative bodies. The members of the original sponsoring group then become advocates for the measure. They make persuasive speeches about it and engage in debate with the opponents of the proposal. The consideration of the idea thus passes from the area of discussion to the area of persuasion, complementary procedures in a democratic society.

Learning discussion principles, then, will aid you in the normal activities of organized groups to which you belong. As you grow in knowledge and responsibility, you may also wish to participate in business, community, professional, and political activities involving both the formation of proposals and efforts to win acceptance for them by large organizations or society as a whole. In either case, you will soon confirm the principle that effective discussion presupposes informed participants, orderly procedures, and objective consideration of all the facts. Without the first, the only result of discussion is pooled ignorance. Without the second, wasted time and inadequate consideration are inevitable. Without the third, inaccurate and false results may be mistaken for sound judgments.

The Thought Pattern of Discussion

For the best development of group thinking, you need to develop group processes in the pattern of intelligent, reflective individual thought. The nature of this pattern has been set forth by John Dewey in his book *How We Think*. Dewey suggests five stages in reflective thinking: "(1) a felt difficulty; (2) its location and definition; (3) suggestion of possible solutions; (4) development by reasoning of the bearings of the suggestion; (5) further observation and experiment leading to its acceptance or rejection; that is, the conclusion of belief or disbelief." Later we shall see how this pattern may be developed into an outline to guide the thought processes of a group.

Reflective Thinking and Intentional Thinking

Reflective thinking begins with a problem and seeks to arrive at a solution. Intentional thinking, on the other hand, begins with a solution and seeks to determine the best means of persuading others to accept it. If your group is to follow the pattern of reflective thinking, you need to phrase the subject for discussion as an open-end question rather than as a proposition for a debate or a persuasive speech. A discussion group considers, "How may this state best provide advanced educational facilities for its high school graduates?" A debate team, on the other hand, argues, "Resolved, that the California plan of junior colleges should be adopted by our state." Both deal with the same issue, but the discussant's question invites reflective thinking whereas the debater must think intentionally. To

---

THE UTILITY OF DISCUSSION

Men are never so likely to settle a question rightly as when they discuss it freely.

— ROBERT SOUTHEY

be sure, debaters may sometimes use the reflective process in analyzing the proposition, and discussants may sometimes engage in vigorous advocacy, particularly in the latter stages of the thought process; but the distinction between the methods is in general valid.

Subjects for Discussion

You will have a better discussion if your subject is well-phrased, but good phrasing is not a guarantee of a good subject. What about the content of the subject? Are some kinds of subjects better suited to discussion than others? What limitations are imposed by the nature of the group itself?

Interest

Clearly your group should select a subject in which they are interested. Otherwise the discussion will be perfunctory, dull, and meaningless. Nevertheless as students in a college dedicated to expanding your fields of interest, you should not reject subjects too readily. As we pointed out in Chapter 2, interest may be stimulated by knowledge, and knowledge may be acquired. For this reason you ought to consider not only subjects about which you know much, but those about which you ought to know more.

Significance

Although as a member of the social committee of your fraternity you might properly participate in a discussion to determine the nature of your next house party, such a subject would hardly be appropriate in a college class room. If discussion is to make a contribution to your education, it should deal with a subject of broader significance than your immediate social group. You need not, of course, settle the future of the United Nations in every discussion, but to be worth the time spent in a college class room, a subject should deal with an issue affecting a group at least as large as your student body. Even such a subject should have implications beyond the borders of the campus. "Should our college get a new football coach?" is both too narrow in wording and too provincial in content. "How may our college become a national football power?" is better in wording but too limited in significance. "What kind of intercollegiate sports program should be conducted on our campus?", on the other hand, opens the whole question of athletic philosophy and poses a question which is of much broader significance than its application to the local campus. Yet the question still allows room for those who wish to fire the coach or hire athletes.

Difference of Opinion

We have already said that some subjects offer only a single proposition which may be accepted or rejected but not varied. But you cannot guarantee a multi-faceted discussion merely by avoiding debate propositions and choosing open-end questions. If the group itself is committed to a particular point of view, the wording of the question has little bearing on the course the "discussion" will take. The Holy Name Society could hardly discuss the question, "Under what circumstances is profanity permissible?" The National Collegiate Athletic Association could get little value from considering, "What professional basketball players ought to be included on the American Olympic team?" The political party of an incumbent first-term President would not need a discussion on the subject, "Which candidate of our party has the best chance of success?"

Although these are extreme examples, it is apparent that discussion is of most value where some difference of opinion exists. On the other hand, there must also be a measure of agreement possible on basic goals and values. The Holy Name Society might have vigorous differences of opinion as to the best means of eliminating profanity, but their agreement on basic goals would encourage objectivity and compromise. The NCAA might reject all compromise with professionalism, but their common interest in superior athletic achievement would foster a profitable discussion on ways of improving American Olympic teams. Russian and American scientists had an amicable discussion about nuclear testing so long as they were dealing with technical methods of discovering distant tests. Problems arose only when the conflicting goals of their respective governments were brought into the discussion.

Types of Problems: Fact, Value, Policy

In addition to limitations on profitable discussion caused by the nature of groups, some questions of *fact* are properly matters for investigation and scientific determination rather than for discussion. "What was the population of the United States at the last decennial census?" Clearly this is not a subject for discussion. Modern scientific statistical techniques make a discussion of the probable population at the next census equally futile. A Congressional committee sought to answer the question, "To what extent have racketeers infiltrated labor unions?" But their method was the taking of testimony from informed persons rather than discussion among themselves. A discussion on such a subject by students who had informed themselves by studying a number of original sources would not be completely unprofitable, but investigating committees are better equipped to get the facts.

Some questions of *value* offer more promise for discussion than questions of fact. Your American Public Address class, applying rhetorical standards learned in the course, might discuss the question, "To what extent was General MacArthur's address to Congress on his return home from Korea a great speech?" On the other hand, many questions of value are matters of personal preference and can hardly be discussed at all. The relative merits of French, Dutch, and Danish pastries offer subject matter for delightful conversation, but they are hardly suitable for discussion.

The most profitable type of discussion centers on questions of *policy*. Such questions require a thorough knowledge of facts and a measure of agreement on values in order to produce sound conclusions. But the values to be chosen for this type of discussion are usually more basic than mere tastes. For this reason, we suggest that for the purposes of this class, you limit your practice to policy questions.

Research on Discussion Subjects

Most of what we said in Chapters 2 and 4 about research for public speaking applies to discussion as well. Still you may profit from having a few concepts specifically pointed out in reference to research for discussion. Good discussion subjects may be found both in areas about which you already know much, and in areas requiring extensive reading before you could be considered an informed discussion participant.

Subjects Growing Out of the Experience of Participants

1. How should our college deal with the problem of cheating?
2. What kind of intercollegiate sports program should be conducted on our campus?

3. How may student government be improved?

4. How may student-faculty relationships be used to improve the quality of education?

At first glance it might appear that the four subjects above require little research for participation in discussion. Yet it would be an error to dismiss research too lightly merely because you already know much about the problems of your campus. To be sure, your research would not be primarily in the library. You would gain more by interviewing members of the faculty, or the coaching staff, or the student council. They in turn might refer you to some written materials, and you would naturally wish to explore the *Readers' Guide* and the card catalogue for relevant material on other campuses. Perhaps you would write to your friends at Slippery Rock, or Yale, or UCLA for information about the same problems there. Whatever material you derived from these research methods, you would integrate with your personal experience and plan your discussion with the insight derived from both experience and research.

Subjects Requiring Intensive Research

1. How might criminal justice in murder cases be improved in our state?

2. How may the narcotics traffic best be controlled?

3. What program may be devised to reduce juvenile delinquency in our city?

4. What changes might profitably be made in our method of choosing presidents of the United States?

In this group of questions, your problems are quite different. Your research must of necessity be primarily in the library. You might interview professors who know far more about the subject than you do, but much of their information comes from printed material rather than personal experience, and you might profit more from reading the same source material. If you could secure an interview with a political leader or a police official, you might get some valuable first-hand information. In the long run, however, your best material must come from printed sources, and your method of research will be much the same as if you were preparing a speech on the same subject.

General Considerations

Since discussion is a cooperative activity, you should not be too firmly committed to any particular solution, even though your study has convinced you that one solution is best. This concept commits you to an even broader research base than you need for preparing a speech. To be sure, no speaker is really prepared unless he knows the alternatives to his proposal. In discussion, however, you may need to modify your position as the views of others become apparent. If you understand all the aspects of the problem, you may be able to discover common ground on which you and your opponents may meet, finding a solution satisfactory to both. Only broad knowledge will make this possible. Moreover, although windy generalizations are inexcusable in either speaker or discussant, the constant challenge to your ideas in discussion makes bold, unsupported assertions untenable. In a group with even one well-informed and thoughtful participant, empty generalizations can lead only to disaster for the ideas you present.

Exercises

1. Formulate five policy questions on which you already have a substantial amount of information from personal knowledge. Rephrase each of them as a debate proposition.
2. Formulate five policy questions dealing with a city, state, or national issue. Rephrase each as a debate proposition.
3. For one question in each of the above groups, list suitable research sources for preparing discussion materials. Indicate what kind of materials you might obtain from each source cited.

Preparing Discussion Outlines

Unlike a speech outline, a discussion outline cannot describe precisely the course a discussion will take, because no one participant (not even the chairman) can tell exactly what will be said. Your discussion outline is, rather, intended to help you and others in the group follow a thought pattern likely to result in a thorough analysis of the question. Unless each participant is adequately prepared, the discussion is almost certain to be little more than a formalized "bull session." For this reason each member of a discussion group should answer in advance a series of questions derived from Dewey's pattern of reflective thinking.

Discussion Outline

I. Felt difficulty
   A. What specific facts (examples, statistics) indicate that a problem exists which needs to be solved?
II. Location and definition
   A. What is the history of the problem? Does it really need remedial action, or will it pass with time?
   B. Who is affected by the problem and in what way?
   C. What are the probable causes of the problem?. Is there a real causal relationship, or is it an accidental time relationship without causal connection?
   D. What are the criteria which must be met in any suggested solutions? Elimination of causes? Avoidance of adverse effects? Others?
III. Possible solutions
   A. What are *all* the possible solutions having any merit?
IV. Reasoned development of solutions
   A. To what extent does each solution
      1. eliminate evils?
      2. remove causes?
      3. avoid adverse results?
      4. meet other criteria?
   B. Is the solution feasible? Can it actually be put into operation?
V. Determination of best solution, and suggestions for putting it into operation.

You should not regard your discussion outline as an inflexible pattern. Nevertheless the discussion will proceed with greater smoothness and less wasted motion if you and your fellow group members are well-prepared within this framework. The importance of this concept will be apparent as we examine the actual process of discussion.

Participating in Discussion

Ideally every participant should take responsibility for the orderly progress of a discussion through the steps of reflective thinking. In practice, however, this is more often the function of a designated leader, whose role we will examine in more detail later in the chapter. But even with a leader, your group will function better if you and your fellow participants assume a share of the responsibility for the progress of the discussion. There will be less need for formal leadership if you will follow a few simple suggestions.

Use of Discussion Outline

A well-ordered discussion should consider each phase of the discussion outline, preferably in sequence. This does not mean that every point on each participant's preparation outline must be considered in detail. If substantial agreement is reached quickly on any individual issue, there is no reason to belabor it. On the other hand, it is important that all points of view be given a hearing. In some cases you may wish to state a concept you do not hold, in order to be sure that there are no unanswered objections to the majority opinion. In a panel discussion before a non-participating audience, this is even more important than in a simple group discussion.

Use of Objective Data

In a well-ordered discussion, contributions should be based on objective data, not unsupported opinion. Discussion without facts is a futile waste of time. It cannot produce profitable results, and the participants would be better off studying the problem in solitude rather than sharing their ignorance with others.

Minimizing Personal Conflict

In a well-ordered discussion, contributions should be phrased in language designed to reduce rather than to sharpen personal conflict. "A soft answer turneth away wrath, but grievous words stir up anger." Note what different effects are produced by these phrases:

ON CONFLICT

It is an excellent rule to be observed in all discussions, that men should give soft words and hard arguments: that they should not so much strive to silence or vex, as to convince their opponents.

— JOHN WILKINS

Personal Conflict	*Discussion of Issues*
That is the most ridiculous statement I have ever heard.	I wonder if I understood you correctly. Did you say — ? Doesn't that imply that — ?
If you had bothered to read the lead article in *Harper's* on this subject, you would know —	You have made an interesting point, but there is some recent evidence that points to an opposite conclusion.
Do you have to keep bringing up the same stale arguments?	I wonder if we haven't considered this point as fully as is practical in the time we have. Shouldn't we move on to the next point?

We could make a much longer list of such phrases, but the point is obvious. Discussion actually moves faster and accomplishes more when participants take a few more words for the sake of conciliating those with opposite views. Hostile remarks stir up counter-remarks and delay the real business of the group. What you are trying to do is to investigate a problem, not analyze the intelligence, industry, or emotional balance of the participants.

Avoiding Ambiguity

In a well-ordered discussion the language used by the participants should be free from vagueness and ambiguity. An incredible amount of time is wasted in discussion by ambiguous language. How many times have you suddenly become aware that the real difference between you and an opponent was a difference in the meaning of terms; on the substance of the problem you were in agreement. For this reason it is better to run the risk of over-defining than of vagueness, and it is better to explore an opponent's statement with a question than to launch an attack. With understanding, the conflict may disappear.

Voicing Ideas Effectively

In a well-ordered discussion contributions should be spoken with the same directness, vigor, and spontaneity as in good extemporaneous speaking. Adjustments should be made for the size of the room and the number of listeners, but these should be adjustments of degree, not of kind. If the adjustments are difficult for you to make, the chances are strong that your public speaking delivery is lacking in directness and spontaneity. In any case review the suggestions about delivery in Chapters 3 and 7, and apply the same principles to the conditions you find in your discussion group.

The Discussion Leader

As we noted earlier, an ideal discussion group would not need a leader. Each participant would from time to time exercise the role, and the discussion would move through its various stages without the designation of a formal chairman. In practice this ideal is seldom attained. It is therefore wise for the group to appoint one person who has the special responsibilities of leadership. In an experienced group he will have little to do. But whether exercised by one person or by the group members in turn, there are certain functions of leadership which are essential if discussion is to be profitable.

Reflective Thinking

The effective leader will guide the group through the process of reflective thinking. You have no doubt been a member of a committee in which one of your colleagues has insisted on solving a problem without really knowing what it was. When he presented his solution, he sincerely believed it to be an appropriate answer to the question the committee had been asked to study. Possibly he was right. But to be sure of the accuracy of the solution, a wise chairman encouraged the group to explore the problem itself in some depth. Even though the ultimate solution was the one proposed in the first five minutes, the fact that the committee had reasoned through all the implications meant that the report could have unanimous and enthusiastic support from all the members.

Wide Participation

The effective leader will encourage participation by all the members and tactfully discourage those who seek to dominate the discussion. It is true that some members of the group may be silent because they have no ideas. If so, this will soon be apparent. But there are others with useful views who are merely timid. A good leader makes sure that all useful views are heard. In some cases, he may wish to restate ideas that are not clearly phrased, or draw out a hesitant or confused participant by carefully-worded questions.

Diverse Points of View

The effective leader will seek to insure that all points of view are represented in a discussion. To maintain his impartiality he ought not to identify himself with one of the parties to sharp conflict. Nevertheless, he may on occasion frankly and openly play "devil's advocate" for a neglected point of view, phrasing his statement in such a way as to avoid identification with the concept. For example, he might say, "Some people favor this opinion," or "Nobody has mentioned the viewpoint of Samuelson on this issue. He contends that —." In this way the leader can insure a full discussion of all phases of the question.

Good Will

The effective leader seeks to prevent aimless discussion based on ambiguity, to reconcile personal conflict, and to point out and develop common ground between contending participants. His aim is to secure agreement if possible, or if not agreement, then compromise. Failing in both of these, he seeks to maintain good will among the discussants so that a new basis for agreement may be found.

Evidence and Reasoning

The effective leader seeks to bring out not only the points of view represented, but the reasons for those views and the evidence on which they are based. If he performs this function effectively, the discussion will have the same framework of supporting material that would be present in a well-developed persuasive speech. Examples, statistics, analogies, and authoritative opinions all have a place in a discussion as in a speech. If the participants do not bring them in, the leader should ask *what, why,* and *how* questions which will elicit appropriate evidence.

Summaries and Transitions

Discussions, like speeches, need a clearly-defined framework. The effective leader will make an introductory statement to launch a discussion and from time to time will intervene with suitable transitions and objective summaries. In this way he can contribute to an orderly progression of ideas.

Special Forms of Discussion

So far in this chapter we have been concerned primarily with *face-to-face* discussion groups, in which only the participants in the discussion are present. There are, however, other groups in which selected individuals present materials within the general framework of discussion for the benefit of an audience. Some writers on discussion term these *co-acting* groups. The most common forms of co-acting discussion include the *panel* and the *symposium.* A third form, the *forum,* occasionally has an independent existence but more often is combined with a lecture or with the panel or the symposium.

The Panel

In a panel discussion a small group of four to eight persons representing diverse points of view present a planned discussion for an audience on a subject of concern to the group. Normally the panel is seated in a semi-circle in front of the audience, often around a table, with the leader in a central position. If the audience is large, a platform should be used. If microphones are needed, they should be numerous enough so that the spontaneity of the panel members is preserved.

Panel discussions are often used at conferences and conventions as a means of presenting differing opinions. Properly conducted, they are effective in covering the most significant aspects of a sub-

To be successful, a panel must have at least three elements: a topic of interest, members who are well-informed and articulate, and a leader who can give pace and direction to the discussion.

ject. Improperly handled, they can be the most boring and wasteful periods of a conference program. Knowing this, let us examine some of the requisites for success.

INTEREST. An effective panel should deal with a subject of wide interest to the members of the audience. Given time to develop a theme, you may create interest by skillful handling of materials in a speech. But in a panel you are limited to the give and take of the discussion format. While interest may develop out of conflict between the participants or arise as a result of an effective short contribution, the inherent attention value of the subject itself is the best guarantee of success.

PREPARATION. An effective panel should make specific preparation before facing an audience. Your group may meet in advance and plan the direction the panel will take, or you may make individual preparation from an agreed outline. If you do not prepare specifically, the panel may bog down in trivia, or one member may ride a special hobby at the expense of the progression of ideas. Or you may bore the audience by arguing about definitions which ought to have been agreed upon before the program began. On the other hand, your group should not be so completely rehearsed that spontaneity is destroyed and the participants appear to be operating from a script.

DELIVERY. If you are to be an effective panelist, you must speak not only to your fellow panel members but to the persons in the farthest corners of the room. If you do not use a platform, make a special effort to be seen by the audience when it is your turn to speak. Do not be deceived by the nearness of other panel members; it is the audience you must reach. Without ignoring your fellow panelists, use the strength of voice and energy of participation that you would use in good informal public speaking in a room of the same size.

LEADERSHIP. When you act as leader of a panel, you will need to make short introductory and concluding statements, furnish internal summaries and transitions, keep the discussion moving by asking occasional questions, and act as a link with the audience. When a forum follows, the effectiveness of a panel may be judged in part by the quality of audience comments and questions. As leader, you can stimulate this portion of the program by breaking off the panel when interest is high. Close observation of the audience will help you to pick the right moment.

The Symposium

A symposium is a series of speeches around a common theme seeking a solution to a problem. It differs from a two-sided or many-sided debate in that the participants are cooperating rather than competing, thinking reflectively rather than intentionally. Often the speeches in a symposium may be pegged to the steps in the reflective thinking process. On a five-speaker symposium, for example, the first speech might discuss the nature of the problem, and the second, causes and criteria for satisfactory solutions. The last three might outline three possible solutions and relate them to the aspects developed in the first two speeches. At other times each speaker might present an independent case for a particular program.

The key to a successful symposium is the attitude which you and your fellow speakers take toward the subject and toward each other. If each of you regards his particular solution as the last word on the subject, while all other speakers are heretics, only debate is possible. On the other hand, if each is seeking a solution and is ready to consider ideas advanced by others as well as his own, the program will have the characteristics of a symposium.

The set speeches of a symposium are often followed by a panel discussion period in which the participants question each other about the ideas developed in the speeches. With or without the panel step, the symposium usually concludes with a forum.

The Forum

As we have noted, panel discussions and symposia are often followed by a question period. In addition, questions are often asked by the audience following a lecture by a single speaker. Occasionally an open meeting is held in which there are no speeches — only an announced subject, with audience participation from the beginning. Such meetings are called forums. In relatively small groups, with or without the panel-symposium-lecture format, great freedom may be allowed, including the right to make short speeches on the sub-

---

THE VALUE OF INQUIRY

It is error only, and not truth, that shrinks from inquiry.

— THOMAS PAINE

The chairman of a forum plays a vital role — in keeping questions from the floor relevant, in preventing digressions or harangues, and in closing the forum before interest lags.

ject under discussion. In most forum periods with larger groups, the audience is limited to asking questions of the speakers.

When you act as chairman of a forum, you should explain to the audience the rules governing the asking of questions. On a subject with lively interest or strong division of opinion, you may decide to require questions to be submitted in writing. An editorial committee can then group the questions and select the best-worded and most significant one from a group dealing with the same theme. This procedure may easily subject you or your editorial committee to the charge of censorship, and it would be easy for you to exercise it. But if you are both fair-minded and tough-skinned, you will discover that written questions offer the best way to insure that the question period remains relevant to the announced subject and that it deals with the ideas in which the largest number of audience members are interested.

When questions are taken from the floor, procedure is more informal, but it is still wise to state and enforce a few simple rules. Here are some which work in practice.

1. Questioners should not make long speeches, but should come directly to the point.
2. Questions should be relevant to the subject matter of the panel, symposium, or lecture. Although this should not bar questioners from inquiring about the reasons for significant omissions, it should be used to prevent the asking of completely irrelevant questions.
3. The same person should not be allowed to ask a number of questions when there are others waiting to be heard.

4. When several questions have been asked of one speaker, or on one phase of the subject, preference should be given to a person who wishes to direct his question elsewhere.

In all large forums, and often in smaller ones, the chairman should repeat questions before referring them to the appropriate speaker for an answer. This serves a dual purpose: it makes certain that members of the audience hear the question; and it allows the chairman to clarify questions which are badly worded. The chairman's role in the forum is thus an active one.

When you act as chairman, you should not allow the forum to continue beyond the scheduled hour for adjournment. If interest lags and the audience becomes restive before normal adjournment time, bring the forum to a close, thank the participants, and suggest that those who wish to pursue questions further may do so on an individual basis.

Public Speaking and Discussion

To be successful, participants in either group discussion or panels and symposia must cultivate the same qualities of good communication that are needed in public speaking: clarity, believability, and interest. Discussants need the same skills in discovering materials, organizing them, wording them, and delivering them that characterize good speech in any medium. On the other hand, public speakers may learn much from discussion about analyzing and responding to cues in the audience, for in discussion visible cues are supplemented by audible ones. In addition there are some public speaking situations in which the best organization of ideas may follow the pattern of reflective thinking. In the symposium-panel-forum situation, the significant elements of each type of communication are blended. Only a person skilled in both can be fully effective.

Exercises

1. If you are in a relatively small class, your instructor may wish to have you participate in at least one discussion involving the entire class. If so, the class may select a subject on which all will do research. It might be one of the ones submitted in the exercises earlier in the chapter. When the subject has

been selected, use the same general research methods you would for a speech. (See Chapter 4.) Prepare a discussion outline according to the suggestions on pages 246–247. On the basis of this preparation, participate in the class discussion according to the suggestions given in the chapter.

2. Divide the class into groups of four to six members. Select one member to act as chairman. Select a suitable policy question, and prepare discussion outlines. Have the panel meet in advance to agree on definitions and general procedures, but do not stereotype the discussion by a complete rehearsal. Present the panel discussion for the class. If possible, allow time for audience participation.

3. Using the same groups, but a different chairman and a different question, plan a symposium along the lines suggested on page 254. Each of the speakers should be familiar with the outline the others intend to follow so that there will be no unnecessary duplication. As you present your portion of the program, adapt your remarks to those which have preceded yours. If possible, leave time for audience questions.

4. A three- or four-man symposium is well-adapted to a final speech assignment, with speeches of approximately eight to twelve minutes. If your instructor agrees, work with other class members to develop your final speech in this pattern.

Criticizing Discussion

Discussion may be analyzed in part by the same principles of speech composition and delivery developed in earlier chapters. Read again the suggestions for criticism given in other chapters and select those points most relevant to discussion. In addition, ask:

1. Were the speakers well informed; had they thought through all the implications of the problem? Or was this merely pooled ignorance, or a "bull session"?

2. Did the speakers deal with the problem in a cooperative rather than a competitive framework? Did they reason reflectively as they spoke?

3. Did the participants make me interested in the problem and eager for the forum period?

11 ORAL READING

Oral reading is neither a private activity nor an exhibition of vocal skill; it is a communicative art akin to conversation and public speaking.

ORAL READING is a practical skill which everyone uses. Parents read to children at bedtime; husbands read to wives from the evening paper; wives read anecdotes from the *Reader's Digest* to husbands. Secretaries read minutes and committee chairmen read reports. Preachers read from the Bible and politicians read speeches. Radio announcers read scripts and television performers read cue cards. Anyone who can read at all sometimes reads aloud. Unfortunately, only a few read well.

Some readers fail because they do not understand the ideas with which they deal. Much of this chapter is designed to help you avoid this problem. In other cases readers are ineffective because they assume that oral reading is necessarily different from other forms of communication. Nothing could be farther from the truth. The reader is first of all a communicator, and techniques of speaking which are effective in one form of communication are effective in another. We need, therefore, to become aware of the similarities between conversation, public speaking, and oral reading.

Oral Reading and Public Speaking

As in public speaking, the goal of oral reading is the communication of ideas. When you read, you must, of course, have material written in such a way that it can be delivered effectively. If you have written it yourself, your failure to communicate, if it occurs, is entirely your responsibility.

But even when you are reading material written by others, you cannot abdicate responsibility for content. The intelligent selection of oral reading material parallels the process by which you select and organize material for a speech. If for any reason you think you cannot present material in a clear, believable, and interesting manner, do not read it aloud.

Ideas in Oral Reading

Whether you are delivering a speech from manuscript, reading a quotation to illustrate a point, or reading *Alice in Wonderland* to the children with whom you are baby-sitting, your first responsibility is to understand the meaning of what you read. While this may appear simple, and often is, there are times when analysis of meaning is a very complex process. For the moment, let us forget the easy passages and concentrate on ways of making sure you understand the more difficult ones. If you do not comprehend what you read, your listeners will have little chance of doing so. They are entirely dependent on the cues you give them, and if they miss a point, there is no way for them to go back and read it again.

Understanding the Passage as a Whole

The first step in preparing to read aloud is to grasp the general meaning of the passage as a whole. Perhaps you can do this through silent reading followed by a silent or oral summary of its content. As a beginner, and even as an experienced reader of difficult materials, you may do better to write out one or more of the following content analyses.

OUTLINE. For a long expository passage or for a manuscript speech, an outline helps you to point up key ideas and see the relationship of the parts to the whole. If you have written a speech, you may have used an outline as one step in preparation. (See Chapter 6.) If you are using the material of others, your ability or inability to outline it clearly is a measure of the probability of audience understanding. If you cannot outline expository or argumentative writing, the fault may be yours or it may lie in the material itself. In either case you have little chance of making an audience understand what is not clear to you.

For more subjective or literary materials, you may find the précis or the paraphrase more useful than the outline as a method of analysis.

PRÉCIS. A précis is a brief, clean-cut statement of the essential facts or points of a passage. It is comparable to, although somewhat longer than, the statement of the central idea of a speech, as suggested in Chapter 6. You will find the précis of greatest value in analyzing relatively short passages. Writing it focuses your attention on the key idea the author had in mind. You can then search for the words or phrases in the passage which most fully express this idea and stress them in your reading. You should be aware, though, that a précis which *misses* the essential points of the selection is worse than no analysis at all.

PARAPHRASE. To paraphrase is to rewrite or restate the sense of a passage in your own words. A relatively close paraphrase is of more value to the oral reader than one which differs markedly from the paragraph and sentence structure of the original. When you find synonyms which are true to the intent of the author, you increase your understanding of the passage. Because of this you can communicate more fully with your listeners. In many ways paraphrasing orally is like practicing an extemporaneous speech from outline; in both, the point is not to memorize the language but to fix the ideas in mind.

Mastering Shades of Meaning

You may understand the gross meaning of a selection and still miss much that is significant. To be sure of complete understanding of complex material, you need more than an outline, a précis, or a paraphrase.

THE EXACT MEANINGS OF WORDS — DENOTATION. In casual silent reading you may often understand the general meaning of a term in its context. The fact that you cannot define it exactly may not trouble you, and perhaps you do not bother to look it up. When

Words, like glasses, obscure everything which they do not make clear.

— JOSEPH JOUBERT

---

you read to others, you must be more precise. Every word in a passage which you cannot define, and every word of doubtful pronunciation should be checked in a good dictionary. Such definitions are said to deal with *denotations,* the literal meanings of words. You must know denotations precisely if you hope to project clear meanings to your listeners.

ASSOCIATIONAL MEANINGS — CONNOTATIONS. If words were like mathematical symbols, possessing a single meaning to all who speak or read a language, life would be much simpler, although perhaps far less interesting. The fact is that even the simplest words in English have many subtle and implied meanings, or *connotations.* The denotative meaning of *man* is clear enough. But in a connotative sense the word suggests the qualities of nobility, courage, and virtue. "Be a man, my son!" *Roget's International Thesaurus* lists ten approximate synonyms for the word *gift* in the sense of a donation, and five in the sense of a talent. Yet for one of the synonyms, *bequest,* only two alternate words are given.

But the problem does not end here. What does the phrase. "All men are created equal," mean? Calhoun thought it did not include Negroes; Lincoln thought it did. What does a writer mean when he uses the word *communist?* Is he talking about an economic system, a political system, or is he just being abusive? What is a *liberal?* Is he one who believes in laissez-faire economics, or one who believes in increased control of business by a democratically elected government? Is a *communist* an extreme *liberal?* Is a *liberal* merely one who favors a relaxation in the moral code? Or one who does not accept traditional theology? What is a *conservative?* Is the word synonymous with *reactionary?* Is a *conservative* one who seeks to save the best elements of existing society while making progress on social fronts?

These and other words in the language are used so loosely that you can seldom be sure exactly what connotations the author intended unless you study the meaning carefully. By the same token you cannot read material containing these words intelligently unless you know what the meanings are.

Even words which are usually regarded as rather exact in meaning may have widely different connotations. To one man the word *home* may be merely a denotative synonym for *house*. To another it may bring to mind a whole series of pleasant and warm human relationships. On the other hand, to a man in the midst of divorce proceedings it may be a synonym for *hell*. To one man a *desert* may be a bleak, waterless, sandy waste. To another it may connote unusual beauty. To a hardened sailor the sea may mean adventure and beauty; to a nauseated neophyte it may suggest only the need for dramamine. You must seek to discover these overtones and reveal them to your listeners.

STUDYING THE INTENT OF THE AUTHOR. Problems of connotation are difficult enough in expository or argumentative materials. But they are compounded in literary selections where the author may deliberately seek to create moods and feelings by suggestion rather than by direct statement. Paradoxical, ironic, and symbolic passages offer a particular challenge to the reader. The Bible is filled with paradoxical and figurative statements which are nonsense if you take them literally: "He that loseth his life shall save it." "Cast thy bread upon the waters, for thou shalt find it after many days." If you read *Gulliver's Travels* to children, you may treat it as a simple story, but for an adult audience you must recognize it as a satire on eighteenth century political life. When you give a literal interpretation to ironic, satiric, or symbolic language, you pervert the intent of the author and fail to communicate his meaning to your listeners.

Sometimes you can grasp the author's intent merely by reading the material carefully. At other times detailed research may be needed. How does the particular passage you wish to read fit into the context of the whole or into the author's experience or purpose? How did Winston Churchill's knowledge of history influence his statement that, "If the British Empire . . . shall last for a thousand years, men will still say, 'This was their finest hour.' "? How did Herbert Spencer's training as an engineer influence his *Philosophy of Style?* For what purpose did the author of an economics textbook introduce a particular example? Are you entitled to read it to develop a portion of your speech, or does it have a different meaning from the one you imply when you take it out of context? In literary selections such as *Moby Dick,* does the passage you have selected help the listener to understand the deep-seated hatred of Captain Ahab toward the white whale? The nature of the complete work and the background of the author may give the clue which will enable you to understand a passage more fully and thus to read it more intelligently.

Exercises

1. Find a newspaper text of a speech by a prominent political figure, or choose one from *Vital Speeches*. Outline the speech to study its structure. What problems, if any, does the outline reveal for an oral reader?

2. Select an expository passage of 200 to 300 words from one of your textbooks. Write a paraphrase of the passage, using a thesaurus if you need it. What words in the original passage will be most difficult to communicate to an audience?

3. Select a passage from a newspaper editorial, a speech, or an essay in which the opinions expressed are forcefully worded. Write a précis of the passage. What words in the passage carry heavy connotations? Are these reflected in the précis? What other methods of analysis will bring them out?

The Effect of Structure on Meaning

The importance of words to meaning varies widely with the function of the words in the sentence. Nouns and action verbs are the workhorses of the language. Without them communication would be reduced to gesture. Obviously then, you will find a large number of nouns and verbs important enough to deserve strong emphasis in reading. Next in importance are pronouns, adjectives, and adverbs. Together these five categories of words are called *content words*. They carry the basic meaning of sentences.

Other words in the language serve a structural function. They show relationships among the content words but seldom add to the basic meaning. In this category of *structural words* are conjunctions, prepositions, articles, and auxiliary verbs. Only rarely do words of this kind deserve special emphasis in oral reading.

NEW IDEAS AND ECHOES. Even content words may have differing importance in different parts of the same passage. When an idea is introduced for the first time, you need to stress it more than when it is repeated. Repeated words, or *echoes* as they are called, may be modified in their second appearance. If so, you will need to emphasize the difference as you read. In the same way, when a contrast or comparison is read, it is the words which point up the comparison which you must stress. Consider this passage from Sir James Jeans' book, *Through Space and Time*. Note the new ideas, echoes, and comparisons.

These are restless days in which everyone travels who can. The more fortunate of us may have travelled outside Europe to other continents — perhaps even around the world — and seen strange sights and scenery on our travels. And now we are starting out to take the longest journey in the whole universe. We shall travel — or pretend to travel — so far through space that our earth will look like less than the tiniest of motes in a sunbeam, and so far through time that the whole of human history will shrink to a tick of the clock, and a man's whole life to something less than the twinkling of an eye.[1]

The key to effective reading of a passage of this kind is to sharpen the new ideas by stressing them and by subordinating the echoes. The word *travel,* or a variant form of it, appears five times in the passage. It should be stressed only on its first appearance. In the later echoes the new meanings are carried by modifying and qualifying phrases such as *outside Europe, strange sights, longest* and *pretend*. It is these phrases rather than *travel* which you would emphasize in reading. In the parallel passages of the last sentence, the words *space* and *time* are key words, introduced by the identical structural words, *so far through*. The latter should be subordinated, the former stressed.

RHYTHM AND MEANING. In spoken American English almost every word of two or more syllables has an accent. Words of three or more syllables often have two accents, although one may be distinctly secondary. In the flow of speech we usually accent nouns and action verbs of one syllable, but do not stress one-syllable structural words. One-syllable adjectives and adverbs vary in accent according to their importance in the context. As a result of these natural stress patterns, spoken English tends to alternate stressed and unstressed syllables. An exact alternation is not difficult to achieve, and indeed often occurs in poetry and poetic prose, as we noted in the chapter on style. *"Life* is a *narrow vale* be*tween* the *cold* and *bar*ren *peaks* of *two* e*ter*nities,"* said Robert G. Ingersoll at his brother's grave.

But such rhythm patterns, whether natural or contrived, present

[1] Sir James Jeans, *Through Space and Time* (New York: The Macmillan Company, 1934), p. 1.

problems in meaning. Consider the accented syllables marked by italics in the passage from Ingersoll cited above. Read the passage with exactly the same amount of stress on each accented syllable. You will find that you have created a drumbeat rhythm but very little meaning. To create meaning you will need to reduce the stress on the second syllable of *between* and on the last syllable of *eternities.* You will also probably increase the stress on *life, vale, peaks,* and the second syllable of *eternities.* By doing this, you will retain the rhythmic effect but make it less mechanical, and the meaning will emerge. Notice that it was the nouns which gained special stress. The sentence does not contain an action verb.

Like all aspects of oral reading, your use of natural rhythm depends upon understanding the meaning and feeling the emotion of the passage. Your analysis of details of structure should sharpen this meaning by stimulating your sensitivity to the elements which symbolize it.

PHRASING. The thought unit of speech is not a word or a sentence, but a group of closely related words which we shall call a phrase. This is not necessarily the same as the grammatical unit known as a participial phrase or a prepositional phrase. It is relatively easy to divide a sentence into short sections, each of which has a certain grammatical unity. Here, for example, is a sentence from the speech by John Jay Chapman in the Appendix. We have divided it into a subject phrase, a predicate phrase, and three prepositional phrases.

> The true starting point/for the world's progress/will never be reached/by any nation/as a whole.

If you insert pauses at each of the vertical lines, you will merely create a jumble of disconnected ideas, even though there is a logical reason for the insertion of each line. If you place pauses anywhere else, you will distort the meaning completely. You must decide, therefore, which grammatical units may be combined with others into meaningful thought groups which may be readily grasped by the listener. The sentence above is short enough so that you might treat it as a single phrase, or you might prefer to use a slight pause after *progress.* Either reading would retain thought unity.

The problem of phrasing is admittedly governed by subjective judgments. There is seldom only one correct way. If you will experiment with several possible thought groupings and evaluate each

Using a tape recorder is one of the best ways of perfecting your skill in oral reading. With practice, you can come ever closer to communicating the author's true meaning.

in terms of your analysis of the author's intent, you should be able to select the most effective arrangement of phrases to convey the meaning to your listeners.

Centering

By this time you are aware that some words are far more important to meaning than others. When you read aloud you will need to recognize these words and give them the central emphasis they deserve. What are these words? Clearly they will be those which are most closely related to the central thought of the passage. Beyond this, they will reflect the changes in emphasis and mood as the idea develops. The selection of these words is by no means a mechanical process; indeed, it is in part a matter of subjective judgment. Still it may help to indicate what kinds of words are likely to carry key ideas. Some of these we have mentioned earlier, but there is value in gathering them together. When you can recognize them, you will learn to center your thinking upon them as you read and give them the special stress they deserve.

1. Words conveying new ideas, not dealt with previously in the selection.
2. Words with strong connotative meanings.
3. Content words, as distinguished from structural words.

4. New modifiers of echo words.

5. Words in parallel construction.

6. Words expressing contrast or comparison.

7. Words expressing the climax of a long sentence, or whole phrases expressing the climax of a longer development of an idea.

8. Refrains — repetitions for emphasis or ironic effect, as "Brutus is an honorable man." Each repetition of the phrase intensifies its impact.

By contrast there are other words which are nearly always subordinated — given less emphasis than other parts of the sentence or paragraph.

1. Parenthetical expressions.

2. Structural words.

3. Echoes.

4. Implied concepts which are not direct echoes, but which grow directly out of ideas previously stated. "The *kennel* in the rear of the lot housed a dog." *Dog* is the expected word and requires no emphasis. *Cat* or *husband* would be an unusual twist and would require emphasis.

In the foregoing pages we have tried to give you advice on the analysis of meaning and the selection of key words and phrases requiring special emphasis in reading. But there is no secret formula for finding and interpreting the meaning and feeling of a passage you wish to read aloud. No computer will ever replace intelligent judgment and keen sensitivity to human values. We can help you organize your search for meaning with greater technical skill, but your ultimate success as a reader will depend in large part on the degree to which you think the thoughts and feel the sentiments of the author as you stand before the audience.

Exercises

1. Select a passage of five hundred to a thousand words of lively and well-written expository material. Analyze the material according to the following plan:

   a. Write either an outline or a précis.

b. Look up the meanings and pronunciations of all words about which you have the slightest doubt. If there are many such words, write a paraphrase of the passage.

c. Write a statement indicating how the author's background may be relevant to a proper understanding of the meaning of the passage. In the same way, how does the intent of the larger work from which the passage is chosen affect the meaning of the smaller selection?

d. What words or phrases are heavily loaded with connotations?

e. Divide the passage into phrases suitable for easy comprehension by an audience.

f. Mark the key words of the passage which need to be made the centers of meaning in each phrase.

2. Read the passage aloud, concentrating on thinking the thought rather than on the individual words of the selection.

3. Follow the same procedures in analyzing a passage from a strong persuasive speech by a speaker of established reputation. Suitable materials may be found in collections like Parrish and Hochmuth, *American Speeches;* Baird, *American Public Addresses;* Goodrich, *Select British Eloquence;* Brewer, *World's Best Orations;* Lee, *The World's Orators;* and Brandt and Shafter, *Selected American Speeches.*

Delivery in Oral Reading

In most of the preceding section we have deliberately used an undefined word, *stress,* to indicate a change of emphasis in oral reading. Obviously stress can be obtained by many techniques. These are precisely the same in oral reading and public speaking, although they may differ somewhat in application. As we noted at the beginning of this chapter, a good speech and a good oral reading should sound much alike, and both should resemble animated conversation.

Use of Specific Techniques

Since we have already discussed most of the oral reader's delivery tools in Chapter 7, we present them here in brief form, with a few notations as to differences from public speaking usage.

BODILY ACTION. When you read, you need the same qualities of alertness and spontaneity which characterize a good speaker. Probably you will use a little less gesture and a little more inner physical response to key words, which you can anticipate more easily in reading than in speaking.

EYE CONTACT. In reading, your manuscript will limit your eye contact with the audience, but you must not permit the reading situation to destroy your relationship with your listeners. You should be familiar enough with the manuscript to look at the audience more than half of the time. Typing your material double or triple space will help, as will using an oversize typescript. Be wary of old books with small print unless you are so familiar with the material that you hardly need to refer to it at all. In any case, with practice you should be able to show the same sensitivity to the audience that characterizes a good speaker.

LOUDNESS. Basic loudness and loudness for emphasis present the same problems when you read as when you speak. If you have any difficulty making yourself heard in a speech, you will compound the problem by keeping your head down and looking at the script instead of at the audience. Loudness for emphasis is the easiest of all methods of stress, but we hope you do not use it to the exclusion of all other methods. Such monotony of technique wearies the listener and is completely unnecessary. When you read, you have the opportunity for experiment and practice which enables you to make more use of the subtler devices of pitch and time changes.

DISTINCTNESS. Your problems of distinctness will be the same in both reading and speaking. In reading, however, you have greater opportunity to correct them by practicing the combinations which give you difficulty.

PITCH CHANGES. Identical techniques are appropriate in both forms of communication. Again, the opportunity for practice should make you use them more effectively in reading, but you must concentrate on the idea rather than the technique when you face your audience.

TIMING — RATE, PAUSE, DURATION. The pause is a mark of phrasing and indicates to the listener the nature of the thought units as you conceive them. As in pitch changes, you must be careful of artificiality in the use of timing, but the basic needs are the same in both reading and public speaking.

*There be players that I have seen play, and heard others praise,
and that highly . . . that . . . have so strutted and bellowed that
I have thought some of nature's journeymen had made men and
not made them well, they imitated humanity so abominably.*

— WILLIAM SHAKESPEARE

INTENSITY — VOCAL QUALITY. Except in heavily loaded emotional material, you do not need great changes in vocal quality to read effectively. To a large extent quality changes may be effected by the physical responses which you make to your material. If you take time at pauses to assume appropriate physical attitudes, numerous changes in vocal quality will follow.

Delivery and Meaning

We have noted earlier that no amount of technical knowledge about analysis can take the place of intelligent judgment and keen sensitivity to human values. In the same way, neither knowledge of delivery techniques nor practice in reading can take the place of a vivid sense of the meaning and mood of a selection *at the moment of utterance.* There is danger as well as merit in practice. If you allow the mechanics of loudness, timing, pitch, or quality to dull your awareness of the thought and feeling you wish to communicate, you will sound artificial and affected. Though you may win praise for your melodious voice and clear articulation, your ideas will not emerge as clear, interesting, and believable.

Similarly you must be aware that you are interpreting ideas, not acting a part. You need not ape Churchill's mannerisms to read one of his speeches, but you must be faithful to the thoughts and feelings portrayed in what you read. Attempting an exact imitation may lead you into caricature, and the ideas may be lost in the process.

Using Oral Reading to Improve Public Speaking Delivery

Because the basic delivery skills of oral reading and public speaking are the same, oral reading is a useful tool for the improvement of public speaking. Since you are not concerned with formulating language at the moment of delivery, you can concentrate on making the most of the language before you. If you keep ideas and feelings rather than techniques in the foreground, you should improve your

271

vocal delivery, not only in reading but in extemporaneous speaking as well. If you have genuine skill as a reader, you can make a manuscript speech sound as direct and communicative as an extemporaneous speech; at the same time, you can make marked improvements in style and in shades of emphasis which might be missed in extemporaneous delivery.

By the same token, even extemporaneous delivery may be improved through oral reading. When you read, you become aware both of possible pitfalls in delivery and of the value of special skills in pitch, timing, and intensity. If you are sensitive and intelligent, you can transfer these skills to extemporaneous delivery. In turn, your reading may benefit by a study of the normal inflections and time patterns of communicative extemporaneous delivery. When you can detect them, you can refine them for sharper delineation of meaning in reading without losing the communicative touch of the speaker. In this way, the clarity, believability, and interest of speaking in both media may be improved.

Exercises

1. The passages given below are typical of materials which you can profitably read to the class. Analyze them by some of the methods suggested in earlier exercises. Then read them in such a way as to take full advantage of the qualities of communicative delivery outlined above. If possible, practice reading with a tape recorder. Where you are not satisfied, read the passage again and compare recordings. When you are confident that you have the best reading of which you are capable, read the passage to the class.

   a. During one of my last nights with the battery we were routed out of our blankets an hour before dawn to put down a barrage preceding an infantry attack. Every other battery for miles around was firing. Batteries were dug in close together and we got the blasts and concussions from other guns as well as our own. Every gun threw up a fiendish flame when it went off, and the black night was pierced like a sieve with the flashes of hundreds of big guns.

   Standing there in the midst of it all, I thought it was the most violent and terrifying thing I'd ever been through. Just being on the sending end of it was staggering. I don't know how human sanity could survive on the receiving end.

   When it was all over and daylight came with a calm and unnatural quiet, a rainbow formed over the mountain ahead of us. It stood out radiantly against the moist green hillsides and drifting whitish-gray clouds. One end of it was anchored on the mountain slope on our side of the valley, while the other disappeared behind a hill on the German side. And, as we watched, that other end of the rainbow became gradually framed by a rising plume of white smoke — caused by the shells we had just sent over. The smoke didn't obscure the rainbow. Rather it seemed to rise enfoldingly around it, like honeysuckle climbing a porch column.

Men newly dead lay at the foot of that smoke. We couldn't help thinking what a strange pot of gold that beautiful rainbow was pointing to.[2]

b. What is a treaty, says the German Chancellor, but a scrap of paper? Have you any five pound notes about you? Have you any of those neat little Treasury one-pound notes? If you have, burn them. They are only scraps of paper. What are they made of? Rags! What are they worth? The whole credit of the British Empire! Scraps of paper! I have been dealing with scraps of paper in the last few weeks. We suddenly found the commerce of the world coming to a standstill. The machine had stopped. Why? The machinery of commerce was moved by bills of exchange. I have seen some of them; wretched, crinkled, scrawled over, blotted, frowzy; and yet those scraps of paper moved great ships, laden with thousands of tons of precious cargo, from one end of the world to the other. The motive power behind them was the honour of commercial men.

Treaties are the currency of international statesmanship. German merchants, German traders have the reputation of being as upright and straightforward as any traders in the world, but if the currency of German commerce is to be debased to the level of that of her statesmanship no trader from Shanghai to Valparaiso will ever look at a German signature again. That is the doctrine of the scrap of paper; that is the doctrine . . . that treaties only bind a nation as long as it is to its interest. . . . It is the straight road to barbarism.[3]

c. To convert what they have for sale into what they want to buy, people sell for money or its equivalent and use the money to buy what they want. The dollars we sell for and buy with are our universal *medium of exchange*. Economists sometimes say that

---

[2] Ernie Pyle, *Brave Men* (New York: Holt, Rinehart, and Winston, Inc., 1944), p. 116.

[3] David Lloyd George in *British Historical and Political Orations*, Everyman's Library Edition (New York: E. P. Dutton & Co., Inc.), pp. 342-343.

"basically" we swap our personal services for the goods we consume. This idea makes a great deal of sense. Just the same, exchange works as smoothly as it does only because we have a monetary system. Try bartering potatoes for an automobile, needles for a house, shirts for a bicycle, or singing for a haircut! You would be very lucky to find somebody who wanted what you had and had what you wanted — let alone to match up the amounts offered in a way satisfactory to both.

Even more fundamental is the function of the dollar as a *unit* of *account*. Comparison of values is made workable by stating them in a common unit. If the seller of shirts who wanted a bicycle found one bicycle seller calling for twenty bushels of potatoes, another for two auto tires, and a third for a weekend at the seashore, it would be a job in itself to figure out which was the best offer. . . . Still further, we need *debt* to enable us to do business without having to make too many separate payments. While it is no inconvenience to deal on a strict cash-and-carry basis for groceries and shoeshines, we draw the line at dropping six successive pennies into the gas meter while the roast is cooking or queuing up every hour at the pay window to collect our last hour's earnings. Practically, we have to let obligations pile up for a while as dollar debts, to be settled at convenient intervals.

The use of money symbols penetrates deeply into our society, and every individual learns to think in money terms.[4]

2. Follow the same procedure with a selection of your own choice: an essay, a descriptive passage from a novel, part of a speech by Winston Churchill, Franklin Roosevelt, or a distinguished contemporary speaker. Or choose a passage from one of the speeches in the Appendix.

3. Write out an introduction for a persuasive speech you would like to give, or for the last speech you gave in class. Read it to the class from the manuscript.

4. If your instructor is willing, try preparing and delivering a complete speech in manuscript. In your preparation, try to put into effect the advice of the chapters on style and delivery as well as what you have learned here about oral reading.

Criticizing Oral Reading

Read again the suggestions for criticism at the ends of Chapters 2

[4] Paul T. Homan, Albert G. Hart, and Arnold W. Sametz, *The Economic Order* (New York: Harcourt, Brace & World, Inc., 1958), p. 58.

and 7. Nearly all of them are relevant to oral reading and should be applied in your criticism. Beyond this, ask these questions:

1. Did the reader demonstrate a complete understanding of the material he read. Did he pronounce words correctly and appear to know their exact meaning? Was he sensitive to connotations, irony, and symbolism?

2. Did he utilize the natural rhythms of his material without surrendering meaning to rhythm? Was he aware of words which needed to be subordinated as well as those which needed to be stressed?

3. Was the reader successful in responding fully to his material without losing contact with the audience? Was he both natural and effective?

APPENDIX

JOHN JAY CHAPMAN
The Unity of Human Nature

A NISEI STUDENT
Our Greatest Wartime Blunder

MARK TWAIN
New England Weather

DWIGHT D. EISENHOWER
A President Campaigns, Oct. 8, 1954

ADLAI E. STEVENSON
Adlai Stevenson Replies: Hollywood Bowl, Oct. 9, 1954

The Unity of Human Nature

By John Jay Chapman[1]

*This address by John Jay Chapman (1862–1933) was deliv-
ered before the Phi Beta Kappa Society at Hobart College,
Geneva, New York, on Commencement Day, June 20, 1900.
The principles developed by the speaker are ageless; only the
examples are dated — though some are oddly prophetic. Some
parts of the original text have been omitted, but the main
theme of the speech has been left untouched. As you read this
speech, determine the central idea and phrase it in one or two
concise sentences. How does this idea apply to you, more than
a half century later?*

*Study the speech to find instances of speech techniques dis-
cussed in this book. Can you find undeveloped examples, developed examples, direct and rhetorical questions, parallel structure, variety in sentence structure within a paragraph, contrast
and comparison, and other devices? How do these techniques
help the speaker make his idea clear, interesting, and believable?*

If one could stand on the edge of the moon and look down
through a couple of thousand years on human politics, it would be
apparent that everything that happened on the earth is directly dependent on everything else that happened there. . . . Constitutional
government in England qualifies the whole of western Europe. Our
slaves were not set free without the assistance of every liberal mind

---

[1] First appeared in *Modern Eloquence,* Edited by Thomas B. Reed, The
University Society: John B. Morris Company, Philadelphia, 1900.

in Europe; and the thoughts which we think in our closet affect the fate of the Boer in South Africa. That Tolstoi is to-day living unmolested upon his farm instead of serving in a Siberian mine, that Dreyfus is alive and not dead, is due directly to the people in this audience and to others like them scattered over Europe and America.

The effect of enlightenment on tyranny is not merely to make the tyrant afraid to be cruel, it makes him not want to be cruel. It makes him see what cruelty is. And reciprocally the effect of cruelty on enlightenment is to make that enlightenment grow dim. It prevents men from seeing what cruelty is.

The Czar of Russia cannot get rid of your influence, nor you of his. Every ukase he signs makes allowance for you, and on the other hand, the whole philosophy of your life is tinged by him. You believe that the abuses under the Russian Government are inscrutably different from and worse than our own; whereas both sets of atrocities are identical in principle, and are more alike in fact, in taste and smell and substance than your prejudice is willing to admit. The existence of Russia narrows America's philosophy, and misconduct by a European power may be seen reflected in the moral tone of your clergyman on the following day. . . .

Let us for the moment put aside every dictate of religion and political philosophy. Let us discard all prejudice and all love. Let us regard nothing but facts. Does not the coldest conclusion of science announce the fact that the world is peopled, and that every individual of that population has an influence upon the conduct of all the rest, an influence as certain and far more discoverable than the influence of the weight of his body upon the solar system?

A . . . [Chinese immigrant] lands in San Francisco. The Constitution of the United States begins to rock and tremble. What shall we do with him? The deepest minds of the past must be ransacked to the bottom to find an answer. Every one of seventy million Americans must pass through a throe of thought that leaves him a modified man. The same thing is true when the American lands in China. These creatures have thus begun to think of each other. And out of their thoughts grows the destiny of mankind.

We have an inherited and stupid notion that the East does not change. If Japan goes through a transformation scene under our eyes, we still hold to our prejudice as to the immutability of the Chinese. If our own people and the European nations seem to be meeting and surging and reappearing in unaccustomed roles every ten years, till modern history looks like a fancy ball, we still go on muttering some old ignorant shibboleth about East and West, Magna Charta, the Indian mutiny, and Mahomet. The chances are that England will be dead-letter, and Russia progressive, before we have done talking. Of a truth, when we consider the rapidity of visible change and the amplitude of time, — for there is plenty of time, — we need not despair of progress.

The true starting-point for the world's progress will never be reached by any nation as a whole. It exists and has been reached in the past as it will in the future by individuals scattered here and there in every nation. It is reached by those minds which insist on seeing conditions as they are, and which cannot confine their thoughts to their own kitchen, or to their own creed, or to their own nation. . . . There have always been men who in their daily life have fulfilled those intimations and instincts which, if reduced to a statement, receive the names of poetry and religion. These men are the cart-horses of progress; they devote their lives to doing things which can only be justified or explained by the highest philosophy. They proceed as if all men were their brothers. These practical philanthropists go plodding on through each century and leave the bones of their character mingled with the soil of their civilization. . . .

Every one knows that self-sacrifice is a virtue. The child takes his nourishment from the tale of heroism as naturally as he takes milk. He feels that the deed was done for his sake. He adopts it; it is his own. The nations have always stolen their myths from one another and claimed each other's heroes. It has required all the world's heroes to make the world's ear sensitive to new statements, illustrations and applications of the logic of progress. Yet their work has been so well done that all of us respond to the old truths in however new a form. Not France alone but all modern society owes a debt of gratitude to Zola for his rescue of Dreyfus. The whole world would have been degraded and set back, the whole world made less decent and habitable but for those few Frenchmen who took their stand against corruption.

Now the future of civil society upon the earth depends upon the application to international politics of this familiar idea, which we see prefigured in our mythology, and monumentalized in our hospitals — the principle that what is done for one is done for all. When you say a thing is "right," you appeal to mankind. What you mean is that every one is at stake. Your attack upon wrong amounts to saying that some one has been left out in the calculation. Both at home and abroad you are always pleading for mercy, and the plea gains such a wide response that some tyranny begins to totter, and its engines are turned upon you to get you to stop. This outcry against you is the pressure of your effectiveness. If you imitate Zola and attack some nuisance in this town tomorrow you will bring on every symptom and have every experience of the Dreyfus affair. The cost is the same, for cold looks are worse than imprisonment. The emancipation is the same, for if a man can resist the influences of his townsfolk, if he can cut free from the tyranny of neighborhood gossip, the world has no terrors for him; there is no second inquisition. The influence is the same, for every citizen can thereafter look a town officer in the face with more self-respect. But not to townsmen, nor to neighboring towns, nor to Parisians in this force confined. It goes out in all directions, continuously. The man is in communication with the world. This impulse of communication with all men is at the bottom of every ambition. The injustice, cruelty, oppression in the world are all different forms of the same non-conductor, that prevents utterances, that stops messages, that strikes dumb the speaker and deafens the listener. You will find that it makes no difference whether the non-conductor be a selfish oligarchy, a military autocracy, or a commercial ring. The voice of humanity is stifled by corruption: and corruption is only an evil because it stifles men.

Try to raise a voice that shall be heard from here to Albany and watch what it is that comes forward to shut off the sound. It is not a German sergeant, nor a Russian officer of the precinct. It is a note from a friend of your father's offering you a place in his office. This is your warning from the secret police. Why, if any of you young gentlemen have a mind to get heard a mile off, you must make a bonfire of your reputation, and a close enemy of most men who wish you well.

And what will you get in return? Well, if I must for the benefit of the economists, charge you up with selfish gain, I will say that you get the satisfaction of having been heard, and that this is the whole possible scope of human ambition.

When I was asked to make this address I wondered what I had to say to you boys who are graduating. And I think I have one thing to say. If you wish to be useful, never take a course that will silence you. Refuse to learn anything that you cannot proclaim. Refuse to accept anything that implies collusion, whether it be a clerkship or a curacy, a legal fee or a post in a university. Retain the power of speech, no matter what other power you lose. If you can, take this course, and in so far as you take it, you will bless this country. In so far as you depart from this course you become dampers, mutes, and hooded executioners. As for your own private character it will be preserved by such a course. Crime you cannot commit, for crime gags you. Collusion gags you. As a practical matter a mere failure to speak out upon occasions where no opinion is asked or expected of you, and when the utterance of an uncalled-for suspicion is odious, will often hold you to a concurrence in palpable iniquity. It will bind and gag you and lay you dumb and in shackles like the veriest serf in Russia. I give you this one rule of conduct. Do what you will, but speak out always. Be shunned, be hated, be ridiculed, be scared, be in doubt, but don't be gagged.

The choice of Hercules was made when Hercules was a lad. It cannot be made late in life. It will perhaps come for each one of you within the next eighteen months. I have seen ten years of young men who rush out into the world with messages, and when they find how deaf the world is, they think they must save their strength and get quietly up on some little eminence from which they can make themselves heard. "In a few years," reasons one of them, "I shall have gained a standing, and then I shall use my power for good." Next year comes, and with it a strange discovery. The man has lost his horizon of thought. His ambition has evaporated; he has nothing to say. The great occasion that was to have let him loose on society was some little occasion that nobody saw, some moment in which he decided to obtain a standing. The great battle of a lifetime has been fought and lost over a silent scruple. But for this, the man might, within a few years, have spoken to the nation with the voice of an archangel. What was he waiting for? Did he think that the laws of nature were to be changed for him? Did he think that a "notice of trial" would be served on him? Or that some spirit would stand at his elbow and say, "Now's your time?" The time of trial is always. Now is the appointed time. And the compensation for beginning at once is that your voice carries at once. You do nót need a standing. It would not help you. Within less time than you can see it, you will have been heard. The air is filled with sounding-boards and the echoes are flying. It is ten to one that you have but to lift your voice to be heard in California, and that from where you stand. A bold plunge will teach you that the visions of the unity of human nature which the poets have sung were not fictions of their imagination, but a record of what they saw. Deal with the world, and you will discover their reality. Speak to the world, and you will hear their echo.

Social and business prominence look like advantages, and so they are if you want money. But if you want moral influence you may bless God you have not got them. They are the payment with which the world subsidizes men to keep quiet, and there is no subtlety or cunning by which you can get them without paying in silence. This is the great law of humanity, that has existed since history began, and will last while man lasts — evil, selfishness, and silence are one thing.

The world is learning, largely through American experience, that freedom in the form of a government is no guarantee against abuse, tyranny, cruelty, and greed. The old sufferings, the old passions are in full blast among us. What, then, are the advantages of self-government? The chief advantage is that self-government enables a man in his youth, in his own town, within the radius of his first public interests, to fight the important battle of his life while his powers are at their strongest, and the powers of oppression are at their weakest. If a man acquires the power of speech here, if he says what he means now, if he makes his point and dominates his surroundings at once, his voice will, as a matter of fact, be heard instantly in a very wide radius. And so he walks up into a new sphere and begins to accomplish great things. He does this through the very force of his insistence on the important of small things. The reason for his graduation is not far to seek. A man cannot reach the hearts of his townsfolk, without using the whole apparatus of the world of thought. He cannot tell or act the truth in his own town without enlisting every power for truth, and setting in vibration the cords that knit that town into the world's history. He is forced to find and strike the same note which he would use on some great occasion when speaking for all mankind. A man who has won a town fight is a veteran, and the country is full of these young men. Tomorrow their force will show in national politics, and in that moment the fate of the Malay, the food of the Russian prisoner, the civilization of South Africa and the future of Japan will be seen to have been in issue. These things are now being settled in the contest over the town pump in a Western village. I think it likely that the next thirty years will reveal the recuperative power of American institutions. One of you young men might easily become a reform President, and be carried into office and held in office by the force of that private opinion which is now being sown broadcast throughout the country by just such men as yourselves. You will concede the utility of such a President. Yet it would not be the man but the masses behind him that did his work.

Democracy thus lets character loose upon society and shows us that in the realm of natural law there is nothing either small or great; and this is the chief value of democracy. In America the young man meets the struggle between good and evil in the easiest form in which it was ever laid before men. The cruelties of interest and of custom have with us no artificial assistance from caste, creed, race prejudice. Our frame of government is drawn in close accordance with the laws of nature. By our documents we are dedicated to mankind; and hence it is that we can so easily feel the pulse of the world and lay our hand on the living organism of humanity.

B

Our Greatest Wartime Blunder

By a Nisei Student

Unless you are older than your fellow students, you will not remember Pearl Harbor, or the evacuation of the Japanese from the West Coast during the months following the outbreak of war. Both this speaker and his audience, many of them veterans of World War II, did remember. In this moving speech, delivered before a class early in 1949, the speaker bitterly condemned the evacuation and appealed to his listeners to avoid similar incidents in the future. As you read the speech, notice the impact of the personal examples; the effective blending of personal and research materials; the use of statistics and quotations; the stylistic devices such as questions, fragments, and variety in sentence length.

December 7th, 1941, just a little over seven years ago, as you all know, Japan attacked Pearl Harbor. At that time most of us were still in our teens. What did you feel? Shock? Anger? Fear? Mixed emotions? Probably so — I too felt as you, perhaps to a greater degree. Japan was the land where my Mom and Dad came from, and I because of my family ties and my appearance, felt the shock of the attack many fold. It couldn't happen — it couldn't. I refused to believe the first reports; I refused because my dreams were stronger — my dreams that my position as an American of Japanese ancestry would yield opportunities for me and others like me to aid in linking the differences between East and West. To me this position of a liaison was most cherished indeed! As the reports filtered over the wires more and more I was forced to believe the awful truth. WAR!

What happened to me in the next four years resulted in what many have termed America's worst wartime blunder. I was uprooted from my home in Berkeley where I was a student. Before I go into the direct causes of evacuation allow me to give you a brief survey of the Japanese in America. The anti-Oriental and anti-foreign agitation can be traced to the cries of the forty-niners. They went like this:

> If foreigners come, let them till the soil and make roads, or do any other work that may suit them, but the gold mines are preserved by nature for Americans only, who possess noble hearts.

Taking into consideration the anti-Japanese feeling which characterizes the history of California with its laws prohibiting Japanese aliens from owning land, the exclusion act, mob violence, and so on, the immigrant alien did quite well for himself. In 1940 the Japanese produced more than $37,000,000 worth of crops. In California alone the aliens produced:

95% of fresh beans
51% of beans for canning
40% of fresh green peas
67% of the tomatoes
95% of spring and summer celery
and so on

In the production of fresh vegetables the Japanese had a near monopoly. The great majority of cut flowers in California were produced by Japanese. The produce markets of Los Angeles alone employed over five thousand men with an annual business of over $25,000,000. Over half of San Francisco's great Chinatown was owned and operated by Japanese.

I speak of the Japanese as such because the second generation, my generation, played only a small part in the economic life of California. It may be interesting to note that the average age of American-born Japanese at the beginning of the war wasn't quite twenty years. So you see, we, the second generation, were still in school, and it was our parents, who barely knew the English language, who had attained this niche in California's economy.

We were justly proud of this economic position of an immigrant group, small in number. But it was this position, plus California's history of anti-Japanese discrimination, that spelled internment behind barbed wire fences for us.

It was not military necessity that put us away in the desert for four years. It was plain ruthless racial discrimination under the film of military necessity. It was the work of agricultural and business interests who envied the Japanese accomplishments. It was the work of lobbyists sent by these interests to Washington who cooperated with the southern "crackers" to keep the Negroes in place, in exchange for support against the Japanese in California. It was the work of newspapers, radios and Chambers of Commerce — Los Angeles being most active. It was election year and anti-Oriental agitation was a strong plank in any platform.

Eugene V. Rostow, professor of law at Yale, called it our "worst wartime mistake." He says:

> The dominant element was race prejudice, not a military estimate of a military problem. One hundred thousand persons were sent to concentration camps on a record which wouldn't support a conviction for stealing a dog.

I ask you, fellow students, was this act on the part of the Government constitutional? At the outbreak of the war, at the very most I expected to be separated from my parents who were aliens through no fault of theirs. By law they were not allowed naturalization; but for two-thirds of the Japanese population, the American citizens to be corralled into virtual concentration camps under a flimsy guise of military necessity just wasn't in the books. Are not we citizens guaranteed the same rights accorded to you? Am I not, too, innocent until proved guilty? There were no charges against me. I had no hearing. As one writer put it: "My only crime is the color of my skin." Dean Monroe E. Deutsch had this to say at the time of evacuation:

> These people who are being evacuated have had no charges against them individually; they are not guilty of misconduct. Personally I feel that our country will some day feel ashamed of its conduct of this entire matter.

But, Dean, General DeWitt who was in charge of this evacuation had this to say:

> The Japanese race is an enemy race and while many second- and third-generation Japanese born on U.S. soil, possessed of U.S. citizenship, have become "Americanized," the racial strains are undiluted.

By this argument every German-American was fighting on Hitler's side and every Italian-American for Mussolini. And our own Mayor Bowron in support of General DeWitt had this to say:

> I may say that I was quite active in getting the Japanese out of Los Angeles.

General DeWitt's claim for the evacuation was that it was for military reasons. I ask you, students, if we of Japanese ancestry are a military threat, how about the Japanese in Hawaii? Was not Hawaii a more strategic military area than California? If the Japanese citizens were to be interned en masse, how about the Germans and Italians? Not that I would support such a case, but why no mass evacuation of them? Any one with any sense will tell you that a German or an Italian would be in a much better position to commit an act of sabotage than a Japanese for obvious physical reasons. But, as you know, there was no mass evacuation of Germans and Italians. It is important also to note that before the mass evacuation of the west coast, to be exact, February 24, 1942, the O.W.I. released a report that no acts of sabotage or espionage by Japanese aliens or citizens in Hawaii had been recorded. A similar report on June 14, 1942, applied to the Japanese on the mainland.

In the spring of '42 this mass evacuation began. Who were some of the people who went or were scheduled to go? I was one, a student of seventeen years. Another was a close friend who was serving his internship at the University of California Medical School. Before Pearl Harbor, some time in October, he had volunteered his services for the army only to be turned down. After Pearl Harbor he again volunteered; again he was turned down on racial grounds. Professor Obata, a name famous in art at the University of California was another. One who didn't make the long trek was Hideo Murata. Having served in World War I, he received his most treasured possession — an Honorary Citizenship Certificate. When he

heard all Japanese were to be evacuated he went to see his friend
the sheriff, to find out if veterans and honorary citizens would be
included in the order. There were no exceptions, the sheriff told
him. Murata hired a hotel room, paid for it in advance, took poison
and died with the certificate of honorary citizenship in his pocket.
There was a man named Schultz who had a Japanese wife, a Farrer,
a Smith — just anyone who had an ounce of Japanese blood in his
veins — all in all one hundred ten thousand of us left, of whom
seventy thousand were women and children. To remain behind one
had to be a hospitalized tubercular, or mad. We were the people —
the majority of us who are American citizens — who never saw
Japan in our lives — were to undergo this four or five years of
humiliation. For us, the younger set, it was not so much the physical
discomforts of internment. It was like a mental slap in the face, or
a low blow, struck when we were down, by the only government we
knew, to be guarded throughout the whole internment by search-
lights, guardtowers, M.P.'s, barbed wire fences, and rifles.

The evacuation was profitable for those who sought to exploit the
troubled Japanese who had to leave home on incredibly short notice.
A legionnaire offered to care for drug store equipment which an
evacuee wasn't able to sell before leaving. The druggist gave the
legionnaire complete power of attorney, but never received any accounting of his possessions. When officials investigated they found
the legionnaire guilty not only in this case but others in which he
sold the property and pocketed the money. The facts were presented
to the Los Angeles District Attorney's office which stated that it
was not interested in filing charges. Innumerable cases similar to
this have been recorded.

In this mass movement our first stop was in a temporary Assembly Center. Santa Anita was one; mine was Tanforan. Hardships
were numerous, but being treated as a criminal by the only government I knew was worse. I was bitter, yes, very bitter. Maybe
I shouldn't have been but wouldn't you be if you were pushed
around, and ended up living in a stable? As I look back at those
gloomy four months my sister's plight comes to me, for she was
pregnant at that time. To see her eat uncomplainingly potatoes,
macaroni, and beans almost daily was almost enough to make me
break. What kind of food is that for a pregnant woman? Starch,
starch, and more starch!

Then after four months we were transferred literally from the frying pan into the fire — to one of the centers, all located in desert areas. I was sent to Utah. The barren desert was bad enough but the constant cyclonic storms loaded with dust and sand were worse. We slept in the dust; we breathed the dust; we ate the dust. Yes, we the American citizens of Japanese descent. My sister at this time gave birth to her baby in this blistering dust bowl. To keep the baby inside the barracks to avoid the dust and heat was of little help. To this day I can picture my nephew crying weakly under the bed which was his inadequate refuge from the heat and dust which were always there.

Our camp in the deep Utah desert was one mile square and twenty miles from any form of habitation. Every fifty yards was posted a watch tower and between towers were barbed wire fences. According to Army rules the fence and guard towers were so erected to protect us from rowdies from outside. In the summer of '43 one evening at 5:00 P.M. Mr. Kashima, a man of seventy, was walking with his dog close to the fence. A few minutes later the man fell dead with a bullet through his heart — a bullet from the M.P. who was in the adjoining watch tower. Why an innocent old man was shot was difficult for us to see. This man wasn't trying to escape; he was shot on his side of the fence. Even if he did try to escape, how far could he get in the desert? Was not, as the Army said, the fence to protect us from elements outside? Or were we to be victims of "pot-shots" if we merely approached the fence? Imagine the psychological effect of just this one incident on us — the young citizens. And then to hear that the soldier went stark free kept us in constant fear and away from the fence.

Then again there was young Joe Okamoto who had a brother in the service who was shot at close range and killed by an M.P. At this incident Secretary of the Interior Ickes issued an indignant radio and press release, calling the shooting *"completely unwarranted and without provocation on the part of the victim."* Feeling in camp was tense, and tenser yet when news came that the soldier was acquitted. Other incidents of similar nature are very familiar to me — but so much for today.

The evacuation of 70,000 citizens has been called by some not only a national blunder but an international blunder as well. It did the United States untold damage in India and southeast Asia. Broadcasts monitored by the Foreign Broadcast Intelligence Service showed how the militarists of Japan used the evacuation to incite hatred among the people of Asia against the white man. A Negro soldier in the South Pacific told me that he heard a special propaganda radio program beamed especially to Negro troops on this subject by the Japanese government. And what a setting it furnished for the United Nations Conference in San Francisco in which to develop means by which men of all races can live together in peace!

The evacuation shouldn't have happened. It didn't need to happen, and it is up to you to see that such an episode doesn't happen again to mar our national and international history.

C

New England Weather

By Mark Twain

Although Mark Twain is best known as a writer of stories about the Mississippi River and the West, he was also much in demand in his own time as a public speaker. He often appeared on the lecture platform, sometimes reading from his books, and was also a popular speaker in the more informal after-dinner situation.

Perhaps his two most famous after-dinner speeches are "Babies" and "New England Weather." In the latter speech, delivered before the New England Society, December 22, 1876, Mark Twain's primary theme is the unpredictability of New England weather. As was his custom on such occasions, he developed his subject with outrageous exaggerations. The humor of the speech, however, lies less in the magnitude of the falsehood than in its recognizable resemblance to truth.

At the end, the speech is given a serious and poetic twist by the description of the beauties of a New England ice storm. Such a conclusion leaves the audience with a warm and positive note, and the barbed humor is remembered only as a background.

Gentlemen, — I reverently believe that the Maker who makes us all makes everything in New England but the weather.

I don't know who makes that, but I think it must be raw apprentices in the Weather Clerk's factory, who experiment and learn how in New England for board and clothes, and then are promoted to make weather for countries that require a good article and will take their custom elsewhere if they don't get it.

There is a sumptuous variety about the New England weather that compels the stranger's admiration — and regret.

The weather is always doing something there; always attending strictly to business; always getting up new designs and trying them on the people to see how they will go.

But it gets through more business in spring than in any other season. In the spring I have counted one hundred and thirty-six different kinds of weather inside of four and twenty hours.

It was I that made the fame and fortune of that man that had that marvellous collection of weather on exhibition at the Centennial that so astounded the foreigners. He was going to travel all over the world and get specimens from all the climes. I said, "Don't you do it; you come to New England on a favorable spring day." I told him what we could do in the way of style, variety, and quantity.

Well, he came, and he made his collection in four days.

As to variety — why, he confessed that he got hundreds of kinds of weather that he had never heard of before. And as to quantity — well, after he had picked out and discarded all that was blemished in any way, he not only had weather enough, but weather to spare; weather to hire out; weather to sell; to deposit; weather to invest; weather to give to the poor.

The people of New England are by nature patient and forbearing; but there are some things which they will not stand. Every year they kill a lot of poets for writing about "Beautiful Spring."

These are generally casual visitors, who bring their notions of spring from somewhere else, and cannot, of course, know how the natives feel about spring. And so, the first thing they know, the opportunity to inquire how they feel has permanently gone by.

Old Probabilities has a mighty reputation for accurate prophecy and thoroughly well deserves it. You take up the papers and observe how crisply and confidently he checks off what to-day's weather is going to be on the Pacific, down South, in the Middle States, in the Wisconsin region; see him sail along in the joy and pride of his power till he gets to New England, and then, — see his tail drop.

He doesn't know what the weather is going to be in New England. He can't any more tell than he can tell how many Presidents of the United States there's going to be next year.[1] Well, he mulls over it,

---

[1] A reference to the Tilden-Hayes election, not yet decided at the time of the speech, six weeks after the balloting was complete.

and by and by he gets out something about like this: Probable nor'east to sou'west winds, varying to the southard and westard and eastard and points between; high and low barometer, sweeping around from place to place; probable areas of rain, snow, hail, and drought, succeeded or preceded by earthquakes, with thunder and lightning.

Then he jots down this postscript from his wandering mind to cover accidents: "But it is possible that the program may be wholly changed in the mean time."

Yes, one of the brightest gems in the New England weather is the dazzling uncertainty of it. There is only one thing certain about it, you are certain there is going to be plenty of weather — a perfect grand review; but you never can tell which end of the procession is going to move first. You fix up for the drought; you leave your umbrella in the house and sally out with your sprinkling-pot, and ten to one you get drowned.

You make up your mind that the earthquake is due; you stand from under and take hold of something to steady yourself, and, the first thing you know, you get struck by lightning.

These are great disappointments. But they can't be helped. The lightning there is peculiar; it is so convincing! When it strikes a thing it doesn't leave enough of that thing behind for you to tell whether — well, you'd think it was something valuable, and a Congressman had been there.

And the thunder. When the thunder commences to merely tune up, and scrape, and saw, and key up the instruments for the performance, strangers say, "Why, what awful thunder you have here!" But when the baton is raised and the real concert begins, you'll find that stranger down in the cellar, with his head in the ash-barrel.

Now, as to the size of the weather in New England — lengthways, I mean. It is utterly disproportioned to the size of that little country. Half the time, when it is packed as full as it can stick, you will see that New England weather sticking out beyond the edges and projecting around hundreds and hundreds of miles over the neighboring States. She can't hold a tenth part of her weather. You can see cracks all about, where she has strained herself trying to do it.

I could speak volumes about the inhuman perversity of the New England weather, but I will give but a single specimen. I like to hear rain on a tin roof, so I covered part of my roof with tin, with an eye to that luxury. Well, sir, do you think it ever rains on the tin? No, sir; skips it every time.

Mind, in this speech I have been trying merely to do honor to the New England weather; no language could do it justice.

But, after all, there are at least one or two things about that weather (or, if you please, effects produced by it) which we residents would not like to part with.

If we had not our bewitching autumn foliage, we should still have to credit the weather with one feature which compensates for all its bullying vagaries — the ice-storm — when a leafless tree is clothed with ice from the bottom to the top — ice that is as bright and clear as crystal; every bough and twig is strung with ice-beads, frozen dew-drops, and the whole tree sparkles, cold and white, like the Shah of Persia's diamond plume.

Then the wind waves the branches, and the sun comes out and turns all those myriads of beads and drops to prisms that glow and hum and flash with all manner of colored fires, which change and change again, with inconceivable rapidity, from blue to red, from red to green, and green to gold; the tree becomes a sparkling fountain, a very explosion of dazzling jewels; and it stands there the acme, the climax, the supremest possibility in art or nature of bewildering, intoxicating, intolerable magnificence! One cannot make the words too strong.

Month after month I lay up hate and grudge against the New England weather; but when the ice-storm comes at last I say, "There, I forgive you now; the books are square between us; you don't owe me a cent; go and sin some more; your little faults and foibles count for nothing; you are the most enchanting weather in the world!"

A President Campaigns:
Denver, October 8, 1954

By Dwight D. Eisenhower

This speech and the one by Adlai E. Stevenson which follows are more or less typical of contemporary political speaking. Obviously, these addresses deal with broader and more complex issues than those you will be handling in class speeches. Yet the principles of audience adaptation, organization, and occasionally of style and delivery, are much the same — in class or before the nation.

There are, however, some obvious differences between these speeches and the ones you should be making. Reassured by the knowledge that partisan audiences ask for little in the way of example and proof, political speakers frequently rely on broad and unsupported generalization. In these two speeches, notice how often the utility of the speakers' generalization depends on the audience's willingness to grant immediate acceptance. Notice also that some generalizations or idea statements are given support, but by undeveloped rather than developed examples. Political audiences either accept undeveloped examples at full value or willingly supply in their own thinking the necessary developmental details.

President Eisenhower delivered the following speech before a Republican rally in the Denver City Auditorium in the fall campaign of the off-year Congressional elections of 1954. During the week before its delivery, the President had been in frequent

*conference with party leaders, including Vice-President Nixon,
Speaker Joe Martin, Congressman Charles Halleck, and National Chairman Leonard Hall. Public opinion polls had shown
a clear need for the Republicans to bring the President's office
and wide personal popularity into the campaign. Thus Eisenhower, in a nationally televised broadcast, appeared before the
electorate and asked for a Republican Congress.*

Governor Thornton, Mr. Vice-President, distinguished leaders of
the Congress, members of this great audience, and my good friends,
over all of America:

Tonight, as I speak to my countrymen, I am privileged to address
myself especially to my fellow Republican workers, gathered here
in Denver and in meetings throughout our land. To each of you
— to your families, to your friends, and to your political associates
— I send my warmest greetings.

All of us are happy that tonight Mr. Nixon, Speaker Joe Martin,
and the other members of our able legislative team are here with
us. Under the leadership of these men, the Eighty-third Congress
made its record of extraordinary success. They have my respect and
admiration for the splendid service they have rendered to the American people.

Tonight, in our meetings over America, we come together as
members of the Republican party. But in spirit we have also with
us the vast army of other Americans who in 1952, and since, have
fought alongside us for the great plans and programs for which
together we stand.

We assemble here, and all over America, proud of our party's
principles — proud of our party's record.

Now, what are these principles and that record, and as Republicans, what is our goal?

That goal is not political power for its own sake, but to advance
the good of 163 million Americans.

To that end, we are dedicated to the maximum of individual freedom, fostered by a government desiring not to dominate but only
to serve — a government kept close to the hearthsides of America —
a government liberal in dealing with the human concerns of the
people, but conservative in spending their money. From Lincoln's
day to this these have been the fundamental aims of our historic
party.

Republicans believe that such government will best preserve liberty and justice, and prosperity and happiness in our land.

Such a government will best promote an enduring peace throughout the world.

These are the convictions that unite us; this is the cause that inspires us — and our friends — to continued and dedicated effort.

Two years ago the people of our country showed their desire for this kind of government.

Remember Election Day 1952. In the early hours of morning, in thousands of precincts over America, our citizens eagerly lined up to vote long before the polls were open.

Do you remember why Americans crowded to the polls on November 4, 1952?

Let's think back.

Two years ago Americans wanted an end to the war in Korea. It was a costly war, allowed to become futile, and seemingly without end.

They wanted something done about our veterans, who suddenly found the country so poorly prepared that they themselves had once again to undergo the dangers of battle, while others remained at home who had never served.

Americans wanted a government thrifty and frugal with the public's money.

They wanted a stop to the endless rise in taxes, taking more and more of the family income to support an overgrown Washington bureaucracy.

They wanted something done about inflation — to end the growing discouragement as day by day pensions and savings and the weekly pay check bought less and less at the corner store.

Americans were determined to eliminate penetration by the Communist conspiracy in our government and in our whole society. They did not consider this menace a red herring.

They wanted clean, honest government.

They were anxious to get rid of the antagonism between the Congress and the Executive which hamstrung the processes of government.

All this America wanted two years ago, and you — you, and those like you throughout this great nation — did something about it.

You remember the telephone brigades of two years ago. You remember the "Get Out the Vote" campaigns. You remember the drive, the enthusiasm that in November 1952, surged forth from our people.

And what happened? You got results.

The people of America established in Washington the kind of government they wanted.

In just twenty months, we have come far.

First of all, with the help of thousands of citizens from every walk of life and from every part of America, we devised a comprehensive, progressive program in keeping with the Republican party's platform and the pledges made to America during the campaign. Fundamentally, that program has but one purpose — to make America stronger and better, with growing prosperity and happiness for all of our people.

Now, that program was made up of many parts affecting every phase of the life of our great nation. Some parts could be accomplished quickly. Others necessarily had to be developed slowly over the months, to assure their fitness and effectiveness. Important sections still remain to be enacted. The program is one, therefore, of continuous and simultaneous study and action. Its completion is essential to the future prosperity, security and peace of the people of America.

So, let's consider this program and what has happened since its inception.

Fourteen months ago, the futile sacrifices in Korea were stopped.

We now have clean, honest, decent government in Washington.

Government spending has been sharply reduced. Stifling controls have been removed from our nation's economy, amid dire predictions of carping critics that inflation would follow and prices would soar out of sight.

In twenty months, this Administration and the Republican-led Congress cut our government's costs by $11 billion.

And at last, we have a tax cut!

Taxes were cut $7.4 billion — the largest tax cut in the history of this nation. It brings benefits to every family in every American home.

At the same time, we smoked out 211 thousand unnecessary positions on the Federal payrolls.

All during this time, our government has been returning to private citizens activities traditionally belonging to private citizens.

It is stopping the roasting of coffee, the baking of bread, the making of paint and clothes. It has stopped running a hotel. It has stopped running a tug and barge business on our inland waterways. In keeping with the philosophy of our whole program, all of these activities have been returned to private citizens — exactly where they belong.

My friends, I could never mention this subject without adverting to a statement of our first and greatest leader, Lincoln. He said, "The legitimate business of government is to do for a people or a community those things which they cannot do at all for themselves, or cannot so well do in their separate capacities; but in all those things that people can do for themselves, the government ought not to interfere."

I think no better philosophy for a free government has ever yet been stated.

Now, Americans wanted a strong national defense at less cost.

We have today the strongest armed forces in our peacetime history. In building them we have saved vast funds. We have cut red tape and eliminated duplication and waste. And let me make this clear: our military strength does not consist of forcibly recalled veterans who have already served our nation in war.

But, of course, our people also wanted a strong peacetime economy. For this, the Congress took many steps. It passed, for example, a new housing program. It passed an expanded highway program. It passed a new farm program to stop the seven-year decline in farmers' income — a program to promote lasting farm prosperity in an America no longer at war. And that program was designed also to remove the great surpluses that were breaking the back of the program then existing.

The Congress extended old age and survivors insurance to 10.2 million more Americans, and raised their benefits. And at last, my friends, these benefits include farmers who have been indirectly helping to pay the cost of the social security system all these years. The Congress extended coverage of unemployment compensation to 4 million more Americans. It passed tax revisions to encourage small business, and to eliminate inequities in the law.

Due to these and other measures, we have at last an economy whose strength is not sapped by the virus of inflation. It is an economy that doesn't compel the piling up of debts for our children — an economy whose strength is not dependent upon the sacrifices of the battlefield.

Without the economic collapse so widely forecast by professional pessimists, our nation has moved from war to peace.

Nevertheless, I am keenly aware that in some American localities, dislocations and hardships do exist. These are the inescapable aftermath of war and inflation. These problems we are striving constantly to ease. In the localities concerned, as well as in the rest of the country, we are taking concrete action to foster strength in the whole economy.

There was something else, two years ago, that all of us especially wanted. We wanted subversives out of the government service.

This Administration and the Congress are dealing decisively with the Communist menace. Supported by eleven new laws, we are backing to the hilt the Department of Justice and the FBI. There is no vacillation nor inaction on the part of this Administration in dealing with those who, by force or violence, would overthrow the government of the United States.

And abroad, we have an honest, forthright foreign policy concerned with deeds, not merely words. Over the globe our friends know our devotion to freedom. They know that America joins with those who help themselves in the effort to preserve liberty and peace.

Two years ago, war was raging in Korea and Indo-China. All Asia lay exposed to the steady advance of the Reds. Iran, with 60 per cent of the world's known petroleum reserves, was in deadly danger. Suez and Trieste posed constant threats to peace in the West. Europe had foundered on century-old differences, unable to build a position of reliable strength. Even in the Western Hemisphere, Communist imperialism had ominously appeared.

You know of the events that have since occurred.

In London, a few days ago, an agreement of momentous significance was signed that can powerfully strengthen the defenses of the West. Just this week, after almost a decade of anxious effort, Yugoslavia and Italy, with the encouragement and help of the Western world, settled their differences over Trieste.

For the first time in twenty years, there is no active battlefield anywhere in the world.

And, at last, we are harnessing the atom to the work of peace.

As for nations which, despite our best efforts, are still unfriendly, they harbor no delusions about the determination and the growing strength of the free world.

Recently, Communist imperialism discovered that the entire Association of American Republics means business in defending freedom.

First at Caracas, then in ten short, determined days, the Communist beachhead in Guatemala was eliminated.

In all these ways, then, there has been progress of the most tremendous import to the peace and security of the Western world. Much of this progress is due to the richness of experience, imagination and determination of our distinguished Secretary of State. He and his colleagues in the State Department and the Foreign Service are carrying American prestige to new heights in foreign chancelleries.

Fellow citizens, I have recited some of the advances made in many fields in a short twenty months. For the most part, they have grown out of a cordial partnership between the Administration and the Congress. This cordiality has been a welcome relief from the bickering and the suspicion that for so long poisoned relations between the executive and legislative branches. In laws passed, and in heightened respect for their government, this harmony has brought immense benefits to the American people.

And now, let's take a quick look at the future.

Many things need to be done.

We must continue to foster the growth of a free economy to provide more jobs and higher living standards.

We must continue our efforts to cut the cost of government, so we can cut taxes still more.

We must continue each year to improve our peacetime farm program.

We must have a vast new highway program.

We must expand our foreign trade and American investment abroad. We must expand markets for America's farms and factories, if we are to keep prosperity within our own land.

We must write into law a national water resources program.

We must help our people meet their critical health and medical needs, while repudiating socialization of medicine.

We must find ways to encourage communities to provide the schoolhouses they need, and to improve opportunities for their schoolteachers.

We must build a new and effective reserve program for our armed forces.

We must begin to unravel the confused relations between the Federal, state and local governments, and make still more improvements in the organization of the Federal Government.

We must drive through partisan obstructions to achieve statehood for Hawaii, to lower the voting age in Federal elections, and to make our promised changes in the labor-management laws.

We must continue our historic advances in the vital area of civil rights.

We must vigorously push all constructive measures for promoting world peace, always strong and secure, but always fair and conciliatory.

Now, my friends, a cold war of partisan politics between the Congress and the executive branch won't give us these goals.

And this brings up a political fact of life.

You know perfectly well that you just can't have one car with two drivers at the steering wheel and expect to end up any place but in the ditch — especially when the drivers are set on going in different directions. By the same token, you cannot have efficient Federal government when the Congress wants to follow one philosophy of government and the executive branch another.

In our system of government, progress is made when the leaders of the executive branch and the majority of the Congress are members of the same political party. The unsurpassed record of the Eighty-third Congress is shining evidence of this truth. Moreover, in no other way can Americans hold one party and one group of people responsible either for success or lack of success.

History shows that when the executive and legislative branches are politically in conflict, politics in Washington runs riot. In these conditions, the public good goes begging while politics is played for politics' sake. Meanwhile, in the eyes of the world, we appear divided in council and uncertain in purpose.

These are the reasons — the compelling reasons — why the completion of your great program requires the election of a Republican-led Congress.

In our effort to keep the kind of government we want, you citizens are on the political front lines — the precincts of America. There you are as much a part of government as the sincere, hard-working men and women in Washington today who are trying to give you the kind of government you want.

As leaders and workers in your precincts, you know that the members of our party cannot carry this battle alone. We must enlist the spirited support of friends and neighbors, regardless of party, who believe in the same principles and objectives. Happily, we have been blessed with millions of such sturdy allies. For the cause in which we believe is bigger than any political party. To this cause, all Americans, regardless of party, can give their enthusiastic support.

And in this struggle, I know you will have the same determination — the same enthusiasm — the same drive — as you had two years ago.

For only through your effort can our program continue to advance.

Only through your effort will we continue to have the kind of America all of us so earnestly desire.

Together, my friends, we shall forge ahead in this great work we have so well begun, determined to keep America strong and secure — determined that this land of freedom, under Almighty God, will not rest until we see in the world a lasting peace with justice. Together we shall forge ahead to build in our America a steadily growing prosperity and happiness that will bring an ever brighter future for our people and for those who, after we are gone, must carry forward the banner of freedom.

That, my fellow Americans, is our kind of America.

Working together with those millions who have made common cause with us in this effort, that is the kind of America we shall have.

Thank you — thank you — and good night to all of you.

A POLITICAL SPEECH: ANALYSIS OF
WRITTEN AND SPOKEN TEXTS

E

Adlai Stevenson Replies:
Hollywood Bowl, October 9, 1954

ADLAI E. STEVENSON[1]

The day after President Eisenhower's Denver speech, Adlai Stevenson was scheduled to address a Democratic rally in Los Angeles. Forced by the President's remarks to discard the major portion of a speech prepared earlier for the occasion, Stevenson wrote an almost completely new speech between the time of his arrival in the city late on the evening of October 8 and the following evening. He worked on it until 4:30 A.M. of October 9, and during the intervals of a day he described as "hopelessly crowded with an appalling schedule," including hand-shaking, public appearances, a luncheon, and a dinner.

As given in the following pages, the speech offers a rare opportunity to study the response of a practiced speaker to an audience and situation. At the left is the script from which Stevenson read, with his underlinings for emphasis and last-minute changes in longhand. At the right is a transcript of what he actually said. For ease of comparison, additions and substitutions are italicized, and deletions and audience responses are in brackets.

Mr. Stevenson was introduced by Dore Schary of Metro-

---

[1] The speech is reproduced from Ralph Richardson, "Adlai E. Stevenson, Hollywood Bowl, October 9, 1954: His Preparation and His Speaking Manuscript," *Western Speech*, May, 1955. The article contains a detailed account of the circumstances of preparation and an analysis of the occasion and the audience.

Goldwyn-Mayer. As he began, Stevenson gave no hint of the point at which he concluded his preliminary remarks and turned to his prepared speech. Throughout, he demonstrated his interest in his audience by maintaining eye contact at least 75 per cent of the time. The same attitude was shown by the changes he made as he spoke. These were toward greater directness (the use of contractions, repetition, and the insertion of articles), identification with audience and occasion, and increased energy and color in language. In all there were 249 changes from the typed script of the 38-minute speech, of which 204 were made at the moment of delivery. There were 82 audience responses during the speech, and many of the changes came during or just after these interruptions.

Mr. Schary, Distinguished Guests, and Ladies and Gentlemen:[5]

Perhaps I should tell you at once that I'm not running for anything. [Medium laughter 5 seconds] I'm profoundly grateful to you, Mr. Schary, for your most gracious introduction. While I can't agree with everything you said about that man, [Light laughter 2 seconds] I like what you said, [Medium laughter and applause 4 seconds] and I'm sure the Chamber of Commerce of Libertyville, Illinois, will take due note of what you said.

I should say, Mr. Schary, that after the performance that has just preceded us, I should think we could well dispense with my speech, [Medium laughter and "Noes" 3 seconds] because our—my talented friends have told, indeed they've enacted, the Democratic story far better than I could; and to them I should also like to pay my respects.

I'm deeply moved by this vast gathering and the warmth of your greeting to the Democratic candidates and to myself here this evening. I am grateful for your presence and for this reaffirmation of your faith in a great political party—a party that has long endured because it has tried to serve the general welfare of all of the people rather than the special interests of some of the people. [Medium applause 6 seconds] And wedded to that principle the Democratic party will endure as long as democracy endures. [Medium applause 4 seconds]

I am deeply moved by this vast gathering and the warmth of your greeting to the Democratic candidates and myself. I am grateful for your presence and for this reaffirmation of your faith in a great political party -- a party that has long endured because it has tried to serve the general welfare of all the people rather than the special interests of some of the people. And wedded to that principle the Democratic party will endure as long as democracy endures.

That you are here in such numbers tonight -- (and have even paid admission!) -- I count as affirmation of that principle as much as respect for these candidates, or even curiosity about this visitor from Illinois.

Thank you Mr. Schary for your most precious introduction - while I sympathize with all you said - I share it.
— Fellow friends

Now that you are here in such numbers tonight—(and have even paid admission!) [Medium laughter 2 seconds] I [Light laughter by Stevenson] *I* count as *an* affirmation of that principle as much as respect for these candidates *and indeed* curiosity about this *traveler* from Illinois.

I wish the world could see this meeting so that it could better know this country for what it really is—not just a greedy economic giant crouching fearfully behind its walls—*and* not just a panoplied warrior nervously fingering *its* weapons—and not a televised sordid civil war between the officers of our government—but as this—as a people who gather together in thousands to give a people's government its essential vitality. [Heavy applause 9 seconds]

And some day, *my friends*, the world will see again—as it does not now, I regret to say—*it will see again* the vision of the real America—the vision that becomes real in a meeting such as this. And when it does it will be a brighter day for international understanding, for confidence and for peace on earth.

[6] During the time he was being introduced, Governor Stevenson was in the wings of the Bowl. The plate above has been made by superimposing a sheet of pencil tablet paper, on which he jotted notes for response to Schary, above the first page of his reading typescript.

-2-

I wish the world could see this meeting so that it could better know this country for what it really is -- not just a greedy economic giant crouching fearfully behind its walls -- not just a panoplied warrior nervously fingering his weapons -- and not a televised sordid civil war between the officers of our government -- but as this -- as a people who gather together in thousands to give a people's government its essential vitality.

Some day the world will see again -- as it does not now I regret today [to say] -- the vision of the real America -- the vision that becomes real in a meeting such as this. And when it does it will be a brighter day for international understanding, for confidence, for good will and for peace on earth.

So I'm glad [Light applause 2 seconds, produced by paragraph immediately before] *I'm glad to be here tonight. I'm glad to be here in this famous Hollywood Bowl which has become a national institution. And I'm glad to be back in California*—where so many people come to live, while I'm in the unique position of *having been* born here and left. [Medium laughter 3 seconds] I can only plead, *however,* that my departure at the age of 5 was involuntary. [Heavy laughter 3 seconds] I seem to have had, *indeed Mr. Schary,* no more influence on my parents than I had on the voters two years ago. [Heavy laughter 4 seconds]

And it is reassuring to find that there is no truth in the *common* rumor back East that 20 months of Republican performances in Washington have put Hollywood out of business. [Heavy applause 8 seconds] [Disillusionment, it seems, is no substitute for entertainment;] Nor, *I could add,* is showmanship an alternative *for* statesmanship. [Medium laughter 6 seconds] Indeed, the voices *one hears* traveling across the land these days *are* familiar—they sound Democratic—and they even sound that way in California where, for

---

in This famous Hollywood Bowl which has become a national institution

-3-

So I'm glad to be here tonight and to be back in California -- where so many people come to live, while I'm in the unique position of one who was born here and left. I can only plead that my departure at the age of 5 was involuntary. I seem to have had no more influence on my <u>parents</u> than I had on the <u>voters</u> two years ago.

And it is reassuring to find that there is no truth in the rumor back East that 20 months of Republican performances in Washington have put Hollywood <u>out</u> of business. <u>Disillusionment</u>, it seems, is no substitute for entertainment; nor is showmanship an alternative to statesmanship. Indeed, the voices you hear traveling across the land these days sound familiar -- they sound Democratic -- and they even sound that way in California where, for the first time in forty years, the Democratic party has nominated a complete *set* of state and Congressional candidates. [Medium applause 6 seconds] *And* what's more, the only state candidate who received the nomination of both parties was a Democrat, your Chairman tonight, *the* Attorney General, Pat Brown; [Medium applause 8 seconds] *and* only Democrats received both nominations for Congress—and *that's* something new and very heartening. *I have a strong feeling indeed that California is on the eve of a political renaissance.* [Medium applause 4 seconds]

Now I suggest that it's in democracy's finest tradition that we are here tonight to endorse the candidacy of [other] men who are fully qualified for the serious business of government—and I mean Democrats like Dick Graves and Sam Yorty. [Heavy applause 7 seconds]

As a Democrat I particularly envy Californians the opportunity to elect as their Governor a man cast in the mold of [his political mentor and][6] this state's leading

---

[6] Apparently a deletion required by the cross-currents of California politics. The Democratic gubernatorial nominee, Richard Graves, had only a few months before his nomination changed his registration from Republican to Democrat. Prior to that time he had been a close associate of Republican Governor Warren. Sensitive political feelings, it would seem, were best not riled by identifying Graves with his "political mentor." And for the same reason. Stevenson had written in the phrase "as a Democrat," here on page 4, and again on 5.

-4-

the first time in forty years, the Democratic party

has nominated a complete slate of state and

Congressional candidates. What's more, the only

state candidate who received the nomination of both

parties was a Democrat, your Chairman tonight,

Attorney General, Pat Brown; and only Democrats

received both nominations for Congress -- and that

is something very new and very heartening. *[handwritten: I have a strong feeling indeed that]*

[handwritten: California is on the eve of a political renaissance.]
It is in democracy's finest tradition that

we are here tonight to endorse the candidacy of other

men who are fully qualified for the serious business

of government -- and I mean Democrats like Dick

Graves and Sam Yorty.

[handwritten: As a Democrat]
I particularly envy Californians the opportunity

to elect as their Governor a man cast in the mold

of ~~his political mentor~~ and this state's leading

citizen, Chief Justice Earl Warren, whom I [Light applause 1 second] am proud to call my friend, and who also convinced me long ago that there were some very lonesome men in the Republican party. [Heavy laughter and applause 7 seconds] Dick Graves, whose [most] unusual background and intimate knowledge of the problems of government at all levels in this vast state I hope is familiar to every Californian, will, *as a Democrat*, bring back that broadminded, *that* forward-looking leadership which left Sacramento so abruptly with Governor Warren.[7] [Medium laughter and applause 5 seconds]

And I am no less happy that at a time when representative government is under such close and *such* critical scrutiny the world over, we may have the sane counsel and *the* straight thinking in the United States Senate of your fellow townsman— Sam Yorty. [Medium applause 6 seconds] *You know*, as they say elsewhere, if not here, *Mr.* Yorty could

---

[7] A reference to Graves' opponent, Governor Goodwin J. Knight who, as Lieutenant Governor, succeeded to the higher office upon Warren's appointment as Chief Justice of the United States.

-5-

citizen, Chief Justice Earl Warren, whom I am proud to call my friend, and who also convinced me long ago that there were some very lonesome men in the Republican party. Dick Graves, whose *his* unusual background and intimate knowledge of the problems of government at all levels in this vast state I hope is familiar to every Californian, will *as a Democrat* bring back that broadminded, forward-looking leadership which left Sacramento so abruptly with Governor Warren.

And I am no less happy that at a time when representative government is under such close and critical scrutiny the world over, we may have the sane counsel and straight thinking in the United States Senate of your fellow townsman -- Sam Yorty. As they say elsewhere, if not here, Yorty could put at rest the widespread notion that California is a province of Formosa.[8] [Heavy laughter, and applause 6 seconds]

But candidacies gather significance not only from the men themselves but from their political environment. Behind the candidacy of such men as [Dick Graves and Sam Yorty] *these* and the other distinguished *gentlemen who have been introduced to you here* this evening, and more like them all across the nation, there loom important public questions upon which the people will express— wisely *and* soberly, we hope—their convictions this fall.

Now there are doubtless many, *perhaps there are many here this evening,* who have not made up their minds. Some *of them may even* be like *that* old man down in the Ozarks [I heard about the other day. He was standing to one side,] *who was* listening *so* attentively to—*uh—one* of those heated political *debates* outside the [village] *country*

[8] A not too oblique reference to Senator William Knowland's identification of interest with Nationalist China.

-6-

put at rest the widespread notion that California is a province of Formosa.

But candidacies gather significance not only from the men themselves but from their political environment. Behind the candidacy of such men as *these,* ~~Dick Graves and Sam Yorty,~~ and the other distinguished candidates who are here this evening, and more like them all across the nation, there loom important public questions upon which the people will express

-- wisely, soberly, we hope -- their convictions this fall.

Now there are doubtless many who have not made up their minds. Some may be like the old man down in the Ozarks I ~~b~~ *who was* listening attentively to a heated political debate outside the village store. And when one of the combatants *turned to him and* said: "Well, Uncle Lafe, what's your opinion," *he* said: "Well, I'll tell you, son; I ain't made up my mind [yet] how I'm *gonna* vote—but [I can tell you this:] when I *do you can be sure I'm gonna be mighty* bitter. [Medium to heavy laughter 8 seconds]⁹

Well unhappily, bitterness and nonsense have grossly debased our *public* debate in these days when sense and sobriety were never more important. And in the extensive catalogue of Republican sins we might rate in first place the vindictiveness, the reckless words, the personal abuse and the stained and dusty epithets and accusations which are not a substitute for discussion of America's problems. [Heavy applause 9 seconds]

We remember the ugly [shouts] *advice* of Governor Dewey of New York—to think of Democrats when you think

---

⁹ The extensive changes suggest that Stevenson merely glanced down, recognized the anecdote, and gave it a live telling.

-7-

store. And when one of the combatants said: "Well, Uncle Lafe, what's your opinion," the old man said: "Well, I'll tell you, son; I ain't made up my mind yet how I'm going to vote -- but I can tell you this: when I do I sure am going to be bitter."

Unhappily, bitterness and nonsense have grossly debased our political debate in these days when sense and sobriety were never more important. And in the extensive catalogue of Republican sins we might rate in first place the vindictiveness, the reckless words, the personal abuse and the stained and dusty epithets and accusations which are not a substitute for discussion of America's problems.

We remember the ugly ~~charges~~ advice of Governor Dewey of New York -- to think of Democrats when you think of American boys *murdered* in Korea, and to remember the Democratic party as the party of treachery. [Loud "boos" 2 seconds]

And we recall, too, that President Eisenhower's close adviser, *the* Attorney General [Brownell], *the chief law enforcement officer of the United States*, maligned and impugned the very loyalty of a former President of the United States—a man, by the way, who has done more to fight communism on all *of* the fronts of the, *of the* world than all *of* the Republican politicians put together. [Very heavy applause 13 seconds.].[10]

Nor did the Republicans elevate the political dialogue *of our country* or honor our intelligence when their national Chairman set the theme *of their celebration of the birthday, if you please,* of Abraham Lincoln as "20 years of treason".—20 years, by the way, during which General Eisenhower emerged from the obscurity of the Army, and Secretary Dulles from the obscurity of Wall Street. [Medium laughter 6 seconds]

[10] The words, "and I mean Harry S. Truman," were not necessary for recognition and were not spoken.

-8-

of American boys killed in Korea, and to remember the Democratic party as the party of treachery.

We recall, too, that President Eisenhower's close adviser, Attorney General Brownell, maligned and impugned the very loyalty of a former President of the United States -- a man, by the way, who has done more to fight communism on all the fronts of the world than all the Republican politicians put together -- and I mean Harry S. Truman.

Nor did the Republicans elevate the political dialogue or honor our intelligence when their National Chairman set the theme for their celebration of the birthday of Abraham Lincoln as "20 years of treason" -- 20 years, by the way, during which General Eisenhower emerged from the obscurity of the Army, and Secretary Dulles from the obscurity of Wall Street.

And now the Republican Chief of Staff, the Vice President of the United States, [Loud "boos" 6 seconds] the heir apparent, [Heavy laughter 6 seconds] has pitched the Republican *congressional* campaign on the high level of corruption, communism, controls and Korea. *You know what the advertising boys in the high—in the G.O.P. high command call it? They call it the East "C3K1."* [Medium laughter 6 seconds] And since Hurricane Maine [Heavy laughter and applause 9 seconds] even, *even* President Eisenhower has begun to talk about communists in government and red herrings, after assuring us months ago that his administration's record was the only issue.[11]

Well, to all such ugliness, *such* bitterness and nonsense I have no intention of replying in kind— *either* here or anywhere else. Indeed, [Heavy applause 8 seconds] *indeed* I am proud of the manner in which the Democratic party has refused to be diverted by irresponsible and incessant attacks. I am proud of the manner in which the Democratic party has supported the President's congressional

[11] The phrase "C3K1" in the manuscript is set off in parentheses because there apparently was some question as to whether it would be used. William Blair, in releasing type copy to the press, had enclosed the phrase, believing it should be cut because it would not be understood. It does not appear in the press release text. "Hurricane Maine"—a pun identifying a New England storm with a surprise Democratic victory in Maine.

-9-

And now the Republican Chief of Staff, the Vice President of the United States, the heir apparent, has pitched the Republican ₍congressional₎ campaign on the high level of corruption, communism, controls and Korea -- ⟨Model K₁C₃ the GOP High Command calls it.⟩ And since Hurricane Maine struck, even President Eisenhower has begun to talk about communists in government and red herrings, after assuring us months ago that his administration's record was the only issue.

Well, to all such ugliness, bitterness and nonsense I have no intention of replying in kind -- here or anywhere else. Indeed, I am proud of the manner in which the Democratic party has refused to be diverted by irresponsible and incessant attacks. I am proud of the manner in which the Democratic party has supported the President's congressional program *wherever* and *whenever* it has seemed to be in the public interest. If, [Medium applause 5 seconds] *if* we have helped to give [the President] *him* a batting average of which he cares to [brag] *boast*, while his own team seemed bent on sending him to the showers in the first inning, [Light laughter 2 seconds] *well* we can be proud of that too—for we are Americans first, and *we are* partisans second. [Heavy applause 8 seconds]

And do you think our Republican friends would do the same and feel the same about a Democratic administration? [Scattered "Noes"] Well, you'll find your answer in 20 years of implacable, stubborn opposition and abuse, and in the current rash of epithets and intemperance.

And now after 20 months of the Great Crusade [Medium laughter 3 seconds] the time, *the time* has come for another accounting at the polls, and speaking from this platform our President *recently* gave us an accounting which he repeated again last night. Now, while I don't want to appear captious, there are just a few comments I should like to make about [a few] *some* of President Eisenhower's remarks. *And* besides, he [expressly] invited, *and I quote him*, "the most rigid scrutiny of the record." [Light applause 3 seconds]

-10-

program whenever and wherever it has seemed to be in the public interest. If we have helped to give *him* ~~the President~~ a batting average of which he cares to *boast* ~~brag~~, while his own "team" seemed bent on sending him to the showers in the first inning, we can be proud of that too -- for we are Americans first, and partisans second.

And do you think our Republican friends would do the same and feel the same about a Democratic administration? Well, you'll find your answer in 20 years of implacable, stubborn opposition and abuse, and in the current rash of epithets and intemperance.

But now after 20 months of the Great Crusade the time has come for another accounting at the polls, and speaking from this platform our President *recently* gave us an accounting which he repeated again last

But first before I do that I must read to you two sen—ten—sentences from a telegram sent this afternoon, a copy of which has just reached me within the last few minutes here in the Hollywood Bowl, sent to the President by the—Senator Lyn-don Johnson, the Minority Leader of the Senate, and Congressman Sam Rayburn, the Minority Leader of the House of Representatives. It's a long telegram. Let me read you only a couple of sen-tences.[12]

"Mr. President: Your statement of last night is un—an unwarranted and unjust attack on many Democrats who have done so much to cooperate with your administration and to defend your pro-gram from attacks by members and leaders of your own party. Nevertheless, we assure you as leaders of the Democratic party in Congress *that* there will be no cold war conducted against you by the Demo-crats when we gain control of both houses of Con-gress. [Heavy applause 11 seconds]

---

[12] These two pages have been set up by editing photographic negatives before engraving was done. Upon receipt of the telegram, Stevenson had his secretary type a copy. It took three pages. Stevenson read it and underlined those portions he planned to use. Page two of the telegram script had no underlined material and he did not take it to the speaker's stand. In the engraving, page 11 of his script has been cut at the point of insertion. It resumes in the lower frame below the underlined telegram. In the speech, however, Stevenson had carried the insert material along separately.

---

night. Now, while I don't want to appear captious, there are just a few comments I should like to make about [handwritten: any] ~~the few~~ of President Eisenhower's remarks.

Besides, he expressly invited "the most rigid scrutiny of the record." *[handwritten: But first let me read you this underscoring.]*

Copy of telegram to President Eisenhower sent Saturday, October 9, 1954, by Senators Lyndon Johnson and Sam Rayburn.

Your statement of last night is an unwarranted and unjust attack on many Democrats who have done so much to cooperate with your administration and to defend your program from attacks by members and leaders of your own party. It may be that you have been placed in your new position of rigid, unswerving partisanship by the frantic pleas of your political advisers to come to the rescue of a party fearful of repudiation of the voters. Nevertheless, we assure you, as leaders of the Democratic party in Congress, as far as we are concerned there will be no cold war conducted against you by the Democrats when we gain control of both houses of Congress.

"In the future, *Mr. President*, we shall meet each problem as it comes before us in the 84th Congress, not on the basis of what will give us partisan advantage, but in the spirit of what is best for America. It is our hope that whatever the outcome of the election may be, you will be able to achieve from all of the members of your own party the same fair treatment." [Medium applause and laughter 4 seconds]

Now I shall not discuss but a few of the things that the President said. I shall not discuss his *most interesting conclusion, voiced here the other night,* that by reducing support prices for farmers from 90% of parity his program will enable farmers to receive *a 100% of parity in the market place.* [Light laughter 2 seconds]

He also *proudly* stated that there has been no scandal or corruption in his administration. [Light laughter] *Now* we must assume, I suppose, that he has forgotten that he [hand] picked a chairman of the Great Crusade, a chairman of the Republican National Committee, from his own State of Kansas who was hardly installed before a scandal broke about his head and he *was obliged to resign.* [Light applause 3 seconds]

In the future, whether we are in the minority or in the majority, we shall meet each problem as it comes before us in the 84th Congress, not on the basis of what will give us partisan advantage, but in the spirit of what is best for America. It is our hope that whatever the outcome of the election may be, you will be able to achieve from all of the members of your own party the same fair treatment.

I shall not discuss his interesting conclusion that by reducing support prices for farmers from 90% of parity his program will enable farmers to receive 100% of parity in the market place.

He also proudly stated that there had been no scandal or corruption in his administration. We must assume, I suppose, that he has forgotten that he picked a chairman of the Great Crusade, a chairman of the Republican National Committee, from his own State of Kansas who was hardly installed before a scandal broke about his head and he resigned.

We wonder, too, if the President has forgotten already that one of the officers of his own Inaugural Committee somehow got involved in [an] attempted [percentage] *influence peddling* [deal] and has been indicted.

And surely *somebody* must have told him about [the] *his* Housing Administration Commissioner [whom he appointed and] whose resignation was accepted because he was aware of the scandalous situation in the Housing Administration and did not act.

Nor have we yet heard, *I dare say,* the end of the Dixon-Yates contract [Scattered exclamations] which the President himself ordered without competitive bidding and over the objection of both government agencies involved. But *I think* we have heard enough [of this deal] to at least suspect that what *is* good for Dixon *and* Yates is not good for the country. [Medium applause 7 seconds]

-12-

We wonder, too, if the President has forgotten already that one of the officers of his own Inaugural Committee somehow got involved in an attempted *influence peddling* deal and has been indicted.

And surely someone must have told him about *his* Housing Administration Commissioner ~~whom he~~ ~~appointed and~~ whose resignation was accepted because he was aware of the scandalous situation in the Housing Administration and did not act.

Nor have we yet heard the end of the Dixon-Yates contract which the President himself ordered without competitive bidding and over the objection of both government agencies involved. But we have heard enough of this deal to at least suspect that what's good for Dixon-Yates is not good for the country.

[To say these things] *Now to enumerate these incidents* is not pleasant nor is it to excuse, *to condone or to over overlook the evil-doers that crept into public positions during Democratic administrations. Rather it is to suggest that self-righteousness *should* be tempered with [reality] *candor,* and to remind our Republican friends that pride goeth before a fall, [Light laughter 2 seconds] and on the basis of 20 months their prospects are not good for beating the Democratic record of public probity *for* during 20 years of depression, *of* war, and *of* vast expansion of government responsibility and expenditure.

Now [Very light applause] *Let me move on.* Aside from ungraciously taking full credit for tax reductions previously enacted by the Democrats, the President [had] *made* this *curious fiscal* comment: [Light laughter 2 seconds] *He said, and I quote him,* "We flatly reject the idea that, for America to stay prosperous the government must always spend more

---

-13-

Summit this wisdom

To ~~say these things~~ is not pleasant nor is it

to excuse, condone or overlook the evildoers that

crept into public positions during Democratic

administrations. Rather it is to suggest that self-

righteousness *should* be tempered with ~~reality~~ *candor*, and to remind

our Republican friends that pride goeth before a

fall, and on the basis of 20 months their prospects

are not good for beating the Democratic record of

public probity during 20 years of depression, war

and vast expansion of government responsibility

and expenditure.

Aside from ungraciously taking full credit

for tax reductions previously enacted by the

Democrats, the President *made* this fiscal comment:

"We flatly reject the idea that, for America to stay

prosperous the government must always spend more

than it has." *Well!* I don't know whose "idea" it is that he is flatly rejecting, [Light laughter 2 seconds] but I can't overlook, as he did, that just a week before that utterance it was announced [in Washington] that the estimated deficit for this year *will be four billion six hundred million dollars.* [Light laughter and applause 3 seconds]—*and that* recalled *to me some* rather glib talk *that* I heard a couple of years ago about balancing the budget with one hand tied behind their backs. [Light laughter 2 seconds]

But *the President* also said: "Yes, we have a prosperous economy," *those were his words and that* will be interesting news to a few million people looking for work [Light laughter] and to a lot of farmers who don't overlook *the fact* that we have the highest living costs and the lowest farm prices in a long while *and* at the same time, [Light laughter] *and that I suppose is what you kill—call killing two birds with one stone.* [Medium laughter and applause 5 seconds]

The President stated a couple of other conclusions, also without supporting evidence, which

-14-

than it has." I don't know whose "idea" it is that he is flatly rejecting, but I can't overlook, as he did, that just a week before that utterance it was announced in ~~Washington~~ that the estimated deficit for this year would be $4.6 billion -- which recalled some glib talk I heard a couple of years ago about balancing the budget with one hand tied behind their backs.

But he also said: "Yes, we have a prosperous economy," which will be interesting news to a few million people looking for work and to a lot of farmers who don't overlook that we have the highest living costs and the lowest farm prices in a long while at the same time.

The President stated a couple of other conclusions, also without supporting evidence, which amazed me. He seemed to be "especially happy," to use his words, about the bi-partisanship [in our foreign problems] *these days* when the facts are that not only have no Democrats been appointed to policy [making] positions in the State Department and our foreign activities, but they don't even want Republicans who worked for the Democrats, [Light laughter 1 second] regardless of competence. *And* surely, *surely* President Eisenhower must have heard that under President Truman a Republican was Secretary of Defense, a Republican was High Commissioner to G-Germany, a Republican was Ambassador to *Great* Britain, a Republican was administrator of our foreign aid program, many of the Assistant Secretaries of State were Republicans, and I could go on and on. I could, indeed, even remind him that Mr. Dulles served under President Truman much longer than he has under

-15-

amazed me. He seemed to be "especially happy," to use his words, about the bi-partisanship *[that long,]* when the facts are that not only have no Democrats been appointed to policy making positions in the State Department and our foreign activities, but they don't even want Republicans who worked for the Democrats, regardless of competence. *And* Surely President Eisenhower must have heard that under President Truman a Republican was Secretary of Defense, a Republican was High Commissioner to Germany, a Republican was Ambassador to Britain, a Republican was administrator of our foreign aid program, many of the Assistant Secretaries of State were Republicans, and I could go on and on. I could, indeed, even remind him that Mr. Dulles served under President Truman much longer than he has under

President Eisenhower. [Medium applause 4 seconds] *And I wonder if he's forgotten that his own exalted appointments came from Democratic Presidents?* Yet, [Light applause 1 second] *yet if you can believe it,* he talks of bipartisanship "unmatched in previous administrations!" [Light laughter 2 seconds]

I hope I don't *seem* frivolous [Medium laughter 4 seconds] when I say that the fact of the matter is that they haven't even *succeeded in establishing* bi-partisanship within the Republican party, [Heavy laughter and applause 10 seconds] and your Senator Knowland, the Republican leader in the Senate, ["Boos"] takes a pot shot at the President's policy every few days.

I won't comment on the President's interesting assertions that we are somehow stronger for spending less on defense and *for* cutting first our Air Force and then our Army, which, incidentally, accounts for most of the budget savings to which he points with such pride.

But there are just a couple of other statements that I can't overlook. He said, if you can believe

---

but I'm sure he hasn't forgotten that his own exalted appointment -16- came from own President.

President Eisenhower. Yet he talks of bi-partisanship "unmatched in previous administrations"!

I hope I don't sound frivolous when I say that the fact of the matter is that they haven't even been able to establish bi-partisanship within the Republican party, and your Senator Knowland, the Republican leader in the Senate, takes a pot shot at the President's policy every few days.

I won't comment on the President's interesting assertions that we are somehow stronger for spending less on defense and cutting first our Air Force and then our Army, which, incidentally, accounts for most of the budget savings to which he points with such pride.

But there are just a couple of other statements that I cannot overlook. He said, if you can believe it:[13] "For the past 20 months," *I quote him, "for the past 20 months* there has been harmony, unprecedented in our time, [Medium laughter 4 seconds] *there has been harmony unprecedented in our time,* between the Executive and the Congress." [Medium laughter 3 seconds] *Now* the fact is that in the squalid McCarthy-Army spectacle, which delighted our enemies and revolted our friends, *in the* Greek ship deal, the almost daily contradictions of administration policy by [administration] *Republican* leaders in *the* Congress, *in the* demoralization of our far flung foreign service, *in the* Republican fight for the Bricker amendment, their challenge of the Bohlen appointment, and many others, *that these* are only the public revelations of the extent of the collisions and the invasions of the executive domain and *of* the President's prerogatives. Yet, what the political scientists have been calling the [gravest] *greatest* constitutional crisis in many years, President Eisenhower calls "harmony unprecedented." [Very light laughter 2 seconds]

-17-

it: "For the past 20 months there has been harmony, unprecedented in our time, between the Executive and the Congress." The fact is that in the squalid McCarthy-Army spectacle, which delighted our enemies and revolted our friends, the Greek ship deal, the almost daily contradictions of administration policy by [Republican] administration leaders in Congress, the demoralization of our far flung foreign service, the Republican fight for the Bricker amendment, their challenge of the Bohlen appointment, and many others, are only the public revelations of the extent of the collisions and the invasions of the executive domain and the President's prerogatives.

Yet, what the political scientists have been calling the gravest constitutional crisis in many years, President Eisenhower calls "harmony unprecedented."

[13] This is not the page which had been released to the press. In reworking his copy Stevenson made so many changes that retyping was apparently necessary.

And I was surprised and *I was* a little saddened when the President referred to "the useless shooting" and "the futile sacrifices" in Korea—*those were the words.* I had not thought that those were his views of [that] *this* greatest collective effort to halt the communist imperialism. *And* likewise, his apparent satisfaction with the peace in Indo-China perplexes me in view of his earlier opinion that a truce in Korea would be a fraud if it helped the Communists to advance elsewhere, not to mention the fact that his administration evidently thought the security of Indo-China so important that it seriously considered armed intervention *by our country.*

But I've saved for the last, or almost the last, the most extraordinary words of all. *Listen to this:* "Over the world we have brought strength where there was weakness. We have brought realism where there was wishful thinking. We have brought frankness, candor

---

-18-

And I was surprised and a little saddened when the President referred to "the useless shooting" and "the futile sacrifices" in Korea. I had not thought that those were his views of that greatest collective effort to halt the communist imperialism. Likewise, his apparent satisfaction with the peace in Indo-China perplexes me in view of his earlier opinion that a truce in Korea would be a fraud if it helped the Communists to advance elsewhere, not to mention the fact that his administration evidently thought the security of Indo-China so important that it seriously considered armed intervention by our country.

But I've saved for the last, or almost the last, the most extraordinary words of all: "Over the world we have brought strength where there was weakness. We have brought realism where there was wishful thinking. We have brought frankness, candor and force to foreign policy which at last insists on distinguishing words from deeds."[14]

I wish it were so. And I suspect *that* the President [also] wishes it were so. [Medium laughter 4 seconds]

But what they have brought is pronouncements instead of policy, clamor instead of candor, and impotence instead of force as the sequel of a long procession of ringing slogans that lie forlorn but [unhappily] *happily* not forgotten, along the winding path of *these* past two years— "liberation," "unleashing Chiang Kai Shek," "seizing the initiative,"—*while the Communists were seizing Indo-China,* [Light laughter 2 seconds] "massive retaliation," the "new look," *"agonizing reappraisal," "more bang for a buck,"* [Light laughter 3 seconds] *and I could go on.*

[14] Because of extensive changes, pages 19, 19a, 20 and 21 were retyped after the release of the press copy.

-19-

and force to foreign policy which at last insists on distinguishing words from deeds."

I wish it were so. And I suspect the President also wishes it were so.

But what they have brought is pronouncements instead of policy, clamor instead of candor and impotence instead of force as the sequel of a long procession of ringing slogans that lie forlorn but, unhappily, not forgotten, along the winding path of the past two years -- "liberation," "unleashing Chiang Kai Shek," "seizing the initiative," "massive retaliation," the "new look," etc.

a growing reappraisal, more laughter & huzza

Yet the President *proudly, even seriously* talks of realism where there was wishful thinking, of distinguishing words from deeds.

Now, to be sure, *it's* not his fault that his *partly,* his party is so sadly divided on foreign policy that the Senior Senator from *his* great state talks of war with China while *the* President talks of co-existence with the Communists; *it's not his fault, I suppose,* that he didn't get a single Republican vote for his foreign trade policy, or that the statements and contradictions from the White House, from Secretary Dulles, and from the part-time Secretaries of

-19a-

Yet the President talks proudly , ~~and~~ seriously of realism where there was wishful thinking, of distinguishing words from deeds.

To be sure, it is not his fault that his party is so sadly divided on foreign policy that the Senior Senator from this great state talks of war with China while his President talks of coexistence with the Communists; that he didn't get a single Republican vote for his foreign trade policy; or that the statements and contradictions from the White House, from Secretary Dulles, and from the part-time Secretaries of

State, *curiously enough both from California,* Nixon and Knowland, [Light laughter and "Boos" 3 seconds] have bewildered us Democrats, let alone our friends around the world. The harsh fact is that in 20 months of bluff and bluster, confusion and contradiction, we have lost influence and friends faster than at any time since Warren Harding and the Republican repudiation of international cooperation after the first [world] war. [Heavy applause 8 seconds] All around the world—*and I can take no partisan satisfaction in it—all around the world* [American prestige—our good] *the* name and the respect of both friend and foe has suffered and any pretense to the contrary is misleading and dangerous.

-20-

State, Nixon and Knowland, have bewildered us Democrats, let alone our friends around the world. The harsh fact is that in 20 months of bluff and bluster, confusion and contradiction, we have lost influence and friends faster than at any time since Warren Harding and the Republican repudiation of international cooperation after the first world war. All around the world American prestige -- our good name and the respect of both friend and foe -- has suffered and any pretense to the contrary is misleading and dangerous.   PAUSE

You know, after reading those speeches and the President's proud recitation of [Republican achievements] *unsupported conclusions*, I was reminded of the classic remark of the lady juror to her feminine neighbor *sitting* in the jury box during the *t*-trial of a lawsuit. *She said,* "You know, my dear, I don't listen to the evidence. I like to make up my own mind." [Medium to heavy laughter and applause 10 seconds]¹⁵

But finally, *finally* I must comment *briefly* on the President's conclusion. He says that a Republican Congress is necessary to complete his great program; that you just can't have—*and these were the words, you just can't have* one car with two drivers and end up anywhere but in the ditch. *Well, Sir,* I'll resist the temptation, [Heavy laughter and applause 10 seconds] *I'll resist the temptation* to discuss the proposition that you can't have two elephants with one driver and end up anywhere but in the ditch [either]. [Medium laughter 3 seconds]

---

¹⁵ The anecdote is not in the first draft released to the press.

-21-

You know, after reading those speeches and the President's proud recitation of *unsupported* ~~Republican~~ *achievements* — I was reminded of the classic remark of the lady juror *nsnash* to her feminine neighbor in the jury box during the trial of a law suit: "You know, my dear, I don't listen to the evidence. I like to make up my own mind." PAUSE

But, finally, I must comment *briefly* on the President's conclusion. He says that a Republican Congress is necessary to complete his great program; that you just can't have one car with two drivers and end up anywhere but in the ditch. (I'll resist the temptation to discuss the proposition that you can't have two elephants with one driver and end up anywhere but in the ditch either.)

Instead, let me point out that except on the give-away and on tax revision where the Republicans stood together as usual, no important legislation passed in the last two sessions of Congress without serious Republican defections made up by Democratic support. And what will happen when a Democratic Congress takes over is that the give-away will end and a lot of committee chairman-ships will change hands. [Heavy applause 9 seconds] *And you know that may be at least two reasons why some of the more emotional Republican campaigners are talking about a Democratic victory this fall as a "crucifixion," "chaos," "confusion" and "the obituary of a free nation." You know what they say is that we must have a Republican Congress to do what they couldn't do—with a Republican Congress.* [Medium laughter 4 seconds] *But the greatest prophet of doom and gloom of them all is Vice President Nixon.* [Medium "boos" 5 seconds] *You know what he said in Ohio the other day? He said that a Democratic victory would be the doom of the Republican party.* [Heavy laughter and applause 9 seconds] *I suppose that's been said every two years since 1864.* [Medium laughter 2 seconds]

-22-

Instead, let me point out that except on the giveaway and tax revision where the Republicans stood together as usual, no important legislation passed in the last two sessions of Congress without serious Republican defections made up by Democratic support. And what will happen when a Democratic Congress takes over is that the giveaway will end and a lot of committee chairmanships will change hands -- which may be at least two reasons why some of the more emotional Republican campaigners are talking about a Democratic victory this fall as "crucifixion," "chaos," "confusion" and "the obituary of a free nation." But the greatest prophet of gloom and doom is Vice President Nixon, who sees Democratic victory as the doom of the Republican party--which we've heard every two years.

you persun what they say is that we musthave — with a Rep Congress.

6 Rep Congress to do what theycouldnt do — with a Rep Congress.

Now the sober fact, of course, is that when the President denounces the Democrats as enemies of his program he must know that on many key measures—*on* foreign trade, *on* housing, *on* health, *on* the conduct of *our* foreign relations—the Democrats were far better supporters than the Republicans.

Of the arguments that a President is *in* some way entitled to a Congress of his own political *koom-koom* complexion, *it's* at least interesting that this is the first time in 20 years that any Republican leader has preached this doctrine. [Medium laughter 3 seconds]

The American system is deliberately and purposely designed to permit the people to review their *government* policies and *its* effectiveness not every four years, but every two *years*.

-23-

The sober fact, of course, is that when the President denounces the Democrats as enemies of his program he must know that on many key measures -- foreign trade, housing, health, the conduct of foreign relations -- the Democrats were far better supporters than the Republicans.

Of the arguments that a President is ⁀ some way entitled to a Congress of his own political complexion, it is at least interesting that this is the first time in 20 years that any Republican leader has preached this doctrine.

The American system is deliberately and purposely designed to permit the people to review their government's policies and effectiveness not every four years, but every two.

We shall insist that *it* is as important in 1954 as in any other year that party not be placed above country; that it is more important that candidates for our service be right than that they be Republican. [Medium applause 9 seconds.]

What, after all, *my friends*, does *this* country want in a government? It wants a government which can inspire unity at home, which will provide security abroad and which will maintain a growing, *and a* prosperous economy. A Republican Congress cannot meet *these* tests as we now must know. The real question that the people must decide this fall is whether the Congress will function more effectively under a divided, *a* quarrelsome, *a* squabbling Republican regime than it will under the proved leadership of the Democratic party.

-24-

We shall insist that ^it^ is as important in 1954 as in any other year that party not be placed above country; that it is more important that candidates for our service be right than that they be Republican.

What, after all, does the country want in a government. It wants a government which can inspire unity at home, which will provide security abroad and which will maintain a growing, prosperous economy. A Republican Congress cannot meet those tests as we now must know. The real question that the people must decide this fall is whether the Congress will function more effectively under a divided, quarrelsome, squabbling Republican regime than it will under the proved leadership of the Democratic party.

That is the real issue this fall, and it is *the* one which the Democratic party confidently submits to the people for decision.

But beyond, [and] beneath today's confidence are principles and great objectives. Our aim, *I suggest*, is not the concentration of authority in the hands of feudal overlords or of a totalitarian state but the diffusion of power as well as of well-being among all *of* the people. We strive to enable free competitive enterprise to withstand [the machinations of] monopolistic *and* cartelized power. We strive to enable honest *savings* and investment to protect itself from fraud [chicanery, and overreaching]. We seek to enable the farmers and the workers to maintain a *free* and equal bargaining position on the markets for their products and for their labor.

-25-

That is the real issue this fall, and it is one which the Democratic party confidently submits to the people for decision.

But beyond and beneath today's confidence are principles and great objectives. Our aim is not the concentration of authority in the hands of feudal over-lords or of a totalitarian state, but the diffusion of power as well as of well-being among all the people. We strive to enable free competitive enterprise to withstand ~~the machinations~~ ~~of~~ monopolistic or cartelized power. We strive to enable honest saving and investment to protect itself from fraud, ~~chicanery, and over-reaching~~. We seek to enable the farmers and the workers to maintain a fair and equal bargaining position on the markets for their products and for their labor.

This is the New Freedom which seeks the prudent use and husbandry of the nation's resources and their—*uh*—*protection from ruthless exploitation* and despoilation [sic] at the expense of future generations. [Medium applause 7 seconds]

It strives *I say not only* to conserve our material resource but our human resources *as well*—*the* self-respect, *the* dignity of all members of our free and independent society. It demands protection *for* every individual and his dependents from the unavoidable hazards of old age, *of* sickness, and unemployment. Our new freedom would give—*uh*—*to* every individual without regard to color or religion or age or wealth or physical handicap a stake in freedom—*a stake* worth defending.

This is no doubt [Light applause 2 seconds] *there's no doubt, I say,* that we are living in a changing world. Progress in science and technology

---

-26-

This is the New Freedom which seeks the prudent use and husbandry of the Nation's resources and their protection from ruthless exploitation and despoilation at the expense of future generations.

It strives to conserve not only our material resources but our human resources -- the self-respect and dignity of all members of our free and independent society. It demands protection of every individual and his dependents from the unavoidable hazards of old age, sickness, and unemployment. Our new freedom would give every individual without regard to color or religion or age or wealth or physical handicap a stake in freedom worth defending.

There is no doubt that we are living in a changing world. Progress in science and technology has awakened the hope for a better life and *for* increased well-being everywhere *in the world*.

The Kremlin tells *us*, *tells all of* those *people* throughout the world yearning for *a* change that our free system has nothing to offer them, *nothing but exploitation and oppression,* and would leave things *changeless* as they are; that only imperial communism offers them a hope for a change and *for* a better life.

But we believe that we have a better way—*that we have* the way of consent instead of force. And we must give proof that our way of life is not [with a new freedom bringing] *inflexible but will bring* a greater degree of continuing wellbeing to all our people than has been enjoyed in all history by any people.

And I beg you, my friends, not to be discouraged. The struggle with evil, *with* error, *with* tyranny is everlasting, but never vain.

-27-

has awakened the hope for a better life and increased well-being everywhere.

The Kremlin tells all those throughout the world yearning for change that our free system has nothing to offer them and would leave things *[handwritten]* as they are; that only imperial communism offers them a hope for a change and a better life.

But we believe that we have a better way --

the way of consent instead of force. And we must *[handwritten: inflexible but will]* give proof that our way of life is not ~~with a new~~ *bring* a greater degree of continuing well-being to all our people than has ever been enjoyed in all history by any people.

And I beg you, my friends, not to be discouraged. The struggle with evil, error and tyranny is everlasting, but never vain.

And even [Medium applause 7 seconds, produced by sentence immediately before] *and even, we pray —we must believe,* the most fanatical ideology must adjust itself to revealed truth or perish. The job is to cling everlastingly to the truth; to try ever-lastingly to find it in the clatter and *the* confusion of these times—[and] to find it even in the storm of words of a political campaign, *which is at once the symbol and the test of freedom. Thank you.* [Sustained heavy applause and band music]

-28-

And even the most fanatical ideology must adjust itself to revealed truth or perish. The job is to cling everlastingly to the truth; to try ever-lastingly to find it in the clatter and confusion of these times -- to find it even in the storm of words of a political campaign— *which* is at once the symbol and the test of freedom.

INDEX

PICTURE CREDITS

In the following page-by-page list of credits, the pictures are referred to from left to right, top to bottom. Most of the pictures not otherwise credited were taken by Associated Students UCLA.

Idea

1 After preliminary reading, observation, and discussion with others, select a subject that interests you.

2 Make a list of available printed sources and sources for observation and interview.

3 Read several general articles about the subject, keeping careful notes.

4 Determine and write out the purpose of the speech.

5 Evaluate material in terms of purpose and audience and make a preliminary plan.

6 Discuss ideas informally with friends. Note the weak spots and gaps in your information.

7 Read to fill those gaps and to amass a wider selection of details. Conduct observations and interviews to personalize your materials. Select supporting materials which make your speech interesting, clear, and believable.